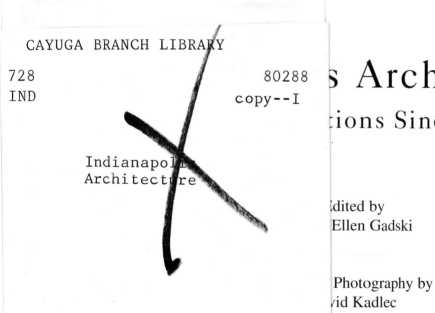

s Architecture:

tions Since 1975

dited by
Ellen Gadski

Photography by
vid Kadlec

apolis, Indiana
Indiana Architectural Foundation
1993

For photographs copyrighted by contributing photographers, see page 193.

Library of Congress Catalog Card Number 93-80478
ISBN 0-96336300-1-6

Design by Eye Blink Studios, Indianapolis.
Maps and index by Constance McBirney.
Copyediting by Paula Corpuz.

Set in Times Roman.
Linotronic output by Douglas & Gayle Limited, Indianapolis.
Printed by Edward Brothers, Ann Arbor, Michigan.
Distributed by Independent Publishers Group, Chicago.

The paper in this book meets the guidelines for permanence and durability
of the Committee on Production Guidelines for Book Longevity of the
Council on Library Resources.

Printed in the U. S. A.

9 8 7 6 5 4 3 2 1

80288- CAYUGA- COPY I

Indianapolis Architecture: Transformations Since 1975

Keystone Contributors:

Lilly Endowment Inc.

Associated General Contractors of Indiana, Inc.,
Construction Advancement Program of Central Indiana

The Indiana Arts Commission

Carlstedt Dickman Inc./Citimark Development Co.

Principal Contributors:
AIA/Indiana
American United Life Insurance Company
Arts Council of Indianapolis
The Associated Group
Bowen Engineering Corporation
F. A. Wilhelm Construction Co., Inc.
Historic Landmarks Foundation of Indiana
In Honor of Rolla E. Willey
Mansur Development Corporation
Ober Foundation
Three-S Reproductions, Inc.
The West Foundation, Inc.

With the support of the
Indiana Arts Commission and
National Endowment for the Arts.

With the support of the
ARTS COUNCIL OF INDIANAPOLIS
and City of Indianapolis

Major Contributors

AIA/Indianapolis
Marbaugh Engineering Supply Co., Inc.
Metropolitan Indianapolis Board of Realtors
McComb Window & Door Co., Inc.

Presidents' Challenge

Bradbury Associates, Inc.
Lee J. Brockway, AIA
William A. Browne, Jr., AIA
CSO/Architects-Engineers-Interiors
Fanning/Howey Associates, Inc.
H N T B Architects Engineers Planners
Indianapolis Chamber of Commerce Foundation
James T. & Marjorie L. Kienle
Craig W. Mullins, AIA
Ratio Architects, Inc.
Schmidt Associates Architects, Inc.
Society of Architectural Historians,
        Central Indiana Chapter

Contributors

American Cablevision of Indianapolis
American Precast Concrete
Architectural Concepts, Inc.
Artekna Design
Blackburn Associates Architects, Inc.
Bohlen, Meyer, Gibson & Associates, Inc.
Brandt Construction, Inc.
Brese Associates
Browning Day Mullins Dierdorf Inc.
BSA Design
Business Furniture Corporation
Calvert*Hoffman Representatives
Charles C. Brandt and Company, Inc.
Charles M. Sappenfield, FAIA
Construction Specifications Institute,
        Indianapolis Chapter
E. F. Marburger & Son, Inc.

Everett I. Brown Company
Gary Weaver, Inc.
Gwathmey Tyler, Tyler Associates
James E. Lingenfelter, AIA
James A. Wurster, American Consulting Engineers, Inc.
Lau & Associates, Inc.
Lilly Industries, Inc.
MAB Paints
Mozingo Williamson Architects
Odle McGuire & Shook Corporation
Prince/Alexander Architects, Inc.
R. L. Turner Corporation
Ralph Gerdes Consultants
Roettger/Selmer Architects
The Rosk Group, Inc.
Rotz Engineers, Inc.
Seward Sales Corporation
Shaffner Heaney Associates, Inc.
Spohn Associates, Inc.
T & W Corporation
Thom Knox, Universal Building Products
Woollen, Molzan and Partners
Angelo & Pam Zarvas

Other Contributors

Aspinall Associates, Inc.
Mr. & Mrs. M. Mazen Ayoubi
B. A. S. E. Architects, Inc.
Baines Builders Products
Beaman Associates, Inc.
Engledow Inc.
G. William Selmer, Architects
Gary David Gaiser, AIA
Goodman Jewelers, Inc.
Dave Halvorson, AIA
Dorothy A. Henehan
John Jelliffe
Kenneth A. Sebree & Associates, Architects
Kosene & Kosene Real Estate Development Management Co.
Kurker & Partners, Architects
McElhiney & Company, Inc.
The Partenheimer Group
Porter Paints
Reid Quebe, Allison, Wilcox & Associates, Inc.
Robert A. Cochran & Associates
David Allen Roettger Architects
Trefzger's, Manufacturers' Representative

Table of Contents

Foreword

by William H. Hudnut, III

Indianapolis is a city of builders, not wreckers, and during the 16 years I served as mayor of Indianapolis, 1976-91, I enjoyed playing a role, either directly or indirectly, in the development of our city's built environment.

When one talks about cities, big and small, great and near great, an image of a particular city comes to mind. It is usually of the city center. New York, Denver, Chicago, Detroit, Newark, Seattle, San Francisco, St. Louis . . . different images flash into focus for each. Twenty-five years ago, you could mention Indianapolis to someone from out of town and either no image would be evoked or one of the Speedway alone. While the latter is a tremendous asset, the former does not say much for the city.

These years probably will be remembered for the effort that was made to create a new city center, a destination you would travel to personally as well as in your mind's eye. The first visible signs of the rebirth emerged in the early 1970s when Dick Lugar was mayor with Market Square Arena, Indiana National Bank, Blue Cross Blue Shield, and Indiana Bell. The bricking of the Circle, the construction of the new tennis facility downtown, and the replacement of the old Sheraton Lincoln Hotel with the Merchants Plaza—Hyatt Regency complex followed shortly thereafter, sending out a loud call that downtown Indianapolis was alive and getting better. So much attention had been given to the suburbs, it was time for the city center to receive new focus. No one building can take all the credit. The collective new skyline reflects the new Indianapolis.

As I look back on my years as mayor now, vignettes by the score flash through my mind. I remember:

• The 17 months of meetings with the American United Life building committee members as city officials worked with them to find a site downtown for their new office building—assembling the 27 parcels of land, vacating part of Indiana Avenue, relocating a sewer, participating in the ground breaking and topping out ceremonies, discussing the design of "Reich's Spike" (a term I dubbed at the 1982 dedication ceremony after CEO Jack Reich), and rejoicing when the finished skyscraper appeared on the Indianapolis skyline.

• The pressure I received and resisted to block the demolition of the venerable Hume-Mansur and Board of Trade buildings to pave the way for the Bank One Center Tower.

• The ground breaking in 1979 for the first single-family residential structure in the Mile Square in over 100 years: new townhouses on East Street.

• The ground breakings on the IUPUI campus for several new buildings that dramatically altered the downtown landscape, during one ceremony for which I spoke, much to the amusement of IU President John Ryan, of "the mutually fructifying" relationship between the university and the city.

• The walk I took with then Secretary of HUD Sam Pierce through Lockefield Gardens, with its broken glass, rusted-out doors, weeds, rodents, and barbed wire, dreaming of what it could become if we formed a partnership between the different entities needed to put the project together.

• The display of designs in an architectural competition for in-fill housing downtown on California Street.

• The luncheon I had with Frank McKinney on the top floor of the old AFNB building when we looked down on the Circle Theatre and wondered if the symphony might like it as a permanent home, assuming it could be refurbished.

• Indiana Theatre's last-minute save from the wrecking ball, followed by the dreams we had for a new hotel going up alongside it with an upper level walkway connecting to the Indiana Roof, which would later be restored.

• The singing of the doxology at the ground breaking ceremony for Goodwin Plaza elderly housing built in collaboration with St. Phillip's Church.

• The time in the late 1970s that I carved my initials in wet cement at the bottom of the Advanced Wastewater Treatment plant, which at the time was the largest public works construction project in the country.

• Hammering nails with Tech High School students as they finished work on houses on Central Avenue that they had built in cooperation with the Chamber of Commerce's Partners in Education program.

• The trips I made to businesses on the Circle, paving the way for the removal of busses and the laying of bricks, and the chastisement I received at a church coffee hour from someone who felt the Circle renovation project was a waste of money, and if I proceeded with it, I would never be elected again to anything.

• The ribbon cutting for Providence Place on the near east side, which turned the old Holy Cross School into apartments.

• The discussions I had with the White River Park folks about my opposition to the erection of a huge tower in the park, and my support for the relocation of the Metro bus facilities and the Washington Street bridge over White River to make the park possible.

• The summer day in 1984 when we inflated the Hoosier Dome, and all Indianapolis watched in fascination.

• The urban homesteading drawings in the public assembly room of the City-County Building, when people who were overjoyed that their name had been drawn for the chance to acquire an old home for a dollar, fix it up, and live in it ran down the aisle and either threw their arms around me, cried on my shoulder, or twirled me around in a dance.

• The meetings we had regularly with the Irvington and Nora Community Councils to resolve concerns about city services in their neighborhoods, trying to achieve a happy medium between "progress" and the preservation of their neighborhood integrity.

• The tours we took in a van with the top brass of Eli Lilly and Company as they shared with us their aspirations for the expansion of their campus on the near south side of town.

• The countless different designs I looked at for the Circle Centre Mall, the difficulties the city had in assembling the land, the delays, the discussions we had with the historic preservation community about which buildings or facades would be saved and which would be sacrificed to make way for this most ambitious and difficult of downtown revitalization projects.

• The Easter Parade in which I marched around Union Station with its developer, Bob Borns, as we celebrated the new lease on life that had been given to this derelict, century-old structure, where the last train had pulled out a dozen years before.

• The push we undertook in our drive to become the "amateur sports capital" of the country, to complete the velodrome, natatorium, and track and field facility in time for the 1982 National Sports Festival.

• The delicate negotiations we engaged in to resolve the thorny issues of the relocation of The Red Garter and Fire Station 13 to make way for the new Westin Hotel and Capitol Commons.

• The efforts we made to provide support services for the tremendous expansion of two industrial giants in the northeast and northwest corners of our city, Boehringer Mannheim and Dow Elanco.

I could go on and on and on with my memories of events that shaped Indianapolis architecture.

I am not an architect, nor am I a student of architecture. As mayor I was concerned with the implementation of certain broad policy goals as we experi-enced the surge of growth during this time period. We wanted to combat urban thanatopsis with urban reinvestment. We did not want our city to become a donut, with all the development occurring around the I-465 belt-way. We needed to reinforce the core, to encourage downtown revitalization without discouraging suburban investment. We involved citizens in our efforts through task forces on downtown and neighborhood planning and revitalization. Our pro-growth policies were designed to create jobs in our Rust Belt city as we coped with the competition from the Sun Belt and the transition from an industrial to an information-based economy.

We believed in quality development, not helter-skelter growth for growth's sake. We understood government's role in building the city to be that of a partner with, not adversary to, the private sector. We were the regulators and enforcer of codes, to be sure; but more importantly, our job was to make things happen, not to prevent them, to facilitate, not to obstruct. We wanted to be sensitive to the concerns of the preservation community and knew it was important to retain the historic as we pushed toward the future. Could we combine the old with the new and steer a viable middle course between the Scylla of progress and the Charybdis of preservation? We hoped so. Our goal was to make Indianapolis a better and more livable city in which to live and work and raise a family.

Did we succeed? Who knows? A city is a living organism. Its development never ends. There is more to do. New changes will occur. But I hope that the epitaph on the period 1975-93 will read: "They effected positive change. They were builders, not wreckers." There is an anonymous poem I used to quote often during my speeches as mayor, which sums the matter up pretty well:

I watched them tearing a building down,
A gang of men in a busy town.
With a ho-heave-ho and a lusty yell,
They swung their beam and the side wall fell.

I asked the foreman, "Are these men skilled,
And the kind of men you'd use to build?"
He gave a laugh and said, "No, indeed,
Just common labor's all I need.
We can easily wreck in a day or two,
What it's taken people years to do."

Well, I asked myself as I went my way,
"Which of these roles have I tried to play?
Am I a builder who works with care,
Measuring life by the rule and square?
Patiently doing the best he can,
Leading his life to a well made plan?
Or am I a wrecker who walks the town,
Content with the business of tearing down?"

Indeed, Indianapolis is a city of builders, not wreckers.

Preface

by Mary Ellen Gadski

Architecture is by far the most public form of art and yet it is often the least known or understood. This guidebook seeks to introduce the reader to the best examples of Indianapolis' architectural work since 1975, the year that the Indiana Architectural Foundation published the first comprehensive guide to the city's architecture. Indianapolis has changed so dramatically since 1975, in new construction as well as the renovation of historic structures, that we now live in a city significantly transformed from the one that existed 18 years ago. Just glance through the old book's pages and see Massachusetts Avenue with derelict, boarded-up storefronts, Merchants Plaza as merely a construction sign, the City Market without wings, or the IUPUI campus without sports facilities, to capture an idea of the city in 1975. During a period of three years between 1987 and 1989, six new high-rise office buildings of over 20 stories were completed downtown. The ever present crane seemed to symbolize the city's process of re-creating itself. Not since the 1920s had the city experienced such a renaissance of new building. Since 1975, 84 individual buildings and 21 historic districts in Marion County have been placed on the National Register of Historic Places—figures that indicate the city's renewed interest in its historic structures.

The first book will always remain as a permanent and valuable record of what the city was in 1975. In its effort to convey its theme, which was that architecture exists in every neighborhood, the old book took a comprehensive approach at identifying buildings of interest throughout the county. The book was a great popular success; its first printing sold out within months, and the book was reprinted twice. Its achievements were all the more laudable in that it was produced by an all-volunteer effort of young architects who wished to bring the work of their profession to greater public awareness.

As with the last book, the scope of this new guidebook covers all 396 square miles of Marion County; however, it is not a comprehensive survey of all structures constructed since 1975 within county boundaries. To focus on the most prominent examples of architecture that transformed the city, a selection has been made of buildings that met the criteria established by the foundation's editorial review board. While everyone has his or her own definition of what architecture is, in our deliberations of representative examples for inclusion we often found ourselves asking the question: "does it go beyond necessity?" Architecture is an extraordinarily utilitarian art form, yet the best examples go beyond the minimum requirements of shelter to express humanistic values and meaning.

To ensure that the new guidebook was as comprehensive as possible, during the spring and summer of 1992 all Indianapolis architectural firms were contacted to solicit their nominations for buildings to appear in the book. The foundation requested that five buildings designed by the firm, as well as five buildings "at large," be nominated. Multiple responses from the individual architects of a firm were encouraged to elicit as many responses as possible. Of the dozens of replies, the three buildings that appeared most often on the architects' lists were the Eiteljorg Museum, the addition to the Children's Museum, and the Bank One Center Tower.

The buildings of over 100 architectural firms—from local single practitioners to some of the largest and most prominent firms in the country—are represented herein. More than one-third of these firms are from outside Indianapolis, which was a surprising discovery made during the course of researching the book. As addressed in the first essay on architectural design, the contributions of out-of-state firms are not easily categorized into either the positive or the negative.

While it is somewhat unusual to comment about a foreword within the context of a preface, William H. Hudnut's writing preceding these remarks deserves attention. Because his terms as mayor so closely parallel the years covered by this book, and because of his personal connection to the history of so many of the buildings presented, his vignettes offer us a glimpse into some of the events that surrounded their construction. Hudnut focused our attention on the center of the city, building an interest and creating a favorable climate for the support of architecture. For the first time published in book form, his remarks here summarize his perspective on the transformations that occurred during his terms of office.

By the very nature of a guidebook, the individual presentation of buildings must be brief. To offer more depth of coverage and to present insights into the ideas and issues in architecture since 1975—and indeed ahead to the future—the book begins with five critical essays. The first four pieces assess the successes and failures over the last 18 years in Indianapolis' architectural design, its planning and urban design, its efforts in historic preservation, and its suburbanization. The last essay challenges us with thought-provoking new ways to think about future architecture.

Following the traditional guidebook format, individual buildings are organized by sections of the city, with numbered photos keyed to maps to help readers find the buildings they are most interested in seeing. A separate introduction to that section of the book will provide an explanation of building entries. (See page 51.)

We hope that the guidebook will prove to be a useful and informative tool for readers to learn more about the architecture they encounter on a daily basis. In the future, the book may be of use as a reference work to a dynamic period in the city's history. We hope that readers will agree that architectural achievements since 1975 have improved the quality of life in Indianapolis and make us feel better about this city as a place to live.

Impressions of Indianapolis Architecture

"Indianapolis does not have many great architectural monuments. Like many Midwestern cities, it tends to have a lot of boiled and shrunken examples of what national firms have done first elsewhere. But what it does have is a pretty consistent, pretty good level of architectural quality."

—Ewing Miller, local architect, 1982

"The curious thing about Indianapolis and so many other places in our country is that one only talks about what was and what will be. One cannot talk about now because now is such a wasteland."

—Michael Graves, noted architect and
Indianapolis native, 1983

"The problem is not that the architecture of this city is much worse than most cities of comparable size. It is not. Indianapolis, however, does not have soaring mountains, lakes, an ocean or a sunnny climate to distinguish it and provide natural beauty. It needs all of the help it can get from the artistic genius of man in the form of architecture to set it apart."

—David Rohn, editorial writer,
Indianapolis News, 1983

"Fashion is not being made here. Design is safely back from the cutting edge—in that broad middle ground of competent, well-made but unremarkable buildings."

—David Dillon, architecture critic,
Dallas Morning News, 1987

"Close to the ideal [city square] is Indianapolis, which was designed on a square-mile plan in 1821 with a circle in the center that radiates axes in different directions toward other public spaces, including the state capitol. People are walking and driving through this circle all hours of the day and night, but it is not necessarily a gathering place, except on special occasions. So it has a special identity, one that captures the wholeness of the city."

—Elizabeth Plater-Zyberk, architect and
town planner, 1990

"The 1975 guidebook's authors noted that "Indianapolis is at a critical point in its life," and the choice was to "recognize that a city is for its people, or it can think only in terms of moving automobiles." At that time, the interstate outer loop was complete but the inner loop was still on the drawing boards. Since 1975 there has been an explosion of new growth. The choice made was to move both people and automobiles. The city has spread to its suburbs and has taken many of its people with it.

"In this day of HDTV and virtual reality, it may seem that there is no need for a city as civilization has known it for a thousand years. However, it seems to me that the concept of "community" remains important to the individual. If downtown becomes only a festival marketplace, what will this mean to our lives? This is something that we all need to think about."

—Lynn H. Molzan, Executive Director,
Indiana Architectural Foundation, 1993

A Critical Look at Architecture in Indianapolis since 1975

by Robert A. Benson, Ph.D.

Indianapolis is the quintessential city of the American Middle West. Spreading out on the seemingly endless plain of Indiana, it embodies that horizontal generosity of space that has been historically synonymous with American optimism and pragmatism. Within that spirit, the Hoosier capital benefited from uncanny foresight on the part of its first planner, Alexander Ralston, who sub-divided the original mile square in 1820 to accommodate the requisite public buildings in a clear, thoughtful arrangement centered on Monument Circle. (All this was done three-quarters of a century before Chicago planner Daniel H. Burnham would admonish his contemporaries to "make no small plans.") Later decisions to develop the five blocks north of Monument Circle from New York to St. Clair between Meridian and Pennsylvania as a series of parks bordered with civic, governmental, and other institutional buildings created one of the finest and most characteristic urban spaces in the country. Its high quality combines strong architectural design and formal pattern with a sense of scale that permits the ensemble to reverberate more sonorously than any individual element. This is an excellent example of the spirit of place that stimulates civic pride and permits public spirit to flourish.

View of the downtown skyline from the west bank of the White River.

But Indianapolis is the quintessential midwestern city for other reasons, as well. To contemporary travelers approaching the city from any direction by freeway, Indianapolis presents an image of mixed character that could only exist on the American prairie. Although urbane high-rise towers dominate the skyline, grain silos rise unabashedly near the capitol building and governmental center. A coal-burning power plant lurks within easy eyeshot of the Hoosier Dome, convention center, and luxury hotels. More important, late 20th-century development has interfered with the density and emphatically challenged the scale of the central business district (CBD), a scale that now decreases abruptly and inconsistently at the edge of downtown to signal an uneasy transition to the surrounding and outlying residential areas. And, although it was hailed as the "Cinderella of the rustbelt" for its energy during the 1980s, Indianapolis nevertheless suffers from the malaise of all major American cities of the postindustrial era. It is trying to reidentify a persona that slipped away when downtown ceased to represent the heart of the city for the majority of its residents. As can be expected, the architectural results of the effort to recoup are mixed, but they are nothing if not interesting.

The most highly profiled buildings of the past 18 years in Indianapolis are, in fact, those found in the CBD. In 1975 the tallest building in Indiana was Indiana National Bank Tower (1970) by Thomas E. Stanley of Dallas with Wright/Porteous and Lowe, a black-and-white modernist box that tipped its hat to its classical neighbors with a ground-level colonnade but stood apart from its context in every other way. Wright/Porteous and Lowe also designed Market Square Tower (1975), a faceless gold reflective glass box at the intersection of Delaware and Ohio streets that could have been built anywhere. In 1975 Indiana Bell Telephone Co., Inc., erected another impervious bluish reflective glass box at 220 North Meridian, designed by Kahn and Jacobs, of New York, with Fleck, Burhart, Shropshire, Boots, Reid and

Associates, Inc. Retrospectively, these buildings seem like unimaginative efforts to keep up with trends rather than energetic efforts to compete aggressively in the architectural arena. They reinforced nothing of what already existed as high quality in Indianapolis, and, typical of late modernist business architecture everywhere at that time, thumbed their noses at local architectural context and traditions.

The CBD was also populated from the late 1970s into the 1980s by a group of new hotels and related commercial structures, in large part to accommodate the sports fans and tourists who would come to the Hoosier Dome and convention center. These buildings undoubtedly served an important economic function; but they were architecturally awkward structures that could have been sited in any city. At that time, hotels with multistory atrium lobbies, balcony overlooks, and exposed elevators, all arranged over a geometric footprint, were mushrooming from Atlanta to Los Angeles, none of them supporting street life outside their own walls (despite their claims to the contrary). Residents of Indianapolis probably felt as though their city was on or near the cutting edge when Merchants Plaza with its Hyatt Regency Hotel went up in 1976. The design by JVIII Architects with Browning Day Pollak Associates takes its inspiration from other atrium hotels rather than from a respect for Indianapolis as a city with a history, form, and character worthy of careful consideration. Although the cross-axial plan purports to address the capitol building diagonally across the intersection of Washington and Capitol streets, the abstract brick angularities of its massing and window projections made Indianapolis more generic than specific in its identity. Oddly enough, however, the rotating restaurant on its top, which resembles a UFO just landed, offers a panorama of Indianapolis that is remarkable and exciting, perhaps the more so because it excludes Merchants Plaza from view.

Merchants Plaza from the capitol lawn.

View down Virginia Avenue toward the Circle.

In the early 1980s, a group of office towers that sprang up to serve a projected growth in white-collar employment downtown also sought to lend credibility to Indianapolis as a place where business, economic, and cultural life was thriving—even if Detroit and Cleveland seemed near collapse. Among them was the American United Life (AUL) tower at One American Square, by Skidmore Owings & Merrill (SOM) of Chicago.

There is much to criticize in the prosaic composition with its bookend props at either side, including the misuse of Indiana limestone cladding as though it were precast concrete. AUL also outscaled the nearby capitol building while turning away from it. Yet, it tried to strengthen the larger urban fabric by orienting its two primary faces toward Indiana and Virginia avenues, two of the four diagonal streets that slice from the center of the Mile Square to its corners. The imposing tower confronts motorists driving into the CBD on Virginia, as if it had unexpectedly turned to greet them. By hiring SOM, Indianapolis developers probably wanted to play hardball in the architectural big leagues, hoping for a landmark design. The 45° cut of its facade across the corner of Illinois and Ohio and the 45° slant of its atrium roof and of the roof above the principal facade were bold moves for a city that had seen little in the way of such geometries. Still, this only calls attention to the dramatic impact of architectural choices by patrons who might not have trusted the same—or better—suggestions from local architects. (Prophets and architects are usually without honor in their own lands, or so it seems.)

In 1986 and 1988, Browning Day Pollak Mullins (BDPM) saw two phases of another office complex completed. Capital Center, on Illinois across from the AUL tower, echoes its geometry in a plan with rotated squares extruded into several interlocking volumes through the height of the two building masses. Some volumes in both project out over entrances, supported by a single leg. BDPM had already experimented with rotated squares in its design for Landmark Center, a smaller office tower at 1099 North Meridian. In both Landmark and Capital Center, granite cladding contrasts with planes of glass curtain wall, suggesting how architects in the 1980s sought, both consciously and unconsciously, to reconcile the conflicting values of modernism—with its concern for abstraction, function, and technology—and postmodernism—with its concern for permanence, tradition, and context. Capital Center's most vital contribution was the placement of glass atria along Illinois Street. Set back from the sidewalk, the atria form a transparent concourse connecting the two towers without completely severing the commercial spaces of the building from the street.

The southwest corner at the intersection of Ohio and Illinois became the site of another building by the same firm. Browning Day Mullins Dierdorf (BDMD) designed 101 West Ohio in a style related to the work of Chicago's Helmut Jahn. The light shaft of the building sports ribbons of matte silver metal paneling and butt-jointed glass that recall Jahn's Xerox Building, while the heavier base is encased by granite in an Art Deco mode reminiscent of his One South Wacker, both in Chicago. The unique feature

Capital Center's glass-enclosed atrium.

of 101 West Ohio is the vertical element at the roofline above the corner that projects a 4,000-watt Xenon upbeam or "lightstick" into the sky at night. During the day, however, it eludes easy interpretation and recalls a smokestack.

In 1988 and 1989, Indianapolis developers went into high gear and erected four major towers in the CBD. Lohan Associates with Ratio Architects designed the Market Tower Building while CSO/Architects with Houston's 3D/International designed First Indiana Plaza. Dirk Lohan's tall Market Tower approaches the scale introduced by the AUL tower but is capped with a hip roof whose shape is described by the exposed skeleton of the structural frame. The slanting members of the frame are marked at the apex by poles that resemble lightning rods. A variegated system of curtain wall articulation in gray and reddish brown granite spandrels with dark aquamarine glass makes the compositional massing of the building difficult to read and thus seems arbitrary, if not bothersome. At street level, Lohan wanted to recall the canted archways from Art Deco towers of the late 1920s such as the Chrysler Building in New York; but, after passing through the large opening, a visitor discovers that the lobby inside is only a cramped, vertical miniature of the entrance to Water Tower Place in Chicago, complete with a lighted fountain, potted flowers, and two escalators.

By contrast, the slightly smaller First Indiana Plaza, by CSO/Architects and 3D/International, works well urbanistically and employs color as a strong, animating design element. First Indiana Plaza is a carefully composed dark rosy brown glass box capped by a glass hip roof with a grid projected from each shiny face in three colors of granite. Dark glass panels in the modules of the grid are recessed at the sides for a more plastic surface. The contrast of grid and glass layers gives the building a strong presence. At street level, the grids form a compositional base by defining arcades and a stepped corner entrance.

First Indiana thus relates to the colonnaded base of the INB building across Ohio Street, to the Federal Courthouse diagonally opposite by virtue of the corner entrance, and to the Market Tower Building with its hip roof. More important, the hip roof and lateral projections on the sides of the tower allude to the Indiana World War Memorial with its pyramidal roof and projecting Ionic colonnades, just two blocks away. The design thus successfully bridges between the technological, self-referential qualities of modernism and the qualities of contextualism and permanence associated with postmodernism. Reflected in the gold mirror of nearby Market Square Center, First Indiana Plaza even gives *raison d'être* to older neighbors and makes them seem less out of place.

The central player in this architectural scenario of the late 1980s, however, is Bank One Center by The Stubbins Associates of Boston. At 48 stories and 700 feet, it is the tallest tower in Indiana. Sited directly opposite the Federal Courthouse, and on axis with the World War Memorial and mall to the north, Bank One Center relates to all its major neighbors in one way or another. This begins at street level where the building connects through a very transparent glass-walled lobby with the sidewalk on Ohio and through pleasant skylit lobbies with Pennsylvania and Meridian on the east and west. Externally, its gray granite surface grid against dark glass and dark brown granite spandrel strips, its proportions, and its profile are compatible with nearby buildings. Moreover, through the stepped pyramid on its top, Bank One Center makes an even stronger allusion to the World War Memorial than does First Indiana Plaza. Although its height is emphasized by two huge antennae that project from its roof like hypodermic syringes, Bank One is understated in color and therefore recedes to some extent in contrast with the more animated First Indiana Plaza.

Bank One Center is not a pacesetter building; it is conservative. Although it dominates the Indianapolis skyline through its height, the designers at The

Skyline view from steps of Central Library.

Market Tower's lobby.

The Stubbins Associates—perhaps in connection with other demands by the developers—were sensitive enough to the urban environment not to overstep the implicit limits imposed by its history and formal character. The best buildings in Indianapolis have always been strong parts of a well-orchestrated whole, as opposed to trendsetting or avant-garde for their own sake. A more dazzling building at the height of Bank One Center, whether in color, material, shape, or concept, would probably have seemed out of place here. At the very least, it would have drastically changed the rules of the game for future planning and development.

Even though each of these buildings to some degree helped knit the urban fabric together, they were all outclassed by a tower that was completed at 300 North Meridian, designed by Haldeman Miller Bregman Hamann of Dallas. Located at the southwest corner of University Park, this building could not possibly compete with any of the other nearby high rises in size or visual prominence. Therefore, the architects opted for an understated tower with rich dark color, subtle detailing, and allusions to older buildings, including the 1926 Chamber of Commerce next door. Three Hundred North Meridian rises as a dark reddish brown granite-clad slab with black glass windows. Entrances on Meridian and New York streets are surrounded in a brownish gray granite, a material also used to emphasize strip pilasters and triangular projections on the building faces above. The delicately modulated surface sweeps up to full height from an almost imperceptible curve above the fourth story with setbacks cut into the volume at the corners. At the top, however, the setback composition becomes a pedestal for an octagonal crown covered in brown standing-seam metal and marked by pilaster strips on the front above Meridian. Along the sides a series of gables leads toward an apsidal termination at the west, also finished in standing-seam metal.

Telescoping skyward, the building is extremely seductive in the skyline from all directions; yet, it offers a wealth of architectural details to the pedestrian as well. Inside, the commodious mahogany-paneled lobby is appointed with leather sofas and oriental carpets beneath large geometric chandeliers. This is the paradigmatic background building that holds its place elegantly and authoritatively without insult to adjacent properties, that becomes a backdrop for the park across the street, and that plays to the character and texture of the urban ensemble, thereby validating and celebrating it.

Other buildings that have contributed well to the urban context include, for example, the Associated Group Headquarters (AGH) at 120 Monument Circle by Ratio Architects. Its facade, finished in flame-cut and polished granite with burnished and polished stainless steel accents, stretches between copper-roofed pavilions at either end. All this defines one edge of Monument Circle and serves as a foil for the neo-Baroque Soldiers and Sailors Monument in its middle. The AGH facade recalls the material, color, and form of Art Deco buildings and thus relates to the idiosyncratic Circle Tower Building directly opposite without competing with it.

On the interior, AGH rejects its Art Deco sympathies by opening up to a white three-story skylit atrium of modernist stepped geometry and floating stairways arranged around a fountain centerpiece. From the exterior its pyramidal skylights form an interesting roofscape against the backdrop of adjacent buildings. However, the fountain is unnecessarily encumbered with weighty chunks of granite and thick plantings that prevent users from experiencing the court from any location but the periphery. This is disappointing since the atrium otherwise offers unanticipated spaciousness and dramatic views of surrounding high rises.

Top floors of 300 North Meridian.

Interior of Eiteljorg Museum.

At the turn of the decade, government and various cultural institutions began to move into new or expanded structures, of which the Eiteljorg Museum of American Indian and Western Art, the Indianapolis Children's Museum addition, and the Indiana Government Center are the most significant. The Eiteljorg Museum, by Browning Day Mullins Dierdorf, is a strong and beautiful design. Its Mankato stone and red sandstone exterior, including the heavy, naturally weathering timber entryway, recalls Pueblo and Hispanic American construction. The square volume of the building interacts with a low circular wall to create garden and patio spaces on the exterior and recall Anasazi Indian structures. The capacious interior is organized around a central light tower and stairway with easy circulation through the colorful exhibits on either side. Elegantly finished in dark wood set against creamy white walls, the museum has the hospitable feeling of a grand hacienda.

But, the location of the Eiteljorg between the Government Center and the grain elevators of the Acme-Evans Flour Company either anticipates some other cultural or architectural context along the White River in the future or unintentionally expresses the pragmatic diversity of the middle west by recalling the desert Southwest in the middle of Indianapolis. Despite the amount of land separating the museum from nearby buildings—and perhaps also because of the suburban overtone of that siting—the Eiteljorg Museum seems unfortunately destined to remain a kind of self-referential curiosity that may never feel completely at home where it is.

By contrast, Woollen Molzan and Partners' addition to the Indianapolis Children's Museum converted a grim brick tomb into a happy, colorful, and welcoming building with a spacious, sunny lobby. The aqua and blue arch beneath a yellow gable at the entrance on the Illinois Street side of the museum is set off by a serpentine wall in dark red brick with playfully scattered punched openings, one of the prominent examples of postmodernism in Indianapolis. The informality of the curved wall hints at the graceful curve of the grand staircase inside that establishes one of several choices for circulation through the new building. The museum design alludes to the tradition of classical buildings in Indianapolis, and because it is sited a mile north of the CBD, weaves that culture of public architecture into the larger metropolitan fabric.

The Indiana Government Center is a very different issue. To add much needed office space for its bureaucracy, the State of Indiana commissioned HNTB to create an office complex on the west or back side of the capitol. Because the Indiana State Library and Historical Building (1932) had established a low height and classical vocabulary that respected the statehouse, it became a reference for the new complex. The government center also incorporated two existing office buildings. One, designed in 1960 as a 13-story Corbusian slab, was remodeled to blend with the new structures: a difficult problem with a compromised solution. The well-groomed Government Center Parking Garage on West Washington by Kennedy Brown McQuiston Architects had been built to relieve parking.

Atrium of Indiana Government Center South.

Capitol Commons looking south.

At an initial glance, the government center seems to do everything anyone could expect of it. Long colonnaded concourses, punctuated by pavilions that echo the corner pavilions of the Capitol, surround the building and line Market Street between West Street and the statehouse. Surmounted by an attic story, the colonnades offer a spatial transition from street to interior and establish a good proportion and scale for the main volume of the building that rises one story higher behind them. They are designed in a reduced classicism of considerable restraint and simplicity. Executed in limestone, they reinforce the traditional language of government here. The colonnades also make a valiant, if frustrated, effort to relate the new building to the remodeled office tower.

However, there are numerous features in the government center that contradict the principles of classicism, the most obvious of which is a cavalier attitude about axial alignments. In several very important places, corridors and other axial elements that govern movement or define formal symmetries lead to a disconcerting shift of axis or a collision with an unsympathetic element. This is true of the misalignment between the new building and the remodeled office tower of 1960; and it is also found in the exterior courtyards of the new building itself, which include symmetrical elements disposed asymmetrically.

Despite this, one of the most striking new spaces in downtown Indianapolis is the skylit atrium that connects the main east-west corridor of the Government Center to the entrance on Market Street. This space, with its colonnade beneath setbacks with borrowed lights at the clerestory level, is a memorable counterpart of the skylit basilican atria of the statehouse wings and proves that interiors of integrity and nobility are still to be found in public places. This stands in stark contrast to suburban office buildings built for speculation in which lobbies are designed to impress through expensive materials and finishes but not to express any shared values on the part of users. Such a lobby can be seen in Three Woodfield Crossing, by Cooper Carry & Associates, in which far more splendid materials are used than in the government center but with far less impact. The effort to create a large, impressive lobby is conditioned here by the real purpose of the building, which is to compete for tenants, not serve a permanent public purpose or express democratic ideals.

Ambiguity between public and private realms is not limited to the suburbs but can also be found in the city. A good example exists in the area of the new Capitol Commons, a park that sits atop a public underground parking structure just south of the capitol building. As an open space, Capitol Commons creates a pleasant and potentially symbolic visual corridor between the statehouse and the expanded Indianapolis Convention Center whose facade, by Plus 4 Architects with Hellmuth Obata Kassabaum, defines the south side of the Commons. Neither the adjacent Hyatt Regency nor the Westin Hotel, by HNTB with Lamson & Condon, create a particularly appropriate edge for the Commons. Although the Hyatt Regency (with its deep triangular cut above a blank brick plane at street level) existed on its site prior to the design for the Commons, the Westin's absolutely unrelieved facade plane is inexcusable and sets up an unproductive tension with its neighbors by claiming the park for itself by virtue of its porte cochere. The Westin's planar flatness is further stressed when, seen from the Indiana Government Center, the facade curves around the corner to meet a series of blank volumes that seem to prop it up from behind. The facade of the convention center, taken by itself, is a fairly eclectic design and can best be explained in terms of the ensemble. It addresses the peculiarities of both hotels through its height, materials and color, and the geometry of its rotated end pavilions, while simultaneously speaking to the formal classicism of the statehouse through its symmetrical composition. It also partially masks the ungainly size of the Hoosier Dome behind it and thus helps it fit into the urban environment more gracefully without completely disappearing.

Narthex of St. Luke's Catholic Church.

Chapel at Christian Theological Seminary.

The Hyatt Regency and Westin hotels, along with the Embassy Suites hotel, by CSO/Architects, represent a phenomenon which can only be described as the suburbanization of the inner city. Each of them is a self-referential building that must be taken on its own terms in a way that only civic, governmental, institutional, or religious monuments—buildings that express communal, collective, or civic values—once were. These urban newcomers can best be compared to the architecture produced in such suburban office parks as Keystone at the Crossing, where office buildings, hotels, and shopping malls stand apart from each other in an open green space that has no purpose except to exhibit the buildings.

At 8888 Keystone Avenue, by 3D/International with Lamson & Condon, the cleverly designed towers of precast panels and mirrored curtain wall read eye-catchingly from the interstate belt. Up close, the combination of materials makes the building seem schizophrenic, unable to decide exactly what it is—glass box or concrete bunker. Entry by bridge from nearby parking structures avoids the dumpster sheds, electrical transformers, and delivery docks that are prominent distractions at ground level. The Emerald City illusion extends into The Fashion Mall where the controlled private commercial world offers tropical decor and climate year-round and no fear of encounters with people of difference in class, income, taste, or more substantive qualities. Because of our lack of faith in the exciting potentiality of authentic public space, the safe illusory world of the privatized commercial realm has become the only kind of public space that many of us ever experience. Our wish to disregard and avoid the broad human spectrum that informs democratic social and political life—not some abstract planning theory or economic formula—in the end, governs the design of all these buildings. Whether in city or suburb, they project who we are and how we want to see ourselves.

It would be impossible to comment on architecture in Indianapolis without mentioning significant educational buildings. Apart from the extensive sports facilities that have been erected along the White River by IUPUI, the IU Medical Research and Library Building, by Boyd/Sobieray Associates, is part of a large campus building program. A series of six pyramid-roofed glass pavilions that step up in height on the diagonal between two brick wings form a transition from the pedestrian to the institutional scale. Locked into the composition on the southeast, the pavilions expose their northwest sides to a triangular entry court and create a contrast between transparency and opaqueness, fragility and solidity.

The Technology Center at the Indiana Vocational and Technical College, by Everett I. Brown, works extraordinarily well within the context of its campus. A reinterpretation of classical architecture, it never resorts to imitation but relies on abstraction to make its statement. Corner quoins, rustication, cornices, and attic stories are treated in brick and stone layers over metal paneling. A triangular projection in metal and glass curtain wall on the Meridian side breaks the brick plane of the building for an emergency exit and implies a high-tech interior through its contrasting materials. The shops and laboratories on the west side of the Technology Center have a more factory-like imagery, but they accommodate a formal entry with a circular light tower on the interior. The surprising shift from a tan and green color scheme on the exterior to a blue palette on the interior further stresses the difference between the traditional envelope and the technological educational program inside.

Public schools in Indianapolis have also profited from excellent design work by local and regional firms. From complicated commissions such as Edison

Johnstone Residence.

Fire Station 13's canal elevation.

Junior High School (IPS 47) to more conventional programs such as the Fox Hill Elementary School, public education has been given superior architectural settings. Woollen Molzan and Partners created a strong sense of presence for Edison Junior High on its site above the White River by using it as a connection between its industrial and residential neighbors. They were also asked to accommodate a kindergarten in the same building with facilities for seventh and eighth graders. Edison's clear internal organization and bold external form, in jumbo brick with a green and white striped roof, created a much needed community focus that reinforces social and educational identity alike.

On a wooded site in northwest Indianapolis, James Architects & Engineers took a conventional program and divided it into four parts, each housed in a separate arm radiating from the central core, for Fox Hill Elementary School. The symmetrical geometry of its form, along with classical references, indicates a very different kind of context and community relationship than Edison Junior High. In this overtly affluent part of Indianapolis, there was no need to establish an identity in contrast to competing interests but rather a need to create an atmosphere of support in harmony with the existing natural environment.

Religious architecture also has flourished in Indianapolis since 1975, as several churches demonstrate. St. Luke's Roman Catholic Church, by Pecsok, Jelliffe & Randall, varies a traditional basilican arrangement by emphasizing its narthex with height and illumination. The brightly lit narthex, which also serves as the baptistery, is seen to best advantage through the gossamer screen of stained glass at the rear of the nave. The smaller and more compact Holy Cross Lutheran Church, by Woollen Molzan and Partners, uses polychromatic brick and surface patterning to enliven its exterior and refresh a conventional ecclesiastical composition. The symbolism of the cross is found not only in the cruciform plan but also in window mullions, especially in the oculus window above the altar.

Of all the recent religious buildings in Indianapolis, however, the chapel of Christian Theological Seminary by Edward Larrabee Barnes is the most

beautifully executed. Although the exterior appears rigid and even uninspiring with its precast aggregate paneling in rectilinear volumes, the interior is serene and calming. The startling effects of light passing through the refractive glass panels of its western windows creates an unexpected symbolism as well as a breathtaking aesthetic effect. Similarly, the use of a skylight on the east above the baptismal tank further reinforces the symbolic presence of light as a participating agent in the architecture and the services that are held there.

The various architectural monuments of Indianapolis exist within a topography that is predominantly residential. Of the many noteworthy dwellings, a few representative examples indicate their high quality and craft. They exist in a wide range of size and concept, from variations on the classical Palladian villa such as 5885 Stafford Way, by Blackburn Associates, with its barrel-vaulted portico, columns, and pilasters, to the radical classicism of 1209 West 64th Street, by Prince/Alexander, with its asymmetries, punched windows, and allusions to quoins in brick and split-face block masonry. Indianapolis residences also celebrate the architectural traditions of the Middle West, as in the addition to the Paul Residence by Muller and Brown, with its ceramic tile and shingled surfaces that recall the organic architecture of the Prairie School; in the house at 6053 Spring Mill Road, by Gordon Clark Associates, Inc., that adapts a stable as a residence, retaining its tower and the charm of its frame structure and detailing; or in the Johnstone Residence, 1065 West 52nd Street, by Kennedy Brown McQuiston Architects, an example of the transformation of midwestern rural vernacular architecture into a disciplined and sophisticated contemporary frame dwelling that meets the ground directly and is equally handsome from all views.

Although Indianapolis, like most midwestern cities, is characterized by neighborhoods of single-family dwellings, developments of the past 18 years have brought an increasing number of multiple family dwellings into existence. Concern about the future of the inner city has spurred the restoration of historic districts and the creation of new residential complexes and condominiums in a ring around the CBD. Canal Square Apartments, by

Sherman-Carter- Barnhart, of Lexington, and Canal Overlook Apartments, by Kennedy Brown McQuiston Architects, have taken advantage of the White River Canal channel in the northwest quadrant of the CBD. There is an unmistakably suburban quality in the scale and form of both complexes, especially in their low height, horizontal composition, and use of gabled elements, all strong contrasts with the nearby government complex and commercial high rises of the CBD. However, they also introduce the urban imagery of towers, bridges, arcades, and quays along the canal frontage in order to increase pedestrian and outdoor life along the water's edge. Surprisingly, Fire Station 13, by Browning Day Mullins Dierdorf, is even more engaging. Its principal facade, in two shades of split-face block with teal trim beneath a small clerestory, fronts West Ohio for functional reasons. Its rear facade, conceived as a series of pavilions, backs up to the canal where it set precedent for the scale and relationship to the water followed by the apartment complexes just north.

To the east and northeast of the CBD, other residential developments, mostly at a low, suburban scale, offer a variety of options. Renaissance Place, by Browning Day, for example, is a group of low-density condominium duplexes arranged on green lawns around short cul-de-sacs that could just as easily be in an outlying subdivision. By contrast, Lockerbie Townhouses, by Archonics Design Partnership, introduce a denser row house with small gardens in front of tall, narrow, and deep units. Lockerbie Townhouses are more urban in concept, though probably no more typical of historic inner-city Indianapolis than Renaissance Place. On the other hand, the introduction of a residential vernacular derived from the Victorian era, as in the seductive house at 627 East Vermont, by Bentley La Rosa Salasky Design, while appropriate as infill in historic districts, comes off more like a stage set, as does the contiguous neighborhood of neo-Victorian houses fronting brick streets.

Much of what is typical about Indianapolis architecture today—the good and the questionable alike—is inextricably tied to the way in which architects, patrons, developers, builders, and government and civic leaders have perceived their relationship and obligations to the urban fabric. The early planners of Indianapolis laid out an arrangement of public spaces seldom equaled in grace and elegance anywhere else in the United States. The inheritors of this master plan really needed to do little more to fulfill its promise than to populate it with appropriate buildings. It was easy for this to happen before the middle of the century but has, for many reasons, been increasingly difficult since then. Inevitable tensions have grown between a city plan suited to a midwestern state capital in the 19th century and the needs, desires, aspirations, and realities of life in the last quarter of the 20th century.

Indianapolis has not escaped the fate of social, political, economic, demographic, and cultural change, despite its traditional demeanor. These changes have brought about pragmatic planning and development in contrast to the classical planning that characterized the city of Indianapolis in its first 125 years. Pragmatic planning has brought the Hoosier Dome into the CBD, but it has also created the huge holes in the urban fabric where radical surgery has cut out an architectural density and historical context that will never be regained, even with substantial new development. Yet,

Construction site of Circle Centre mall.

Indianapolis has managed to produce many significant answers to architectural questions, even when those questions have been difficult. Discrepancies between residential and high-rise scale in the inner city, the question of whether avant-garde architecture can be as appropriate in the urban fabric as conservative design solutions, the avoidance of authentic urban experience versus the attraction of stylish but dated suburban malls and office parks—these and many related issues will continue to be the issues that Indianapolis confronts as the century turns. It will be worthwhile to look back in 2020 to see how these issues are being resolved 200 years after the founding of Indianapolis.

Robert A. Benson, Ph.D., is Chair of the Department of Architecture, Miami University, Oxford, Ohio. He is also a contributing editor of *Inland Architect* and was formerly architecture critic of *The Detroit News*.

Urban Design
in Indianapolis

by Harold W. Rominger with Scott Truex and Robert Wilch

Indianapolis began abruptly in 1820, politically positioned in the center of the state, with a "Mile Square" plan that was drafted to guide its development. Alexander Ralston borrowed and simplified the plan concept from his experience with Pierre L'Enfant who designed Washington, D.C. This story has been repeated many times in Indianapolis as we have fought to carve a dramatic form from a flat landscape, far from ocean, lake, or mountain. The natural environment has proved to be of little consequence in shaping the form of the city. The hardwood forest that confronted the early settlers was not an impediment; it simply provided the material for constructing the new city. White River, which was incorrectly thought to be navigable, was avoided because of mosquitoes and intermittent flooding. As time passed, the river was bridged and sufficiently controlled to allow an uninterrupted flow of streets and development.

During the last 173 years, Indianapolis has grown and evolved primarily through the manipulation of the transportation systems that serve it. Planning bench marks in our evolution have included moving the National Road to pass through the city, creating the first Union Railway Station, hiring John C. Olmsted to develop a park and parkway system, developing the nation's most extensive interurban system, placing the Soldiers and Sailors Monument in the Circle to mark permanently the center of the city, hiring George Kessler to refine the park and parkway plan, developing the World War Memorial Plaza, enacting one of the nation's first zoning ordinances, building the largest number of interstates passing through any one city, being one of the first cities to enact legislation to consolidate planning and eventually government at the county level, and rebuilding the downtown.

Indianapolis is now the center of an urban area of over one million people, located in central Indiana, served by an extensive interstate highway system and an international airport. Its economy is diverse. Pharmaceuticals, electronics, insurance, government, and automobile-related industries dominate. However, in recent years tourism, entertainment, conventions, and service-based industries have grown, replacing job losses in manufacturing. Indianapolis has, to its advantage, historically attached itself to new styles, trends, and economic opportunities.

Indianapolis has continuously grappled with its identity as a city, and there is little evidence that the quest is over. In 1990 as a part of preparing an update of the downtown plan (The 1990 Regional Center Plan), a two-day workshop was conducted to try to focus on a theme for the plan. Dennis Frenchman, who has consulted with many communities across the country and has helped them devise themes for "cultural tourism," was hired as a facilitator. After two days of discussion there were still four themes and little hope of narrowing to just one. And so, Indianapolis is a "Capital City" reflecting tradition and stability, a "Crossroads City" reflecting its historic development and contemporary culture, a "Dynamic City" reflecting the focus on sports, tourism, and competitiveness, and a "Livable City" reflecting the commitment to neighborhood, community, and diversity.

We have always been nervous about our future, always looking outward to make sure that we are competitive. This concern has for the most part served us well. We have usually hired designers with the best credentials to design our public spaces and buildings. The "visions" created by these advisors has often remained a vision. This work has been important in defining the scope and quality of what does eventually get built. Plans not followed that were prepared by Victor Gruen (1965) and Evans Woollen (1975) for IUPUI; by Groves Associates for the Canal; by SOM (Walter Netch) for the Washington Street Corridor; and by HNTB (with Charles Moore, Cesar Pelli, Angela Danadjieva, and others) for the White River State Park have become a part of the context in which incremental decisions have been made (or not made).

There are so many themes that could be pursued when writing about urban design that it is difficult to focus without omitting important pieces of the story. Urban design is an imprecise term. It is used to describe many types of planning and design activities. The range of meaning can include work as grand as establishing regional growth policies and as detailed as designing a single sign. The common thread, however, is that the work focuses on physical design activities in which the general public has an interest. Professional practitioners include architects, landscape architects, and planners. Each profession brings a different set of experiences to the table that filters the worth of a policy or project through different eyes. Architects will probably see the aesthetic and functional relationship of buildings as most important, landscape architects will see the natural and social environment as a priority, while planners will see economics and process as a priority. Many urban design "teams" have members from each discipline.

Urban design is practiced from three different work environments: the public, the academic, and the private. Each of these sectors plays a different role in composing the picture of urban design in Indianapolis.

PUBLIC

The contemporary history of urban design and planning started with legislation in 1955 that created a Metropolitan Planning Department within county government. From its inception, design professionals were hired to manage the Planning Department. Calvin Hamilton, a landscape architect who went on to serve as planning director in Los Angeles for many years, was the first director. John Walls, a planner who had worked for Cal Hamilton in Pittsburgh, returned to Indianapolis to head up the newly formed Greater Indianapolis Progress Committee. The next planning director was F. Ross Vogelgesang, also a landscape architect, who served until 1978. During this period aggressive plans were prepared for the downtown, Lockerbie Square, the City Market, and the White River Corridor. Also, development standards related to landscaping, signage, and parking were adopted, which have dramatically improved the image of the downtown.

During the period from 1955 to 1970 very important groundwork was laid for the changes that occurred in the 1970s and 1980s. Commitments to build an urban university were forged, one of the nation's first historic primary zoning districts was formed for Lockerbie Square, and the Regional Center Zoning Ordinance requiring aesthetic review of all downtown development was enacted. Several design professionals who worked for government went on to carry their concern for the city into their private practice. Notable among this group are Jim Browning, Alan Day, K. P. Singh, and Don Perry.

Development during the 1950s and 1960s was primarily suburban and the downtown continued to lose economic influence as businesses, especially retailers, followed their clientele to the suburbs. Other major changes taking place added temporarily to the negative downtown development atmosphere. In the 1960s interstate highway right-of-way, the site for IUPUI, and the site for Riley Towers were all acquired, displacing lower-income residents and putting pressure on the existing housing stock. The issues surrounding locating IUPUI in the Regional Center is a good example of how difficult it is to "serve the public interest" when making urban design decisions. How could all of the aspirations and needs of the disparate interest groups have been met? During this same period, the development of the City-County Building paved the way for consolidating city and county government, construction of the Convention Center took place, and the discussion of the need for a downtown arena occurred. People were beginning to see an expanded role for downtown.

In 1970 the Consolidated Cities Act created countywide government that recaptured the suburbs and the suburban vote. The Planning Department was made a division of the new Department of Metropolitan Development. Mayor Richard Lugar appointed David Meeker, an architect, director of the new department and named Michael Carroll, a planner, his deputy. The Metropolitan Development Commission that was appointed to oversee the new department had several notable members who were advocates for quality design. Charles Whistler, who headed up the task force that negotiated the redevelopment of Lockefield Gardens and Indiana Avenue and cochaired the 1980 Regional Center Plan Committee; Dr. Frank Lloyd, who serves as a member of the White River State Park Commission in charge of planning and was cochair of the 1990 Regional Center Plan Committee;

Monument Circle.

City Market.

"Niel" Alig, who was a strong supporter of the downtown; and Richard DeMars were among the members of the 1970 Metropolitan Development Commission. From the private sector Fred Tucker and Dan Evans worked to build the momentum necessary to initiate a downtown renaissance. Jim Kittle, Larry Conrad, Don Tanselle, Tom Binford, and many others from the private sector ably supported these efforts over the past 23 years.

The first Regional Center Plan linked to zoning was adopted in 1970. Lilly Endowment committed to help rebuild the downtown. Early projects included the City Market restoration, Market Street beautification, the Indianapolis Sports Center, and the Indiana Theatre. Downtown Indianapolis was in an ideal position to take advantage of the development "boom" that occurred in the 1980s. The *1980 Regional Center Plan* prepared by the Division of Planning provided a strong framework for the downtown growth that took place in the 1980s. Almost six million square feet of office space was constructed, and over 1.8 billion dollars invested in the downtown. The plan was updated again in 1990 because of dramatic change that had occurred. John Walls and Dr. Frank Lloyd were cochairs of the 1990 task force, and planners Harold Rominger, Robert Wilch, John Byrnes, and Laura Wise-Ewing staffed the Regional Center planning office.

Mayor William Hudnut; Deputy Mayors David Frick and John Krauss; Metropolitan Development Directors Robert Kennedy, David Carley, and "Mike" Higbee; and Planning Administrators Nick Shelley and Stu Reller continued the support for downtown during their tenures with the city. The period from 1970 to 1990 can be summarized as a period when strong leadership from the public, not-for-profit, and private sectors collaborated to build a strong downtown.

ACADEMIC

Integral to urban design efforts in Indianapolis has been the involvement of the public in helping designers to create their visions. Students, professionals, and the general public have volunteered their time to participate on committees, in class projects, and in design charrettes.

Cities are the most complex product of our culture. We construct simplified "models" in order to explain the various phenomena that we associate with cities. Urban designers and clients intuitively use criteria related to their own experiences and set of values when making a decision or debating an issue. It is the tension between the following paradigms that makes synthesizing "the right" design solution so difficult. People base their actions upon the belief that:

Cities are holistic organisms that grow and change in predictable ways based on measurable trends. Transportation and economic planners use trend analysis to forecast the future.

Cities are composed of social groups, with definable values, that compete and interact in ways to influence the city's form and function. Participatory decision making, conflict resolution, civil rights protection and minority participation are examples of activities derived from this model.

Cities are economic machines that respond to the public's demands for goods and services, but which must also compete on a regional, national, and global basis for resources, markets, and jobs. Value engineering, "right sizing," flattening the organization, etc. are examples of activities that derive from this belief.

Indiana Government Center North.

Circle Theatre.

Cities are composed of the natural environment, public infrastructure, public facilities, and private facilities, the value and beauty of which can be monitored and modified. This description—supported by scientists, naturalists, environmentalists, urban designers, engineers, and architects—often generates highly detailed data about specific issues that are directed at increasing long-term human viability. Urban design, infrastructure repair, environmental policy, etc. are examples of activities that are generated.

Cities are the product of incremental decisions, discoveries, technology, and inventions. The most obvious evidence of this model would be to track the effect that the internal combustion engine or that electricity has had on the form of the city. At another scale this model would contend that all of our actions and decisions "ripple" through time affecting our future.

Cities are the product of leaders who use their power (derived from wealth, political influence, or the ability to motivate people) to determine the city's form and function. Political leaders, business leaders, and lobbyists interact daily to forge alliances, gain influence, etc.

The way we perceive cities directly affects what we value, what is seen as good or bad. If a project (1) positively affects our economy, (2) favors one social group to the detriment of another, (3) damages the environment, and (4) has a positive effect on our self-image and sense of place, the total value of the project is left unclear. Most urban design activities call for compromise. Interestingly many of the historic urban design projects that we view as good were the products of people who were totally insensitive to the paradigms above. The development of Olmsted's Central Park and Haussmann's plan for Paris uprooted disadvantaged people but dramatically increased the value of land and property. Today it is difficult to imagine Manhattan without Central Park or Paris without its boulevards. In Indianapolis the development of the World War Memorial Plaza in the 1920s uprooted churches, moved apartment houses, and used funds allocated to the state for World War I veterans.

It is critical to devise and communicate a vision for public consideration and debate. In 1967 the University of Illinois prepared the Indianapolis Centrum Study. The model that was constructed for this study was on display in the Observatory of the City-County Building until 1983 and for many years contributed to helping develop people's vision of the downtown.

In 1980 a storefront design center (the City Center) was opened on Monument Circle to encourage public access to the Regional Center Planning Process. A model of the downtown was constructed as a "center-piece" while the plan was being prepared. Thousands of people visited the center, responded to surveys, and talked to planners.

One of the primary methods for establishing a community vision has been the "design charrette workshop." This French term has become synonymous with public participatory activities that engage design and planning professionals with the community. Charrette workshops help refine visions that reflect heritage as well as aspirations for the future. Indianapolis has used charrettes to generate community involvement beginning with neighborhood-based charrettes for the Model Cities area in 1969. In 1980 nationally prominent architects, landscape architects, and planners envisioned a park at the western edge of downtown encompassing the long-neglected White River Corridor. This Park Design Assistance Team (PDAT) generated a new image for the city with the integration of park, recreation, and entertainment activities in the daily functions of the city. The use of charrettes has contin-

Market Street from Alabama Street looking west.

ued through the recently completed Regional Center Plan 2010. A Ball State University class of students, under the supervision of Scott Truex from the College of Architecture and Planning, conducted six public workshops focused on refining the downtown plan. The charrettes included two days of intense design and planning activities. Planning and design professionals, college students, advocacy groups, and neighborhood residents engaged in establishing an agenda for community development in the study areas.

The charrette and the storefront studio have been two very important vehicles for involving the community in planning and design. This type of open-door activity should continue to provide a public interface for the community.

DOWNTOWN (THE REGIONAL CENTER)

Indianapolis is a very cohesive city. The Circle that Alexander Ralston placed in the center of his "Mile Square" plan still functions as the town square. The Soldiers and Sailors Monument has marked this point since 1901, and on pleasant days its steps and walls provide seating for hundreds of downtown workers at lunchtime. The "car culture" youth have chosen it as their main drag in the evening, and the Indianapolis Symphony Orchestra and Columbia Club open their front doors onto the space. Young newlyweds often take a traditional drive around the Circle with their entourage following.

The idea of downtown Indianapolis as the Regional Center was articulated as a part of the 1970 Regional Center Plan. The name is more than a label; it is the vision that has driven our rebuilding efforts for the past 23 years. The goal has been to place those activities that serve the people of central Indiana (and in many cases the entire state) into this downtown location in order to provide better access and to have a focus for the celebration of our culture. Federal government agencies, state government, local government,

regional education opportunities, regional health care, and convention and regional entertainment facilities have been concentrated here to provide a strong service center for our region.

The downtown has a mix of uses that is perhaps unique to Indianapolis. There is prime office space adjacent to the Greyhound Bus Station and public housing in the 400 block of North Meridian Street, our "alpha" street. Although these situations might change, the diversity that is engendered is very positive. The tendency to relegate low-income housing and public transportation activities to the perimeter of the downtown can weaken the entire system. As real estate values increase in the "core," parking lots and service-type uses are also pushed to the fringes. Nearby neighborhoods that could benefit from their proximity to jobs, restaurants, etc. are separated by a wall of parking garages and service buildings.

The ultimate urban design goal is to create public spaces, places, and forums so sublime that the rich and the poor, the abled and disabled, and the young and the old share a common communion when experiencing them. The earth is a sacred place. We all know the power that "place" has; the Grand Canyon, a rugged cliff battered by the ocean, the Aurora Borealis, an empty cathedral with western sun through centuries-old windows are images easily visualized and can stand as metaphors for describing the peak experience to be sought of large-scale urban design. The opposite universal metaphors for small-scale urban design could be the campfire on a cool, cloudless evening or even the bar on the "Cheers" television show. If we expect less of our built environment we are demeaning our own culture.

Among the many excellent urban design activities in the past 18 years, the new Indiana Government Center stands out as being exceptional for a number of reasons. This project transformed a surface parking lot, railroad spur,

Market Street, Indiana Government Center.

and two existing buildings into a critical connection between the business core, IUPUI, and the Canal. The aesthetic strength of this project is that the buildings are used to frame the Capitol Building and adjacent streets. Colonnades are provided to protect pedestrians, and sublevel walkways link the south basin of the Canal to the corner of Illinois and Washington streets. This commitment from Governor Robert Orr to provide new facilities for state government in downtown Indianapolis has reinforced the strength of the Regional Center by providing jobs, state services, and important "connective tissue" to the fabric of the downtown.

John Fleck, Executive Director of the Indiana State Office Building Commission, assembled a large team of local design firms and a 10-member Design Advisory Committee to review the work. Members included: Kendall Cochran, Office of Governor Robert Orr; Howard H. Wolner, Indiana State Office Building Commission; Eleanor F. Bookwalter, Indiana State Office Building Commission; Ken Englund, Indiana Society of Architects; Robert Fisher, Dean, College of Architecture and Planning, Ball State University; Robert Amico, Dean, School of Architecture, University of Notre Dame; M. J. (Jay) Brodie, Pennsylvania Avenue Development Corporation, Washington, D.C.; Elizabeth Plater-Zyberk, Architect, Miami, Florida; and Rudolfo Machado, Machado and Silvetti Associates, Inc., Boston, Massachusetts.

The design firms hired to design facilities were: MSE Engineers and Rundell-Ernstberger for master plan development and site planning; Howard, Needles, Tammen and Bergendoff and associate architects Edmund Hafer and Walter Blackburn for the south building; CSO/Architects and associate architects Cole Associates and 3D/International for the north building; Browning Day Mullins Dierdorf, James Architects and Engineers, and The McGuire and Shook Corporation for the judicial facility (project terminated due to funding constraints); Kennedy Brown McQuiston for the south garage; and Ratio Architects for the north garage.

The Design Advisory Committee helped develop design goals and guidelines and also reviewed and commented on all design work. This process produced a very good project to the credit of all those involved and could serve as a model procedure for other significant public projects. It allows for the primary design work to stay with local firms but provides for national review and expertise.

Keeping the downtown strong and cohesive is a relatively easy job when compared to making the suburbs work better. Over 60 percent of the land and improvements in the downtown are publicly owned. If public agencies are sensitive to the plan for the Regional Center, much of the work can and has been accomplished through public investment. A majority of the downtown literally belongs to the citizens of Indiana and Indianapolis.

The Pyramids at College Park.

SUBURBS AND BEYOND

The suburbs are a different matter; private developers often work to their own detriment as incremental decisions create image and access problems. Pressure to lessen design controls, increase profitability, and increase tax base have helped create suburban conditions that will be difficult to correct. Castleton Square is close to being choked by its own success.

Indianapolis is a low density city (3.1 people per acre). Residential districts and jobs are dispersed throughout the community. Only one in six jobs is located in the Regional Center. People who do not have personal access to a private automobile are separated from job, entertainment, educational, and residential alternatives. This includes not only the poor but also young people, elderly, and many in one-car households.

The move to the suburbs accelerated after World War II due to new household formations and the promise of a less-polluted environment. The 1944 "Post War Plan for Indianapolis" had as major goals to "halt the trend toward decentralization," to "cure the evil smoke problem," and to correct the unequitable tax rates. In the days of coal-burning furnaces, open trash burning, and leaded gasoline the urban air was toxic. Lower densities were appealing. The search for cleaner air, better schools, safer streets, and upward social mobility is still with us today.

Many of the problems with suburban development are not due to poor design. They were created by economically driven consumer choices resulting from a competitive residential marketplace. A gridiron street pattern, sidewalks, and sewers are more expensive to construct and maintain than cul-de-sacs, drainage ditches, and septic systems. Mixed land uses do not guarantee a safe resale value. Small pedestrian-related retailing cannot compete with large centralized supermarkets, drugstores, and hardware stores. The economic values that we espouse, competition and economies of scale, have created the contemporary suburban environment. Reduced residential density, reduced household size, and increased market share required to support our larger shops, schools, and businesses mean that there are few opportunities for neighborhood-scaled shopping or services.

There are some signs that the suburbs can be improved. The new landscaping, curbs, and sidewalks along 86th Street have transformed a totally inhospitable street into a more hospitable one. One hope for suburban salvation is to create public pedestrian-scaled, mixed-use oases for occasional respite. Zionsville is the best older example that we have. The best new example is Keystone at the Crossing. Shopping, hotel, entertainment, dining, and offices are linked with sidewalks, walkways, and landscaping. If apartments were integrated with this development it would provide a reasonable suburban prototype.

If we want to respond effectively to the current growth pattern of low-density residential development and workplace dispersion, it will require changes. Regional government and schools, balanced economic and environmental policies, and equitable taxing policies would all need to be invoked to have any meaningful effect. Communication technology is already allowing further dispersion by allowing employees to work in the home. We are one regional community, and the sooner we deal with the problem of fragmentation and parochial decision making, the sooner we can address important regional issues.

Street scene in the Old Northside.

Obelisk Square.

SUMMARY

What urban design activities have we done well, and what have we done not so well since 1975 when the last *Indianapolis Architecture* book was published? The single most important event in the past 20 years has been the commitment from Lilly Endowment to support public physical development projects and to assist in rebuilding the Regional Center. This commitment started with the City Market in 1973 and has continued uninterrupted for 20 years. This public-private partnership has transformed the downtown in miraculous ways. Without its commitment to quality and its leadership, much of what we have now could not have happened.

The positive image that this commitment provided has created the public expectation that we can complete the job of renewing the downtown. In fact, our expectations are so high that when a project takes longer than expected, such as the Circle Centre mall, we are unsympathetic. One evening, a man on his way to a Monday night football game at the Hoosier Dome was overheard explaining to a friend that those "holes in the ground" for the Circle Centre mall were another one of Hudnut's follies. He did not understand, or had forgotten, how it came to pass that the Colts were playing at a domed stadium in downtown Indianapolis. Risk taking is integral to success.

Downtown, the Regional Center, is increasingly important to the community. It provides a strong central identity point for our own self-image and for purposes of marketing our resources in a very competitive global economy. The existing infrastructure can also be used more efficiently if we focus our resources on renewing the downtown and our older neighborhoods. The downtown still offers the most accessible jobs, and its proximity to lower-income neighborhoods makes it an important link in providing many with access to the American dream.

WORKING BUT UNFINISHED EVENTS (1973-93)

• Failure to complete White River State Park—The Washington Street relocation and landscaping, the Water Company Pump House Restoration (1981), the Indianapolis Zoo (1988), and the Eiteljorg Museum (1991) have all been completed, but the commitments needed to complete this project have been difficult to acquire. The "vision" needs to be refreshed. As time passes and the original design concepts are discarded, there is a much greater chance that incremental decisions will undermine the potential for the park. The park needs to be connected. Washington Street improvements, the Canal Improvement Project, and the Convention Center converge on the "front door" of the White River State Park, but there is no door there. Only a few lunchtime joggers have a pedestrian sense of where the zoo is.

• Failure to complete the Circle Centre mall—Department-store type retailing in the United States has been going through major changes for many years. Consolidations and bankruptcies, combined with sales losses due to recessions, and competition from discount stores and telemarketing have made it difficult to get the commitments to keep this project on schedule. This project forms a critical piece of the "fabric" of the downtown that will connect employment centers with the Union Station and convention facilities.

• Failure to rebuild older neighborhoods—There are some success stories. Several projects by community development corporations and individual home owner investments in historic districts have made progress in improving older neighborhoods, but the resources to make dramatic improvements have not been forthcoming. Recent initiatives by the city to concentrate on "neighborhoods" could improve this situation.

Capitol Commons.

Athenaeum parapet.

• Failure to rebuild infrastructure—The recent report by GIFT (Getting Indianapolis Fit for Tomorrow) outlined the severity of this problem. Indianapolis has 6,618 lane miles of streets, 477 bridges, 2,400 miles of sewers, 9,331 acres of parks, and 6 million square feet of floor space in publicly owned buildings. The report estimates that it will cost an average of $110 million per year for 10 years to repair and rehabilitate infrastructure. Recent initiatives by the city will improve this situation.

WORST EVENTS AND NONEVENTS (1975-93)

• Failure to deal effectively with public transportation.

• Lack of regional growth and environmental policy.

• Failure to beautify interstate highway corridors and entry points.

• Failure to restore the World War Memorial and the Athenaeum and to reuse the City Market Rathskeller.

• Failure to improve the water quality and recreational potential of White River.

• Failure to develop a public observation level at the top of the state's tallest building. The Bank One Tower can be seen from as far away as 15 miles, but when you arrive in the downtown, there is no good public vantage point from which to view the city.

• The untimely deaths of Larry Conrad, Michael A. Carroll, Frank McKinney, Jr., and R. V. Welch.

BEST EVENTS (1975-93)

• Commitment from Lilly Endowment—Tom Lake, Richard Ristine, Will Hays, Jim Morris, Mike Carroll, Gordon St. Angelo, and John Mutz.

• Beautification of public spaces—Obelisk Square (1976), Monument Circle (1978), and Market Street (1980).

• Restoration of landmarks—City Market (1973), Union Station (1986), Soldiers and Sailors Monument (1987; 1990), State Capitol Building (1988), Circle Theatre (1984), Indiana Theatre (1980), Walker Theatre (1982-87), and Lockefield Gardens (1987).

• Designation and protection of historic neighborhoods—Chatham-Arch, Fletcher Place, Fountain Square, Herron-Morton Place, Lockefield Gardens, Old Northside, and St. Joseph.

• Indiana University-Purdue University at Indianapolis—major landscaping, upper level walkways and circulation, and garages. Natatorium, Track and Field Stadium, athletic fields, Science Education and Technology Building(s), Medical Research Facility, Riley Children's Hospital, and Library.

River Promenade on White River Park.

Lower Central Canal looking south.

• Indiana Convention Center and Hoosier Dome—Hoosier Dome (1984), Capitol Commons (1988), and current expansion (1993).

• Lilly Corporate Center—commitment to concentrate corporate offices and research at McCarty Street, new facilities, new entry plaza, landscaping, and garages.

• Methodist Hospital—expansion of facilities at Capitol Avenue, landscaping, garages, Life Leadership Center, community advocacy, and support.

• North Meridian Street—designation as a historic district on the National Register of Historic Places in 1986.

• Indiana Government Center—offices, garages, conference center, and linkage to Canal Basin.

• Lower Central Canal (1987-93)—canal basin, fire station, bridges, and corridor.

• 1980 and 1990 Regional Center Plans and Planning Process—Over 460

people representing various downtown constituencies contributed their time and talents to the preparation of the 1990 Regional Center Plan. This plan was adopted as a segment of the Marion County Comprehensive Plan and is the legal reference for administering the Regional Center Zoning Ordinance (aesthetic review).

Harold W. Rominger is an architect and planner who has worked in both the public and private sectors. He was head of the Urban Design Section of the City of Indianapolis from 1970 to 1983 and a member of the design team at James Architects and Engineers from 1983 to 1989. For the past four years he has been a consultant to the city .

Scott Truex, AICP, who is an assistant professor of Urban Planning at Ball State University, has had extensive experience with neighborhood and community development projects.

Robert Wilch, architect and planner, has been with the City of Indianapolis, Planning Division for 21 years working in the areas of neighborhood, park, and Regional Center planning.

Historic Preservation in Indianapolis since 1975

by James A. Glass

HISTORIC PRESERVATION IN 1975

Historic preservation was one of the chief themes of the 1975 *Indianapolis Architecture*. Although the guidebook included many contemporary buildings, a majority of the entries presented architecture of the past. Because no formal survey of historic buildings in Indianapolis had been published before, the guidebook helped the public discover the rich architectural heritage of the city. There was excitement in the air: after decades of repudiating or ignoring the buildings of the 19th and early 20th centuries, the architectural profession had begun to take an interest in what had preceded post-World War II Modernism. The young architects who collaborated on the guidebook freely praised aesthetically pleasing works of past designers. They also critiqued the work of contemporaries who failed to provide the same degree of attention to detail, scale, materials, and craftsmanship that older buildings often conveyed. The delight that the authors took in the richly detailed elevations and interiors of such landmarks as the Soldiers and Sailors Monument, Maennerchor, Central Library, Athenaeum, and Union Station carried them into repeated endorsements of preservation and expressions of chagrin when the new resulted in destruction of something pleasing of the old.

Lockerbie Street.

Eden-Talbott House in the Old Northside.

In addition to providing the first systematic inventory of the city's historic buildings, the authors were the first to point to the existence of historic districts, i.e., areas with distinctive and cohesive identities that denoted a sense of time and place. The guidebook also expanded the public's concept of historic preservation beyond the limited notion of a few landmark institutional buildings and house museums to the many examples of vernacular architecture throughout the commercial and residential areas of the city. Little workers' cottages in Lockerbie Square and on Fletcher Avenue, dilapidated commercial buildings along Indiana and Massachusetts avenues, and old wholesale houses on South Meridian Street all made their appearance in the pages of *Indianapolis Architecture*.

It would not be an exaggeration to say that the authors of the 1975 guidebook saw historic preservation as part of the future of architecture in Indianapolis. They hoped that the book would awaken the public to the potential contributions to "livability" in the city of the future that architectural landmarks of the past and historic neighborhoods could make. One of the underlying themes of *Indianapolis Architecture* certainly was that the architectural profession and its clients should not continue to build new structures indiscriminately on the sites of the city's historic architecture.

A "BOOM" IN HISTORIC PRESERVATION

Indianapolis Architecture helped launch a boom in historic preservation activity in Indianapolis. At the same time that the guidebook was under preparation between 1973 and 1975, the city administration of Mayor Richard G. Lugar responded to increasing public interest in historic districts and landmarks by persuading the Indiana General Assembly to pass a new statute broadening the authority and jurisdiction of the Indianapolis Historic Preservation Commission.[1] In 1975, shortly before the guidebook appeared, the Lugar administration provided Community Development funds to enable the commission to hire its first staff members, and city sponsorship and encouragement of historic preservation began on a large scale.

The commission's expanded powers and acquisition of staff positions coincided with two other developments that helped spur historic preservation efforts during the next 10 years. First, Historic Landmarks Foundation of Indiana, a nonprofit preservation organization founded by Eli Lilly, assumed an aggressive role in purchasing and restoring key historic properties in Lockerbie Square, the city's first historic district, and in the Old Northside, a potential district north of the downtown area. Under its executive director,

Middle Drive in Woodruff Place.

Union Station waiting room.

J. Reid Williamson, Jr., who arrived in Indianapolis from Savannah, Georgia, in 1974, the foundation created a revolving fund in the Old Northside that soon was purchasing abandoned houses, fixing them up, and reselling them with protective covenants to buyers interested in restoration.

The second development was the local expression of a popular movement sweeping the nation. The so-called "back to the city" movement was made up of young people who worked downtown and liked the idea of living nearby in historic houses. The movement was also conservation-oriented, drawing inspiration from the shortages created by the 1973 OPEC oil embargo and from the growing realization that energy resources were limited. Rehabilitation of existing housing stock consumed less resources than new construction and promised a reduction in gasoline consumption through less commuting between suburban areas and the downtown.

In Indianapolis "urban pioneers" began restoring dilapidated workers' cottages in Lockerbie Square. Together with Historic Landmarks Foundation, the Indianapolis Garden Club, the Junior League of Indianapolis, and the City of Indianapolis, the pioneers started to transform the "blighted" appearance of the neighborhood around James Whitcomb Riley's home into a very attractive urban neighborhood. New street pavements, tree plantings, sidewalks, light standards, and even houses appeared in the district between 1975 and 1980. In the Old Northside, a neighborhood of large residences from the late 19th and early 20th centuries, another group of "pioneers" was restoring Victorian homes with care. In 1976 Historic Landmarks Foundation, the Indianapolis Historic Preservation Commission, and the Junior League helped define the area and give it a name when they nominated the Old Northside to the National Register of Historic Places. Four years

later, the residents obtained designation of the neighborhood as a historic area under the protection of the Preservation Commission.

Designation offered assurance to the residents of historic districts that their property values would be protected. The commission would prevent the demolition of vacant historic residences and ensure that remaining historic buildings would be rehabilitated or restored according to consistent historic preservation standards and guidelines. In 1977 the commission also conducted a countywide windshield survey that identified many additional potential historic districts throughout Marion County, such as the former towns of Irvington and New Augusta, sections of the Meridian-Kessler neighborhood, the cities of Beech Grove and Southport, and a multitude of small possible districts in the downtown area. Some of the downtown residential districts were soon under restoration and came under commission designation and protection in the early 1980s: Fletcher Place southeast of the Mile Square; Chatham-Arch north of Lockerbie Square; Fountain Square, at the southern end of Virginia Avenue; and Herron-Morton Place, north of the Old Northside. One obvious historic neighborhood, Woodruff Place, despite much public attention and restoration activity, never was designated, but became revitalized under the leadership of the Woodruff Place Civic League.

Historic Landmarks Foundation complemented the governmental protections by continuing to acquire, market, and resell threatened houses. The Old Northside Revolving Fund, Inc., which was initially operated jointly by Historic Landmarks and the Junior League of Indianapolis, gradually expanded its efforts into other historic areas. During the 1980s, the foundation renamed the project Fund for Landmark Indianapolis Properties (FLIP),

Sears Building in the 1970s.

Sears, Roebuck and Company Building in the 1930s.

which has steadily added to the momentum toward restoration in the historic neighborhoods and helped ward off demolition of additional neighborhood buildings.

A powerful governmental stimulus to private investment in historic buildings throughout the city and county became available in 1981, when the Federal Economic Recovery Tax Act of that year authorized generous federal income tax credits of 25 percent for rehabilitations of income-producing buildings listed in the National Register of Historic Places. A host of local and out-of-town developers and investors took advantage of the tax credit program during the 1980s, and soon deteriorated commercial buildings, office buildings, industrial buildings, and wholesale buildings that preservationists had despaired of preserving were being rehabilitated.

The most celebrated beneficiary of tax credit financing was Union Station, which was rehabilitated as a festival marketplace by local developers Robert and Sandra Borns between 1984 and 1987. Other downtown historic buildings that were preserved through the tax credits included the Majestic Building, the Century Building, the former Sears, Roebuck and Company Building, the Morrison Opera Place Building, the Merchants Bank Building, the McKee Block and Erwin Building (now the Old Spaghetti Factory restau-

rant), the Circle Theatre, and the Omni-Severin Hotel. A large number of historic apartment buildings in the St. Joseph and Old Northside areas also benefited from the tax credits, as developers rehabilitated them as market-rate apartments. Another tax credit rehabilitation occurred on Indiana Avenue, where the southeastern one-third of Lockefield Gardens, an early public housing complex, was adapted for market-rate rental housing.

Other residential developments resulted from the conversion of historic industrial buildings into condominiums or apartments. These adaptive uses, unimaginable 20 years before, transformed the former Indianapolis Glove Factory in Lockerbie Square into a condominium and apartment complex, converted one of the buildings in the former Real Silk plant on North Park Avenue into condominiums, and changed a former wholesale warehouse, the Murphy Building, into the Harness Factory Loft Apartments. North of the downtown, developers transformed two former public schools, Henry P. Coburn School on East 38th Street and School 80 in Broad Ripple, into apartments. Some owners of historic commercial buildings rehabilitated their structures for a continuation of the existing use. The Business Furniture Building at Pennsylvania and Maryland was the beneficiary of one such rehabilitation.

Circle Theatre.

Walker Theatre.

Government and nonprofit organizations also "re-cycled" historic buildings during the 1970s and 1980s. The City of Indianapolis had already begun the rehabilitation of the 1886 City Market when the guidebook was published. Under Mayor William H. Hudnut, III, the city assisted private developers to rehabilitate the Indiana Theatre, the former H. P. Wasson and Company department store, and Union Station. The State of Indiana restored both the 1878-88 Statehouse and the symbol of Indianapolis, the Soldiers and Sailors Monument. The Lilly Endowment, the largest private philanthropic foundation in the city, assisted the Madame Walker Urban Life Center to restore one of the principal landmarks of the black community, the Walker Building, and provided grants to the Indiana Repertory Theatre and the Indianapolis Symphony Orchestra to help them complete the rehabilitation of the Indiana and Circle theatres, respectively.

In addition to downtown preservation efforts, which were stimulated in part by government and nonprofit programs, the 1980s brought an increased appreciation of historic houses and districts in the suburban areas of Marion County. Some former towns, such as Irvington, Broad Ripple, and New Augusta, attracted new residents who restored or remodeled residences and strengthened the character of each community. Several northside suburbs or subdivisions with distinctive plans from the early 20th century—Meridian-Kessler, Golden Hill, Brendonwood, and Crow's Nest—maintained their aristocratic charm or attracted new residents who rejuvenated them. Generally, throughout Indianapolis, as new house prices rose swiftly during the 1980s, both first- and second-time home buyers increasingly turned to pre-1930 houses with distinctive details, spaciousness, and extensive displays of wood in the interiors.

THE BOOM FADES

Since the late 1980s, much of the boom in local historic preservation efforts has faded. The movement of professional persons and couples to downtown historic neighborhoods has slowed in part because of the loss of downtown shopping, decline in downtown employment opportunities, and a belief by some that center city public schools are inferior to suburban schools. Together with the national 1990-92 recession, which depressed real estate activity of all types, these factors have resulted in a lower demand for working spaces and residences in historic buildings.

L. S Ayres shopping experience.

Historic Landmarks Headquarters.

Wilking Building.

In addition, the federal historic rehabilitation tax credits, which had stimulated the rehabilitation of large numbers of income-producing historic structures in Center Township, lost much of their attraction for high-income investors after changes made by the 1986 Federal Tax Reform Act. As a result, in Indianapolis the amount invested in historic income-producing buildings has fallen dramatically.[2]

In city government, a decline in the number of professional staff at the Indianapolis Historic Preservation Commission since the late 1980s has limited the number of additional historic areas that the commission could designate and protect. In recent years, municipal leadership in preservation has concentrated mainly on conserving the historic character of the six residential historic areas already designated.

An exception to the general slowdown has been the increased preservation activity promoted by the nonprofit Historic Landmarks Foundation, whose financial resources and staff have grown considerably in the last decade. The foundation made a symbolic commitment to the rehabilitation of historic buildings downtown when it rehabilitated the historic Kuhn House on the Central Canal at Michigan Street as its state headquarters. Historic Landmarks has also continued to thwart the demolition of key smaller historic buildings through its FLIP revolving fund.

Another exception has been the ever-increasing number of home buyers who purchase older houses with character and ample living amenities. Consumer demand for affordable quality has proven to be a potent ally of preservation in the residential real estate market.

A LOSS OF DOWNTOWN IDENTITY

Nathaniel Owings said in his retrospective introduction to the original *Indianapolis Architecture* that the capital city still contained a "character and genus" all of its own. In 1975, much of the "character and genus" that made Indianapolis distinctive resided in the center of the city. Since 1975, despite a great increase in preservation of residential districts and individual commercial and institutional buildings, the overall identity of the downtown has eroded considerably.

The Downtown's Identity in 1975

At the heart of the Mile Square in 1975 stood the symbol of the city, the remarkable Soldiers and Sailors Monument. The monument was circumscribed by Monument Circle, the enduring street laid out by Alexander Ralston and Elias P. Fordham 175 years ago. Buildings with curving elevations, limestone facades, and limited heights paid deference to the monument and contributed to the special qualities that distinguished the Circle as one of the great urban spaces in the Midwest.

Washington Street—Owings' "personal main street of America"—was still one of the premier shopping districts in the state. Anchored by the Hoosier retail institutions of L. S. Ayres and Company, the William H. Block

Hume-Mansur Building.

School 5.

Merchants Bank Building.

Company, and H. P. Wasson and Company, Washington Street and its branches on adjacent streets provided a shopping experience that was admittedly inspired by State Street in Chicago, but had an Indiana character and charm of its own. Between the department stores, specialty stores such as Lyman Brothers' Picture Framing, Marott's Shoes, Lieber's Cameras, L. Strauss and Company clothing, Em-roe's sporting goods, and Goodman's Jewelers still sold customers most of the products available in the suburban malls.

Around the corner on Pennsylvania Street were Stationer's Office Supply and the Ober Book Store in the heavily remodeled Ober Building; the Wilking Music Company in the finest remaining cast-iron fronted building, the Vajen Block; and Kittle's Furniture. On Illinois were Rost's Art Deco Jewelry Store, the G. C. Murphy store, and Harry Levinson's hats. Occupying the whole northwest quadrant of Monument Circle were the J. C. Penney and F. W. Woolworth stores in a 1949 retail building custom-designed for the Circle by Skidmore, Owings and Merrill.

To the north, along Ohio Street, could be found the best remaining group of pre-World War I office buildings in the city. At Pennsylvania and Ohio stood the Bankers Trust Building, with a large interior atrium bordered with brass rails. At the center of the block between Pennsylvania and Meridian stood the terra-cotta-covered Hume-Mansur Building, containing the largest collection of physician and dentist offices in the city. On the southeast cor-

ner of Meridian and Ohio was the Board of Trade Building, center of grain trading since the turn of the century.

South of Washington Street, along Meridian, Illinois, Capitol, Pennsylvania, and Delaware, stood groups of nearly vacant warehouses surviving from the Indianapolis wholesale district. At Maryland and Meridian stood the 1862 Schnull's Block, first wholesale building along South Meridian. Next door stood the former Schnull and Company wholesale grocers building, designed by Vonnegut and Bohn. Further down the 100 block of South Meridian stood the 1866-67 building occupied for 70 years by the House of Crane wholesale cigar firm. Two blocks to the west, the former Kiefer-Stewart Wholesale Drug Company Building housed part of the state's Employment Security Division at Georgia and Capitol, while the former Citizens Street Railways "barns" served as a storage structure.

West of heavy commuter traffic on West Street stood remnants of Indianapolis' settlement period and its industrial past. On the east bank of White River above Washington Street a historical marker designated the approximate site of John McCormick's cabin, wherein the town of Indianapolis was laid out in 1821. North of the marker on Blake Street were the post-Civil War brick buildings of the former Brower and Love Cotton Mills, one of the principal Indiana cotton factories of the 19th century. East of the marker was Washington Avenue, the original course of the National Road when it still crossed White River via a covered bridge. At Blackford

J. C. Penney Building.

Journal Building.

and Washington stood the 19th-century office building and 20th-century concrete silos of the Acme-Evans Flour Mills, descendant of one of the early gristmills after the founding of Indianapolis.

The Beveridge Paper Company, one of the last plants to manufacture paper along White River, occupied a complex of early 20th-century brick buildings on the south side of Washington Street; within the L-shaped Beveridge complex stood the 1870s Washington Street pumping station of the former Indianapolis Waterworks Company. South of the Beveridge Company ran several brick-paved blocks of Maryland Street, formerly the principal traffic artery for workers at Kingan and Company, largest meat-packing concern in the city until the 1950s. A remnant of the Eastern European neighborhood that once occupied the area north of Washington Street was School Number 5, a brick and terra-cotta building designed by Robert Frost Daggett which stood at Blackford and Washington streets.

Two diagonal avenues from Ralston's and Fordham's 1821 plan for Indianapolis yet ran unbroken through the Mile Square: Indiana Avenue to the northwest and Virginia Avenue to the southeast. Indiana Avenue had been the principal street of African-American culture in Indianapolis since the turn of the century. Although many of the nightspots identified with "the Avenue's" golden age as the center of jazz music in Indiana had been demolished by the 1970s, several buildings remained on each block. Many of the commercial buildings along the first two blocks of Virginia had already been demolished in 1975, but south of the elevated tracks, 19th and early 20th-century wholesale houses, a freight rail depot, and several retail buildings survived.

The Downtown's Loss of Identity since 1975

The "character and genus" of which Owings spoke resided not merely in old buildings, streetscapes, or city plans. They also consisted of the experiences that people derived from visiting or working in a particular company or institution, in a particular building or setting, over a long period of time. Since 1975 many of the experiences and buildings that made up the identity of downtown Indianapolis have disappeared.

The loss is seen most keenly on Washington Street, where Indiana's Main Street is nearly dead: the three landmark department stores of Ayres, Block's, and Wasson's have closed, and most of the specialized retailers of 1975 are gone. Likewise, the retail branches of Washington on Illinois, Pennsylvania, and the Circle are no more: Rost's, Murphy's, Levinson's, Wilking's, Kittle's, Woolworth's, and Penney's exist only in suburban malls.

North of Washington Street, municipal government and downtown developers have concentrated much effort since 1975 on constructing new office buildings. Some of the new skyscrapers, such as the American United Life and Bank One buildings, displaced the historic office buildings along Ohio Street and other elements of the city's cultural past. Others went up on the sites of parking garages. In either case, construction of the new structures has reduced the economic viability of the surviving historic office buildings. Given that demand for additional downtown office space leveled off in the 1970s, erecting new Class A buildings has had the effect of drawing tenants from the former Class A buildings erected in the 1960s. The latter in turn

Park Street in the Old Northside.

Delaware Street in Herron-Morton Place.

have attracted tenants from the former Class B office buildings (now Class C), many of which are historic structures erected before 1930. With tenant demand for Class C space slumping, the future of Indianapolis' office building heritage is uncertain.

One pocket of the former wholesale district, along the 200 block of South Meridian Street, has thrived due to its proximity to popular restaurants and night spots in Union Station. However, the heart of the district along the 100 block of South Meridian has been removed to serve as part of the site for the future Circle Centre Mall, and the former Kiefer-Stewart and Citizens Street Railways buildings at the west end of the district have been demolished for the site of the Pan American Plaza development.

To the west, the surviving structures and artifacts from Indianapolis' early industrial history are mostly gone. The White River State Park site, largely vacant, and the Indiana University-Purdue University at Indianapolis campus occupy the area where the Brower and Love Cotton Mill, much of Washington Avenue, School Number 5, and old Maryland Street stood in 1975. Across White River, the new location of the Indianapolis Zoo has displaced the 1890s brick "barns" of the former Indianapolis Street Railway Company, home of the city's electric streetcars until 1953.

The two intact diagonal avenues of 1975 have lost much of their character. Indiana Avenue has been truncated, like Massachusetts and Kentucky before it, by construction of a mammoth office building, in this case the 1981 headquarters of the American United Life Insurance Company. The remaining blocks of "the Avenue" are devoid of the buildings that tied the area to black culture and the jazz era, with the exception of a handful of structures at the intersection of Indiana and West Street. Virginia Avenue, although not truncated, has lost all but one of the 19th-century buildings south of the elevated tracks.

Possibly the area that has retained the most identity is Monument Circle, where the Soldiers and Sailors Monument itself has been restored, and the buildings lining the northeast and southeast quadrants have been restored or maintained. The west side of the Circle, however, has lost much of its traditional character. In the northwest quadrant, the smooth Indiana limestone facade of the Penney Department Store has been replaced, first with smoked glass, and later with granite veneer. In the southwest quadrant, although the 1920s Guaranty and Test buildings have been preserved, all but the Renaissance facade of the 1897 Journal Building has been demolished.

HISTORIC PRESERVATION IN THE FUTURE

What will be the role of historic preservation in the future of Indianapolis? Preservation will undoubtedly continue, but in ways different from those of the 1970s and 1980s. The governmental role in promoting preservation will probably continue to decrease, as local government reduces its budget and the federal and state governments face no more than a status quo level of expenditures in historic preservation. Thus, the Indianapolis Historic Preservation Commission may designate few additional historic areas, and there may not be many additional federal or state funds available for preservation grants. The role of Historic Landmarks Foundation of Indiana is likely to increase as it continues to promote preservation efforts by neighborhood groups, private developers, and owners of individual historic buildings.

What types of preservation efforts will predominate? The leading preservation activities will almost surely be rehabilitation and restoration in historic residential areas. The spaciousness, attractive details, and high quality materials found in many older houses will, as before, attract home buyers in both the downtown and suburban sections of the city.

Scottish Rite Cathedral.

Commercial and industrial preservation faces uncertainty during the next decade. Much depends on the degree to which the currently depressed local economy recovers. If the entire metropolitan area economy improves and creates uniform increased demand for office and residential buildings, developers and building owners may rehabilitate some of the many historic commercial and industrial buildings downtown. If the recovery is uneven and favors the suburban real estate market more than downtown, the current trend toward abandonment, dilapidation, and demolition of nonresidential historic buildings will likely accelerate.

The future of the many historic structures associated with nonprofit and institutional organizations is also uncertain. Probably all of the existing historic monuments and museums downtown will survive and continue to attract visitors: the Soldiers and Sailors Monument, the World War Memorial Plaza, the Statehouse, the Indiana State Museum, Central Library, the James Whitcomb Riley Home, and the Benjamin Harrison Home. The many historic buildings occupied by fraternal, religious, and social organizations may not all survive. Masonic temples, historic churches, literary societies, and ethnic organizations all face declining memberships and shrinking financial resources. Some of the most majestic and appealing institutional architecture in the central city may be at risk during the next 20 years. In addition, landmark schools, such as Attucks Junior High and Arsenal Technical High, may experience lower enrollments and the threat of closing.

If the Indianapolis of 18 years from now is not to become a city low in vitality and visitor interest, much needs to be done by the civic and business leadership to promote the rehabilitation of historic commercial and industrial buildings for contemporary adaptive uses and to assist nonprofit organizations to search for ways to use more fully the symbols of Indianapolis' social and religious history.

Notes

1 The commission had been created in 1968 to review land use and design changes in the Lockerbie Square historic district, but had been largely inactive.

2 The situation may be improved soon by the use of a new 20 percent state income tax credit created by the 1993 Indiana General Assembly for the rehabilitation of historic income-producing buildings.

A former historian on the staff of the Indianapolis Historic Preservation Commission, James A. Glass currently serves as director of the Division of Historic Preservation and Archaeology, Indiana Department of Natural Resources. He holds a Ph.D. in architectural history and historic preservation planning as well as an M. A. in the history of urban development from Cornell University.

Suburban Indianapolis—
Living on the Edge

by Valentina G. Williamson & James T. Kienle

"A city . . . is more like a dream than anything else."
> Joseph Rykwert, 2Oth-century architectural theorist

" There is such relief from the clangor and din of the heart of the town. . . ."
> "Lockerbie Street," James Whitcomb Riley

Indianapolis, a prototypical American city with few physical constraints to growth, has always been seeking its edge. Designed in 1820 at the edge of our developing nation, Indiana's capital city was to be anchored with a classically ordered center and contained within a Mile Square. Yet, Indianapolis grew to be a city of suburbs and has few areas with truly urban forms, such as the row houses so characteristic of Baltimore or Boston. After 173 years, Indianapolis is still a young city, in a young nation. As French planners studying American suburbs asked: "What will this thing look like when it grows up?"

Not only economic and environmental forces, but also dreams, drive the built form of suburban Indianapolis. What transformations have occurred since 1975 in our old and new suburbs, described then as composed of diverse neighborhoods? Indianapolis today seems to be somewhere between dreams:

The Meadows Executive Plaza and Shopping Center.

USA Funds building from I-69.

• The Indianapolis of our collective memories hovers ideally somewhere between 1920 and 1955, centered on Monument Circle.

• The agrarian visions of our American founding fathers and mothers encourage us to seek the edge—the edge of settled land, the beginning of country, the land of the tamed wilderness.

• The automobile still promises freedom of movement and access. It promises to allow anyone to be almost any place at any time. Newer techno-possibilities of electronics, virtual reality, and mobile phones promise that anyone can be many places at any time.

What realities govern the design of the buildings and environment of suburban Indianapolis? If we hold a mirror to the face of suburban Indianapolis, what is beautiful, what is cramped and chaotic, what is functional, and what enriches our lives?

NO MOUNTAINS, NO SEASHORE

Indianapolis expanded easily. Unconstricted by great rivers or dramatic terrain, its form was shaped by transportation of the individual to and from work and the activities of daily life. As it grew outward in successive concentric rings, Indianapolis found a continual supply of inexpensive, easily developed land and skipped over sites requiring extensive site improvements. Growth favored the northern direction, first because of flooding Pogues Run, then because of railroads and industry south of Monument Circle.

The city's growth from a population of 105,436 in 1890 to 314,000 in 1920 paralleled the development of the interurban electrified streetcar and the affordable automobile. It became easy to live at the edge of the country and commute to downtown Indianapolis for work or shopping. Post-World War

II financing subsidized new single-family residential growth in the suburbs. More automobiles made very low-density living feasible for the average working family. Both white and black middle-income families took advantage of new "auto-mobility" to seek "better life and better schools" at what was then the suburban edge.

After completion of the interstate beltways during the 1970s, it became possible to drive anywhere in Indianapolis in 25 minutes. Anderson, Danville, Franklin, and Lebanon are evolving from small towns to semidetached suburbs. Their residents live at the edge of the country and commute 25 minutes to jobs on the beltway. I-465, intended to channel traffic around the perimeter of the city, has become a kind of interstate Main Street, lined with new buildings on both sides. Intense growth, and even more intense traffic, is generated on the thoroughfares that feed interchanges such as at the intersection of I-65 with Main Street, Greenwood.

Since 1975, despite modest population growth, the number of cars per family has exploded, fueled by two-wage earner households and scattered locations for work and recreation. Indianapolis' low population density could support mass transportation only in the Castleton corridor. Indianapolis' generous midwestern scale and broad streets were planned for a capital city, but the surrounding country roads were not. Suburban planning commissions now wrestle with whether to retain the charm of the country lane, or seek the efficient traffic flow of a multilane thoroughfare. In most of our new suburban areas we cannot safely walk or ride a bicycle to a shopping area. We demand bicycle trails, yet build streets without sidewalks and drive to our fitness spa.

The real edge of Indianapolis now has little relationship to county lines. The 1993 city map covers an area north to 136th Street in Hamilton County and south to Whiteland in Johnson County.

Black-Eyed Pea Restaurant on 86th Street.

China Coast Restaurant.

The edge of the suburb is exciting, as new buildings grow from cornfields. What of the area behind the edge? The Meadows was a flourishing suburban commercial and office center in 1975, with pedestrian walks to adjacent apartments and ample parking. It was a primary northeast suburban commercial center in its time. The Meadows has been abandoned and deserted since 1982, succumbing to two factors: white flight to the suburbs, coupled with lack of interstate access. Must Indianapolis' expanding edge leave behind a ring of decay in its wake?

THE SHAPE OF THIS SPACE

Before World War II, urban planning theories emphasized visionary "physical planning" concepts in which buildings were sculptural elements in grand public spaces. In the postwar period, planning theory moved to focus on thoroughfares for optimal traffic flow and functional differentiation of land uses. Connections between one area and another were neither required nor encouraged. Missing is the spatial shaping that created Monument Circle, charted the strong geometry of our diagonal avenues, and positioned a series of squares and memorials between Meridian and Pennsylvania streets. The space of our suburbs is two-dimensional, shaped by automobile circulation and disconnected areas on a planning map. What building forms and visual organization are emerging in Indianapolis' suburban environment?

In heavily trafficked suburban areas, a "40-60 mph auto" scale is required for recognition and perception of buildings. Auto-scale buildings are characterized by larger-than-life signage and decorative elements, easily identified forms—sleek and streamlined, nostalgic, or exotic in "theme" with extensive, prominently placed parking. The sheer size of individual suburban buildings is increasing. "Mega buildings" include stores, gas stations, office buildings, schools, even churches and houses. Are these buildings larger because of the economics of labor and overhead, or do they also wish to establish a stronger presence in a diffuse landscape?

Buildings in the Castleton Mall area, executed during the first decade after completion of I-465, turned their backsides to the interstate. By 1990, major new projects, such as the USA Funds Headquarters on I-69, were designed with "front sides" to face the Interstate Main Street, although their real access is from the back side—the access road and parking lot. Multistory buildings at Keystone at the Crossing are spaced almost as closely as new buildings in Indianapolis' downtown, creating almost urban spaces and resembling a city skyline.

THE NEW VERNACULAR

The buildings of Victorian Indianapolis may seem to be the last heyday of design character and unity. Most buildings were vernacular architecture—remarkable for being characteristic and typical, not for being unique. Most of these buildings were created by carpenters, basing their designs on published pattern books, catalog building components, and mass-produced ornamentation in terra cotta, cast iron, and plaster. Although not pure in any academic style, these buildings now seem fitting and charming.

Today, as in the Victorian period, the majority of buildings use the technology of our day: variations on standard or modular plans and premanufactured, standardized building and decorative components. Their appearance is enlivened by reflective glass skins, or preshaped panels, which may simulate the visual character of more "traditional" materials. Wood gingerbread is replaced by highly detailed, nonrotting fiberglass ornament. Whether designed by architect or by accident, vernacular architecture represents and occasionally celebrates the common, everyday design language of our environment, not the exceptional.

What is the new vernacular architecture of our day? It is our most familiar scenery—the fantasy fast-food place, the slick, atrium-filled office building, and the lavish tract house.

Shopping area at 56th and Illinois streets.

McDonald's at I-65 and Main, Greenwood.

A CULTURE ON THE MOVE

The opportunity for self-determination, which is the fabric of our American culture, leads us to lightly rooted and mobile lives. Our choices of food, music, and entertainment are eclectic. Suburban commercial areas have a Disneyland-like visual character, a design response to our need for instant orientation. It is not accidental that the design and menu of a chain restaurant is a familiar constant anywhere in the United States. It is sometimes hard to determine visually whether you are in Indianapolis or Atlanta, much less whether you are on Indianapolis' north or south side.

With some modification in the size of signage, the exterior design and materials of the Black-Eyed Pea Restaurant would fit into the design guidelines for construction in an Indianapolis historic neighborhood. But the site development calls us back to the reality that we are in the heart of the suburban commercial strip. A thin band of landscaping borders the road and softens the base of the building. Ample parking surrounds the building on three sides.

To compound our potential sense of dislocation, what if, next door to the Black-Eyed Pea, we find the equally thoroughly and colorfully detailed China Coast Restaurant? Indianapolis has no historic ethnic districts with this Oriental character. Where are we? We are suddenly confronted with the real Disneyland experience: the American Southland next to Chinatown. The food in both of these chain restaurants is well prepared, but, like its architectural containers, standardized and not quite authentic. We know the kitchens will be new and functional and the quality and quantity of food well controlled. It is safe cultural diversity, popularly priced and mass-media style.

Indianapolis' suburbs have areas of "authentic" ethnic character. Newly arrived Americans today live in older suburban ranch houses and garden apartment complexes, where the American dream of one's own open space can be achieved with relative economy. The most authentic ethnic restaurants in Indianapolis today are owned by new Americans—Vietnamese, Hispanic, Russian—and are in middle-aged suburban shopping centers and in remodeled older fast-food restaurants. The rents are lower and offer entry into the American entrepreneurial dream.

Is suburban Indianapolis now visually different from any otherAmerican city with major development since World War II? Despite the growth of ethnic flavor, the visual character of our suburbs is becoming geographically homogenized and threatens our sense of regional identity.

I'M GOING DOWNTOWN: WHERE IS IT?

In the Indianapolis of our collective memory, each residential neighborhood had its commercial corner at the streetcar stop, with a gas station, a market, and a drugstore. Downtown shopping was reserved for major expeditions. Comprehensive department stores offered goods from bargain basement to designer department. Even in 1975, shoppers either parked their cars immediately outside these downtown stores or stepped conveniently off a bus at the corner. Wm. H. Block's, Wasson's, and L. S. Ayres were the flagships of downtown retailing. Satellite commercial districts, such as Fountain Square, occupied the midrange. Less elegant than downtown, they too catered to riders of public transportation (buses and interurban cars) as well as a family's one automobile. Later, the automobile took us to drive-in movies and drive-in restaurants, such as the legendary Al Green's or the TeePee, now ironically replaced by a parking lot.

"I'm going downtown," but where is it? It's gone to 86th Street, Highway 31 South, Lafayette Road, and East Washington Street. On 86th Street,

Steak 'n Shake Restaurant.

Deer Creek Music Center.

between Castleton and Keystone, enough mixed uses have grown up to become an "Edge City," with more office and retail space than the center of Indianapolis. Where does that leave the center of Indianapolis: Monument Circle and the Mile Square? Downtown remains the governmental, financial, and cultural center for Indianapolis and Indiana. Circle Centre mall will regain major retailing for downtown, but it cannot reverse the decentralized growth that has occurred. It can reinforce the symbolic importance of the Mile Square, center and anchor to a diffuse suburbanized city.

AT 45 MPH, WHICH NICHE IS THIS?

The architecture of commerce has always responded to our transportation patterns, as well as the economics of doing business. Major enclosed suburban shopping malls were created throughout the 1970s and 1980s. Castleton Square, Lafayette Square, Washington Square, and Greenwood Mall became ever larger and more elaborate, with multiple major department store anchors and fashionably decorated interior spaces. The mall has been a teenage hangout, a symphonic performance hall, an exhibition hall for boat shows, antiques, and other vendors, and a gym for indoor power walking. For the buying public, this air-conditioned privately owned space has supplanted the community center and town square. The mall is an interior Main Street, with fountains, sculpture, and enough parking for the Christmas shopping season.

Every new mall has sapped the market for the shopping center at an earlier city edge. As malls have become larger, they have become more inconvenient to enter for brief shopping expeditions. Are enclosed malls an endangered species of retail development? Are they imperiled by their own success and size and by being left behind the moving outer edge of the suburb?

The charm and survival of older neighborhood shopping areas, such as 56th and Illinois streets, is not derived from acres of parking and trendy details, but from broad sidewalks, big windows for window shopping, and curbside parking to promise convenient access.

The newer and better strip shopping center is exemplified by North Willow Commons, where forms, details, and materials—brick and limestone—are intentionally nostalgic and reminiscent of older shopping corners. The buildings are much larger (auto-scaled) and wrapped around much more parking. Happily, the corner commercial building creates a tree-dotted, partially enclosed space—verging on a public square. Adjacent to the North Willow Commons is the handsome Crestview Christian Church, which remained at this location and was built anew during the 1980s, giving 86th and Ditch an all too rare urbane characteristic: a mixture of land uses.

The design goal for high sales, "name brand" businesses is to express an identifiable, consistent image, rather than the building's relationship to its context. A national import chain, Pier One, uses steeply pitched blue metal roofs and heavy timber construction to express West Coast/Pacific Rim trading origins. A new McDonald's, within the chain's design guidelines, uses glass block, a blue metal roof, and streamlined detail to provide a fresh variation on one of our most standard and familiar products.

We once had to travel to New York to buy Brooks Brothers clothing and to London for Laura Ashley decorative fabrics. Now we can go to a "high end mall," a creature of the 1990s, devoted to a collection of stores stocking national lines of expensive and unique items. Shopping becomes an elegant and exotic act of consumption. We now have purchasing choices once only available to the very affluent and well traveled. The design of the Fashion Mall has the hallmarks of this market niche: high style colors and materials in dramatic spaces, and, of course, a Palm Court and a Food Court. Although its design and its brand name stores are predictably similar to those in high end malls elsewhere, a site problem was overcome to create a real sense of place. A pedestrian bridge necessary to connect the east and west wings of this mall is used as the Food Court, creating a view out and a real sense of entry to Keystone at the Crossing.

Middle-aged shopping centers have survived and thrived when they have found a niche and offer more than geographic convenience. Nora Plaza, an

Carmel Civic Square.

Sunny Heights Elementary School.

aging strip shopping center, has been relandscaped and refreshed with new colors, signs, and awnings. It offers gently discounted items and is anchored by Target, a discount department store. The architectural design states clearly "few frills, some style."

Mega stores are new stars of retailing: their niche is the bargain. During the 1980s and 1990s, a difficult economy and labor costs have created these stores in giant buildings operated by limited staff. Best Buys, Sam's Club, and Cub Foods employ a simple set of conventions in their built forms: gigantic, simple block letter signs; plain, squarish concrete block buildings; acres of parking; and the minimum landscaping required by zoning. The driving economic force for the mega store is to provide lower prices. Would more interesting and elaborate exteriors and landscaping be a significant cost in the overall construction budget? Probably not. The austere exteriors are that way by design. The architectural message is: We aren't putting any extra money into the building.

Commercial strips at the interchanges of thoroughfares and interstates seem to defy our desire for visual order. Dreary and unformed by day, at night these strips take on a lively, chaotic, carnival form composed of brightly lit signs. The building itself may become the sign.

Gas stations at interchanges expanded in their roles and presence. Under their spacious, glowing canopies can be found convenience food store, restaurant, and gift shop—almost an entire neighborhood corner shopping area, but inaccessible on foot, and often with no repair services for the automobile.

PRIVATE PUBLIC SPACE IN THE SUBURBS

Indianapolis' unique array of handsome public spaces draws people together—to the Strawberry Festival, the Fourth of July fireworks, La Fiesta, Black Expo jazz concerts, and the 500 Festival parade. Perhaps the most important anchor for all Indianapolis is space itself, centered on Monument Circle, created through 19th-century civic vision, enhanced during the 1970s and 1980s. It is truly civic space. What are its suburban counterparts?

Suburban settings draw large and faithful audiences for both high and popular culture, yet these spaces remain private, not truly the public domain. Deer Creek Music Center, reputedly one of the best spaces in America for large outdoor music concerts and popular shows, is a favorite venue for performers ranging from the Grateful Dead to Bob Hope. At Conner Prairie, 14,000 people may attend a summer symphony concert in a field next to an authentic but artificially assembled outdoor museum.

Municipal governments in Fishers and Carmel have recently completed governmental centers that seek to create a civic focal point for their communities. Carmel's City Hall and Fire Station employ a design vocabulary and materials modeled on Williamsburg, a symbolic civic cradle of our nation. Carmel's governmental buildings are arrayed around a fountain in a circle for summer concerts by the Carmel Symphony.

Suburban Indianapolis abounds with churches of all sizes. Few are major suburban landmarks in the same sense that St. Mary's Roman Catholic Church commands its skyline and helps define our only working square in the European sense—the parking lot of Lockerbie Marketplace. Suburban churches have typically been placed in residential neighborhoods, yet the surrounding streets usually have no sidewalks. The most visible sites tend to be sold for commercial use.

The Gothic limestone forms of Second Presbyterian Church, built in the middle 1950s, have a commanding site, in sweeping view from north and south on North Meridian Street. Its recent additions have extended this design and reinforced its siting and presence. The Church of the Crossing exemplifies a new type of church facility: an interstate-oriented, technically

One Parkwood Crossing.

Castle Creek Corporate Park.

sophisticated auditorium/worship space for its congregation of thousands. It is large and bold enough to make its presence felt on I-465, our interstate Main Street.

The economic advantage of large-scale development seems to appear in all aspects of suburban civic building. Even elementary schools are bigger than in our idealized memory. The Sunny Heights Elementary School tries valiantly to make a very, very large school be comfortable in scale for little children by tucking its voluminous form behind smaller wings and entry canopies.

WORKPLACES—PUTTING THE "PARK" IN OFFICE PARK

Many negative side effects of the workplace, such as smoke and pollution, have been mitigated. Today, offices and industry in the midst of a residential community do not call up the Dickensian images of yesterday, but are low-key, attractive buildings with expansive green lawns. As the popularity of the "home office" attests, a power source and a computer are all the hardware needed for many operations. There is little or no need for many businesses in a typical office development to be located next to each other. The growing use of electronic information and connections allows an increasing dispersion of workplaces. Living places adjacent to office parks and shopping could provide the option of driving less, even of walking or biking to work.

In most instances, office "parks" lack the expanses of lawn and trees that are usually associated with a park environment. Parking lots are typically the most prominent feature of their landscape. There is very little park in office park. Castle Creek Office Park and Allison Pointe are more truly office parks and have capitalized on existing trees and slightly hilly topography to integrate large office and commercial buildings into natural landscape forms and existing trees.

Placing office buildings with almost identical requirements on flat, largely treeless cornfields is a formidable challenge. Instead of trying one design whim after another, the Browning Investment office buildings lining the North Meridian to Carmel corridor used repetition of form, color, and materials—red granite and brick—to design a spread-out, suburban version of the wall of buildings lining Market Street downtown.

No recent suburban project has achieved the striking form and unity between building and landscape that make the Pyramids the landmark-defining image for their northwest corner of the city. From the interstate or from the air, they command their space. Their grand, abstract, stark scale has not been repeated by the office and commercial neighbors that have grown up at their feet in College Park.

INDIANAPOLIS—A CITY OF HOMES

Residential development in Indianapolis has followed a single-family pattern from the early Federal-style frame houses on the Circle, to McOuat's Addition (now known as Lockerbie Square), to Irvington, to the development of Fishers and Avon. At every period and income level, the edge of the developed area has been perceived as the most desirable.

Living on any kind of waterfront is alluring in this landlocked city. New apartments overlooking White River, the mansions at Geist Reservoir, and condominiums and homes at Mystic Bay and Eagle Creek integrate recreation into daily life. Exhausted gravel pits, flood plains, and retention areas

Office buildings at 116th and Meridian streets.

"New Tudor" in Greenwood.

Geist Reservoir home.

have been landscaped to become lakes and landscape features, a neat exercise in transformation, in which leftovers become amenities.

A notable change since 1975 is the disappearance of new ranch houses, once the virtual icons of suburban Indianapolis. Often combining various shades of brick with limestone, the low and occasionally sweeping lines of the ranch house trace their descent from the Prairie School and the work of Frank Lloyd Wright. Development costs have narrowed lot widths, and our needs/desires for multiple garages and baths—and more square footage—have forced new houses upward to two stories. Suburban remodelers are now adding second floors to ranch houses.

Indianapolis seems to have retained a predilection for designs reminiscent of the Tudor Revival houses, perhaps in search of positive associations with Irvington and Meridian Street Tudor Revival-style houses built during Indianapolis' golden period of expansion in the 1920s. New Tudor houses are enlivened with hooded, arched feature windows, soft-toned brick or stone (at least on the front facade), complicated, gabled rooflines, and as much limestone trim as can fit in the developer's budget. Few tract houses are built in what might be termed Modern or Post-Modern architectural style.

Individually designed tract houses are rare. They are generally variations on standard plans from magazines and plan books and incorporate current market-driven features. This year, the new Tudor house will feature a master bath suite; in next year's model the suite may be smaller so a home office can be included. Since 1975 Indianapolis' larger new houses have grown ever larger to include increasing sets of desirable features. The megahouse has 10,000 square feet, with a minimum four-car garage. Narrower lots and bigger houses squeeze attached garages out toward the street, often nearly hiding the front door and freeing the backyard for development as semiprivate outdoor living space.

New suburban development seems increasingly stratified by economic levels. Houses costing $150,000 are not built in the same development as houses costing $80,000. This seems the extension of the theme of commercial

niche shopping. Perhaps in our mobile society it is a way of gaining some information about, and comfort with, our prospective neighbors.

ENCLAVE, SWEET ENCLAVE

Higher income Indianapolis has traditionally lived in enclaves, with imposing masonry pillars and gates, picturesque curving streets, semirural landscaping, and often clustered around the open space and amenities of a golf course, a lake, or a horse stable. This type of residential development moved outward and northward to Golden Hill, Buttonwood Crescent, Crow's Nest, Williams Creek, to Crooked Stick, Bridlebourne, and Geist Reservoir. Valle Vista and other new residential developments have carried this development pattern south to Greenwood and south on Meridian Street between I-465 and Smith Valley Road. One of the newest "patio home" developments is called "The Enclave at Carmel."

The more exclusive the apartment or condominium development, the higher will be its walls and gates, and the more limited will be pedestrian or auto connection with its surrounding neighbors. A restrained palette will be used for the exterior design, materials, and colors of the residential units. Paving resembling brick and generously scaled trees and shrubs create a pleasant setting for quiet walks within the enclave.

New moderately priced housing has followed the enclave development pattern, but with more modest space and amenities. In Pike and Warren townships, the Harcourt Springs developments use smaller masonry gates to define the entrance to residential developments, which are usually surrounded by

Woodmont Condominiums.

Island Club apartments.

wood fences and earth berms landscaped with clusters of trees. The masonry-clad fronts of houses face inward to relatively quiet streets and turn their vinyl-siding-clad backsides to the surrounding thoroughfares.

An alternative atmosphere is the "life-style enclave," as well exemplified by the Island Club development tucked just outside the I-465 west beltway, south of 38th Street. Two- and three-story apartments are tightly packed around the meandering edges of a small lake. Even on a quiet Sunday evening, a pick-up volleyball game is in progress, and small boats float on the lake. Small, white-trellised porches, weathered gray-stained wood, and proportions hint of seaside resort towns. Although the landscaping is generous and well tended, there is very little grass. The message is escape to an active and sociable life-style, not peaceful retreat from the city. Currently, the theme of choice is not New Tudor, but "American resort town à la Cape Cod."

The suburbs are not all affluent. Homeless people can be found here. Some garden apartments that were new in 1975 have become suburban slums. Desperate efforts are being made to salvage Blackburn Terrace, garden apartments built as public housing in inner ring suburbs less than 30 years ago.

At their best, residential enclave developments are clusters of community in what might otherwise seem large, even featureless suburban areas. The least happy aspect of suburban enclaves is the apparent need to visually express defensible living, a circle of covered wagons in an uncertain urban landscape.

Indianapolis' downtown historic neighborhoods are among the most suburban in character of the central core of almost any American city. A look at the Old Northside confirms this. In these neighborhoods the predominant building type is the single-family house with green lawns. Like their suburban counterparts, these neighborhoods have visible identity and contain-

ment. Instead of being defined by the developer's berm, this identity has been fostered by strong neighborhood cooperative efforts and enlivened by variety in the scale of buildings and diversity in the age, social, and economic conditions of residents.

SOLID COMFORT AND CLOSE NEIGHBORS

From Speedway to Sunset Lane, Indianapolis has historically lived in neighborhoods of solid comfort and low density, of gracious, easy living. Perhaps the greatest visible change in residential areas since 1975 has been the infilling of Indianapolis' open spaces. In 1975, open space, woods, and farmland mixed with developed land. This open space, with waterways such as White River, Fall Creek, Crooked Creek, and Pleasant Run Creek, gave the city a pleasantly discontinuous feeling rather like a collection of small towns, separated by interior green edges. Today the fields and open spaces are rapidly filling with clusters of development. Even creek bottoms are being filled in with small residential developments raised on earth berms above flood levels.

Infill development has been cost effective from a public policy perspective, mitigating the cost of expanding city utilities and services. How can we quantify the impact of the loss of interior edges, of a remaining sense of relationship to open country? Has this infill pattern actually accelerated expansion of the outer edge of Indianapolis?

In 1993 the prevailing impression in new residential suburban areas is that of density. The "million dollar" residences fronting on Geist Reservoir and homes in suburban enclaves join their more modest vinyl-clad cousins and new apartment homes in being as tightly clustered as the houses in Irvington or Meridian-Kessler. However, in the new suburbs there are more parking spaces and more cars. Residential developments add common recreational facilities to expand limited individual space. High density is more apparent in development on former farmland. In time, new trees will soften and reduce this impression. New developments such as Oakland Hills, which retained existing hills and established trees, feel more spacious and established.

WHERE WILL IT END?

Will Indianapolis' suburban areas expand forever? During the period from 1975 to 1993, the disadvantages of expansion have not overcome the perceived advantages. The automobile has not become too expensive to own, and technology is hard at work trying to replace gasoline. Indeed, in typical suburban areas three-car garages may be replacing two-car garages as the norm. Unless we raze our buildings and start over, or control extension of infrastructure and land use, our density of development will support mass transportation primarily in limited, traffic-choked areas like 86th Street.

The quandary is not what life is like on the very edge. It is pleasant to live in sight of the country, our American agrarian dream. But today's suburban edge will be in sight only until the next ring of development is built. If what happens behind the edge is an inner belt of decline and decay, even the outermost edge is less desirable and less safe. Not all of us can continually move to the edge.

If our development remains incremental, defined by the needs of the automobile, not of people, our expansion and decay pattern will not change. In trying to control and accommodate the automobile, we have concocted zoning and street planning that hinders the businesses and institutions we wanted to serve. Instead of continually widening traffic arteries and forcing all traffic into a limited number of paths, public policy can prescribe multiple streets that connect major civic and business centers and reduce congestion by creating many options for travel routes. For example, the reason the Hoosier Dome traffic dissipates quickly is that there are many routes provided by the historic downtown grid system. We can alleviate suburban traffic congestion and use the enclave pattern of development to form a connected community, simply by weaving streets, sidewalks, and bike paths between enclaves, civic buildings, and park space. A radical parking solution may be a practical one. We could cease to have any regulation of the number of parking spaces required and let the marketplace dictate the amount of parking needed. We could reward developers who provide parking spaces that can be shared, such as business use during the week and church use on Sunday. By spending less money on asphalt and site utilities, we devote more resources to quality in our buildings and civic space. We can place the automobile in its proper role, to serve the dream of mobility, not to strangle it.

If we are not responsible stewards of the rich Indiana farmland, we and the world will ultimately suffer its loss. In Europe, there are very old, well-established partnerships between people and the environment to protect working landscape. For example, Paris is closely linked with the surrounding farmland, as well as with protected woodland. Here in Indiana, where we highly value individual property rights, we have accepted eminent domain for actions perceived to be in the common good, such as highway construction. We can reward development in which good farmland remains in cultivation and woods and wetlands can be retained and restored.

It is time to develop a new equivalent of Ralston's grand plan for Indianapolis to its outermost edges. We can encourage new points of orientation, like the Circle and the Pyramids, to punctuate and add a third dimension to our landscape. We can encourage connection between places and the creation of real public domain, shaped by private buildings surrounding relatively small areas of park or civic space. Monument Circle was but a line on a map until surrounded by private buildings. The green spaces of the edge can be transformed into a kind of green ribbon that twists into the city and out, bringing the outside to the inside, and vice versa. How much green space is needed to feel like an edge? From Frederick Law Olmsted to Christopher Alexander, urban and park planners have observed and recommended specific widths of green space and walking distances from parks, which create desirable connections to nature. In older Indianapolis, we already have many such connections. Fall Creek Parkway is a natural landscape, wide enough to shelter wildlife. Pleasant Run Parkway is parkland, winding through and connecting neighborhoods from English Avenue to 10th Street. The Water Company Canal is a totally man-made feature, only a towpath width at Broad Ripple. The White River Greenway is an excellent start, as we begin to apply our own experience to a newer Indianapolis. If we will not set boundaries to our growth, we can control its character. We believe that the tool of zoning can be transformed to shape the forms of our space and increase our sense of connection and community.

Within the Indianapolis suburban environment, most of us work, play, sleep, worship, shop for bargains and luxuries, get sick and get well, and are buried. We try to re-create our myth and memory of an America—an Indiana—of friendly small towns and tightly knit city neighborhoods. As we look at new buildings that may alternately remind us of spaceships and of Disneyland's version of the past, we struggle with the concept of what is appropriate reality. Perhaps it is quite simple. Buildings fit to the uses of people and situated to admit light and views to green open space contribute to a sense of community and have a sense of reality.

Civic spaces and greenways cannot substitute for jobs and food, nor can they eliminate crime and other urban ills. However, if accessible to all, they can define the standards we set for our life together as the Indianapolis community. Can we shape spaces that reflect and reinforce new common visions for both new and old suburban Indianapolis?

The very form of Indianapolis shapes the forms of its buildings, the texture of its spaces, and our lives.

Notes: see page 192.

James T. Kienle, AIA, is an architect and principal in charge of architecture for the Indianapolis office of HNTB Corporation. Valentina Gafford Williamson is an architect and principal in the firm of Mozingo Williamson Architects, Inc. Both architects have long been involved in planning and urban design for downtown and suburban development in Indianapolis and other cities.

View to the Future

by Steve Mannheimer

The future? The word itself is a question. For that matter, what all is meant by "architecture?" And how precisely can or should "Indianapolis" be defined? Compounded, they are confounding: what is the future of architecture in Indianapolis?

The question may be asked with wide-eyed curiosity or the focused appraisals of accountants. The answers will be both warranted and laughable, exhilarating and depressing, right for the wrong reasons, unreasonable no matter how right.

In any event, we will be surprised. A prognosticator's main task may simply be to prepare us for that surprise, to pull the rug out from under us before the earthquake knocks us flat. But the future is far more subtle in its approach. It shaves and whittles away at the present so subtly that we think ourselves secure until looking down we see the scars of wounds we had not felt.

Nationally, the future has had a tendency to become *The Future: A Century of Wonder!* No country, no continent ever had a future like America's. We have been and may always be the New World, the world of the new.

Tudor Revival home in Meridian-Kessler area.

In the Midwest, the architectural future has a distinguished history. The year of this writing, 1993, is the centennial of the World's Columbian Exposition of 1893, the signal event in America's conception of the architectural future as the Glorious Past. During its six-month run, as many as 2.5 million people, approximately one out of every five Americans, were dazzled by the patriot's dream and faux-alabaster gleam of the exposition's fabled White City, a Neoclassical spectacle of awe-inspiring, if temporary, pavilions designed by the great American architects of the day.

It was a thoroughly marketed event. Visitors took that vision home with them in memory and memorabilia. It became a song in America's heartland —Oh! Beautiful—and catalyzed the City Beautiful movement, a half century of Beaux Arts aesthetics and grand-scale Baroque city planning. By the time America glanced down from the nearly imperial heights of this chapter in civic architecture, it noticed a large oil stain on the pavement and a honking, smoking, clanking beast waiting at the curb.

After World War II, America inherited Modernism. The future was its cause, in both senses of the word. An architecture trimmed of fat and curlicue suited our postwar self-image to a T-square. With the Baby Boom and the construction boom coming fast, no one had time for carving Corinthian capitals. The future began without so much as a coffee break.

During the first two postwar decades, Indianapolis planners produced a series of well-illustrated and visionary city planning documents. These offered images of a spacious and mostly Modernist city of the future comprised of equal parts Jetson and Jefferson. Yet these were not images of a distant, Utopian future. It was almost literally "The City of Tomorrow," as in about 24 hours from now. This was a city we had better get busy building or we would find ourselves stuck in the past. For all intents, the future was now. This left little if any room for the present. It was blithely assumed that humans would happily learn to behave like next year's new and improved model.

Starting in the 1970s, statistical charts slowly began crowding visionary renderings out of official planning documents. No doubt this reflects a growing concern for demographic and economic determinants over aesthetics. Perhaps it also avoids the political embarrassment of unfulfilled dreams.

Meanwhile, on the national front, Hollywood has taken up the visionary slack with miles of imagery from back-to-back-to-back *Back to the Futures*, from *Blade Runner* to *Star Trek* and its descendents. Architecture has a major role in all of these futures as backdrop, as studio set.

This in itself is nothing new. The White City was simply the largest stage set of its time. Indeed, it may be argued that its success was more due to the persuasiveness of its theatricality and not its architectural sophistication—or—at least that the two are practically indistinguishable in this case. As early as 1937, architectural critic Eugene Raskin suggested that "the best way to build a World's Fair is not to build it at all, but to make a motion picture of it." And animated dioramas such as Norman Bel Geddes' miniature "City of 1960" for the Futurama exhibit at New York's World Fair of 1939—an amazingly prescient image—were basically sci-fi movie sets sans camera.

Aerial view of Park 100 looking west.

For the next half century, bits and pieces of the future appeared in movies and on television. Collectively, these captured the popular imagination and became practically self-fulfilling prophecies. To say that the future had become a movie, or at least a television series, is more than a convenient metaphor. It describes how and where Americans enjoyed their most meaningful, most public visual experience.

Architecture used to provide those experiences.

This point has snuck up on everyone. Other venues of public visual experience have cut into the traditional role of architecture so subtly that, looking down, few notice anything. Having heard for centuries that architecture is the public art, architects have almost forgotten to wonder if anyone was actually watching.

Of course, there are still many people who see the wisdom of engaging an architect to design a home. Others are happy to hire contractors who may or may not work with a registered architect. Many others may delight in rehabs, restorations, and remodeling. One way or another, home ownership makes appreciators of us all.

This is especially the case in Indianapolis, where residential architecture has a distinguished history and social status is associated with specific neighborhoods with specific design identities. This not-so-subtle connection to social

success will probably ensure a respectable future for the city's residential architects.

But the "Art" of residential architecture is unlikely to make great leaps forward in Indianapolis. Local designers have created outstanding private homes, homes that are every bit as sophisticated in their architectural concept and execution as any found in other cities. But mainstream local taste is founded in the generic types and grand historical fabrications of the Meridian-Kessler district. The same taste for historical pastiche runs through their architectural descendants, all the frog-pond chateaus and half-timbered lily pads of the nouveau "burbs." These concoctions, often created by ersatz rather than registered architects, are merely more liberal in their theatrical interpretations, freely combining motifs until every design notion inside and out is essentially a changeable facade in a private stage set. You want Gothic? We got Gothic.

Much the same theatricality affects multiresidential complexes, which view design as a means to an end, that end being a marketable look, the visual equivalent of the development's romanticized name/theme. However much professionals and intelligent consumers decry such creations, it is difficult to believe that such censure will diminish either their popularity or their inevitability.

Nighttime view of skyline from south.

Night lighting of loggia at 10th and Illinois.

Once they step out the front door, the public at large concerns itself with architecture mostly when proximity, newness, controversy, oddity, size, or expense makes some structure remarkable. People care, but generally only about specific buildings, rather than the whole of the designed environment, and with a kind of omnivorous appreciation that does not worry overmuch about distinctions between art and vernacular innovation and off-the-rack.

Probably the greatest contributing factor to this leveling of popular appreciation is the automobile. Where architecture was once a pedestrian, daylight experience, it has become a drive-by experience, often at night. The automobile drastically reduced the amount of time a viewer was obliged to spend on any building and commensurately increased the amount of architecture that might be seen in any given period. For developers and marketers of commercial properties and the general public, this has distilled architecture to image.

Visibility and legibility are what count—numbers of viewers that can immediately identify the image. This is the main power of the Bank One Tower: it can be seen from a hundred blocks away. It has the city's highest Nielsen rating.

All of which is to say that for all intents and purposes, the highways and the airwaves have become practically interchangeable venues of public experience. The same characteristics spell success in both.

Through the high-definition windshield of our portable living rooms, we see the city in all of its winding rhythms of architecture and landscape. We see the downtown skyline loom in the distance as we rush to greet it. We watch the city fade to countryside at least for the few miles before the next pocket of development looms before us. Like the promotional channel for pay-for-view movies in hotel rooms, we watch until we choose to exit, until we have selected today's vision.

Our cities have become TV, our TV has become our city. A century from now, historians will look back at the 1950s and marvel at the simultaneous fluorescence of the interstates and the networks. They will find in this decade the epoch-making origins of their America.

Again, this is especially true for Indianapolis. If America is becoming a loosely woven, tangled mesh of development and green space, of commercial and residential that flows over and around any inconveniences of topography or conceits of governmental boundaries, then ditto and double ditto for Indianapolis.

To the drive-by viewer, we are already an endless string of Shorewood Estates without shores and darned little wood, of Park 200, 300, and so on, with the only park in the -ing lot. Eventually, the city—at least as experienced along our interstates and major thoroughfares—will appear as a chain of chains, a Universal Studio of franchise architecture leading the passenger/viewer in quick fashion past the mock historical and comforting facades of family-style restaurants, the no-frills late-Modernist efficiency of budget motels and spec office buildings, and the total graphic package of service stations pared down to neon geometry, ironically reminiscent of a glow-in-the-dark Barcelona Pavilion. And there in the middle stands an old country church, once a spiritual island in the virgin green scape, now 100 yards from a 16-lane interchange.

Keystone at the Crossing at night.

Bank One Tower from 100 blocks away.

Although many traditional urbanophiles sneer at the image of an endless mall, it obviously has its attractions. It is architecture as typecasting and, as such, reassures the public that things can be taken at facade value:

"Here we serve predictable meals. Here we sell the highest technology. If you were here it would feel luxurious. If you worked here, you would be efficient and business-like."

In an all-too-uncomfortable era, we are comforted by the perception that the world is known and knowable—and, further, that any such knowledge can be reprogrammed quickly if fashion or franchises change. It is an architectural typology shrink-wrapped and neon-labeled to reveal as much information as possible in a five-second look, which is often four seconds longer than necessary.

The lesson is not lost on building owners off the beaten highway. Downtown office buildings are equally susceptible to the attractions of facade-lifts and new tops, most of the time in imitation of the bare-bones Modernism and add-an-arch instant Post-Modernism of the automotive corridors.

The America and Indianapolis of the future will be, in a phrase, Castleton gone ballistic.

For many that hardly seems a threat. The flipside is a developer's dream: a planned and manicured community. If not Castleton, then Keystone at the

Crossing or Woodfield Crossing. These are ultimately pleasant unions of architecture and landscape, quite tasteful if unadventurous in their aesthetics, all carefully maintained and patrolled. If this strikes traditional urbanophiles as unutterably bland, it might be argued that there are a lot worse futures to be imagined. More to the point: any apprehension of the Developer's Dream, any fear of the Disney-izing of America is to a considerable extent a fear of labels, a fear of words. Concepts of safety, cleanliness, design, and psychological harmony (with just the right touch of planned exotica) embodied in this future are undeniable attractions.

Whether designing for the blazing neon thoroughfare or the developer park, architects of the future will increasingly be called upon to produce and/or direct visual experience, to create mood and image, and to manufacture atmosphere and even special effects. There are cinematic expectations, nominally at odds with the values of traditional architectural education, long-standing notions of the architect as gentleman, and the contemporary marketing of architecture as Art (rather than an art)—but hardly in conflict with the elevation of a few practitioners to magazine-cover celebrity.

Looked at another way, most apprehension about the future role of architects is really an anxiety about the future role of architecture. And that is really just a way of saying, the hope of finding a reliable, stable society. And that is another way of saying—for architects as much as if not more than any other profession—the hope of finding a stable, understandably ordered city. In other words: a stable, understandably ordered Indianapolis.

Eli Lilly and Company Corporate Center from I-70.

Traffic congestion on 82nd Street.

Indianapolis, indeed. What is it? Is it the old city limits, mostly within the I-465 ring road, with downtown as its center and soul? That would be a charmingly nostalgic and almost uselessly limited definition.

Is it greater Indianapolis, the city of the Standard Metropolitan Statistical Area, with its population and development spreading out like syrup on a pancake? That encompasses an area too large to analyze practically.

Or is it actually all the territory served by I-465 and its tributary highways? Is this monumental paved pretzel the true skeleton of our body civic? And the Ralston plan an heirloom more treasured than functional?

Is the highway the city's only truly public space, annually sustaining millions and millions of motored miles, every day affording us the largest percentage of our visual experience of Indianapolis and its buildings?

This definition leaves out our lately much-discussed neighborhoods, but even here some reconsideration is in order. A couple of generations ago, before the mall, Lewis Mumford defined a neighborhood as the territory a child might wander on foot in a day. This concept is still useful when it comes to calculating and protecting real estate values. But it is equally useful to think of a neighborhood as that disjointed but linear set of experiences that each of us chooses or is obliged by family responsibilities to connect via car. For instance, your "neighborhood" grocery store may be one of several, depending on the time of day, the traffic, and happenstance.

One advantage of defining the city and its neighborhoods as a set of experiences connected by car is that it allows a clearer vision of the future of downtown. This vision, currently being promulgated by city leadership, pictures Indianapolis as a series of nodes connected by the highway. Downtown becomes the most valuable node, both in terms of real estate investment, cultural activity and historical identity. In this vision, downtown will become the city's center for professional entertainment, complementing the amateur and inadvertent entertainment value of local and state government. At the same time, downtown will achieve parity with outlying nodes as a shopping/consumer center. What's missing is any workable scheme for a broad economic spectrum of housing, either newly constructed or retrofitted into the hundreds of thousands of vacant square feet between I-70 on the south and I-65 on the north.

This lack may prove to be a major drawback if downtown is to be truly revivified. It may never again achieve the primary importance it enjoyed 50 years ago. Already in 1993, the city seems to be growing a new downtown—call it Uptown—along 86th Street. This is a truly linear city paralleled by a leg of interstate for express trips.

If downtown is to compete successfully with uptown, it may have to play up its strength, which, ironically enough, is the potential for widespread design harmony, much like the more successful ringroad developments. With a modicum of public push and private encouragement, downtown's private sector may come to see the wisdom of design control as complete as that already seen in the serene blocks and acreage of the Eli Lilly and Company campus, which, significantly, turns its main facade to an interstate. Presumably much design harmony will be orchestrated among the Mansur holdings in the southeast quadrant of downtown. The state can probably be trusted to continue the design coherence of their campuses—the governmental and the university's—on the west side of downtown. Some great scheme will be needed to meld these two campuses either via the canal or the yet-to-be-determined configuration of the White River Park.

429 North Pennsylvania Street.

Hedlund Hardware, Keystone Avenue.

And there is every indication from the designers of the Circle Centre Mall that they will offer up a design that will successfully integrate the demands of commerce for a well-regulated interior experience and the demands of urbanophiles for a user-friendly streetscape. Together, these "mini-nodes" of downtown design should provide some guidance and context for local architects employed in smaller projects near them.

However, beyond the loose, interstate boundaries of the downtown node, the architectural fabric begins to unravel. The rest of the city, where everyone actually lives, is still stuck at Nora trying to get to Castleton. The rest of the city is still trying to figure out which of the seemingly interchangeable strip malls lining the major routes on the southside is the one they want. The rest of the city is still growing in whatever direction offers the least resistance and greatest profit.

And to that extent, this vision of downtown is ultimately a pessimist's shrug. It implies by omission that the rest of the city will just have to take care of itself. It implies that there is not much we can do when our jurisdiction quits just short of the freeway.

Jurisdiction is the key. Regional, which is to say multicounty, design planning is one possible answer. Certainly regional planning will become essential to

maintain any hope of environmental quality. With luck, some sense of design planning will trickle down from structures and guidelines thus enacted.

Yet, perhaps paradoxically, local or neighborhood planning authorities could prove equally beneficial. Some design control at this level could literally bring home the whole discussion to citizens who otherwise assume that the designed environment is beyond their control and thus their long-term interest. Further, it might even encourage an interesting variety of "towns within a town," so to speak, a blend of local flavors of designscape to lend character and identity to areas and major axes of the city.

Moreover, Indianapolis must reclaim a meaningful voice in the design of its main streets—its interstates. It will be impossible to even minimally nurture an architectural identity for our city without some attention to the highways, their bridges and design details, their entrance and exit ramps and, most important, the visual corridors that parallel them.

The simplest suggestion would be to begin a program of graphic or design identity along our highways, perhaps a set image to symbolize the city. The circle comes immediately to mind, whether carved into a limestone block at major exchanges or paved into major intersections. Other possibilities include a massive program of plantings, symbolic archways, even some regulation of the color of graphics along the various sections of the pretzel. The

Thomson Electronics on U.S. 31 north.

Branch bank on Keystone Avenue.

imagination can run as wild as anyone will let it, which is not all that far around here.

But an architectural identity will not come purely from mass exposure. It will require practitioners with a bred-in-the-bone feel for the city. Some presence must be established in Indianapolis for the state's schools of architecture and landscape architecture. The architectural students who will in so many cases become the architects of Indianapolis must begin to cut their eyeteeth, so to speak, in the best and biggest laboratory in the state, in the total spatial environment that every day would be teaching them the realities of design while they are busy learning the theories. It might even be suggested that the presence of an art school in the same city would facilitate an all-embracing conversation among the visual profession, among the graphic designers and landscape architects, architects and sculptors, industrial designers and architects, and so forth and so forth. If nothing else, this might hasten the realization that a common vocabulary is needed if they are ever to understand each other and cooperate to manage an urban reality far beyond the capabilities of any one profession.

Wishful thinking. Good design in a traditional sense—even, for that matter, celebrity design—just is not that important in Indianapolis, at least to most Indianapolitans.

No more telling demonstration of this is the fact that it took a French-owned company to finally commission international architectural superstar Michael Graves to design a building in his own hometown. Appropriately, that building, the American headquarters of Thomson Consumer Electronics, is sited within eyeshot of the intersection of the main street of the past, Meridian Street, and the main street of the future, I-465. Even then, Graves was only asked to design a new facade for what started out to be a nice, normal stack of bland, banded stories and will remain an awkwardly sited beauty forced to cohabit with a pseudo-Southwestern chain hotel.

In fact, along the great circular main street of interstate, this sort of juxtaposition is quite normal. We may as well get used to the idea. We may even learn to like it. Our children will. And our grandchildren will find it positively charming—that is, if these and every other state-of-the-art building have not been reskinned in liquid-crystal/electrooptical screening that changes the facade's imagery every other week.

Steve Mannheimer has been the *Indianapolis Star*'s visual arts writer since 1982 and has contributed to various regional and national magazines. Since 1976 he has been on the faculty of the Herron School of Art, IUPUI.

Map of Marion County

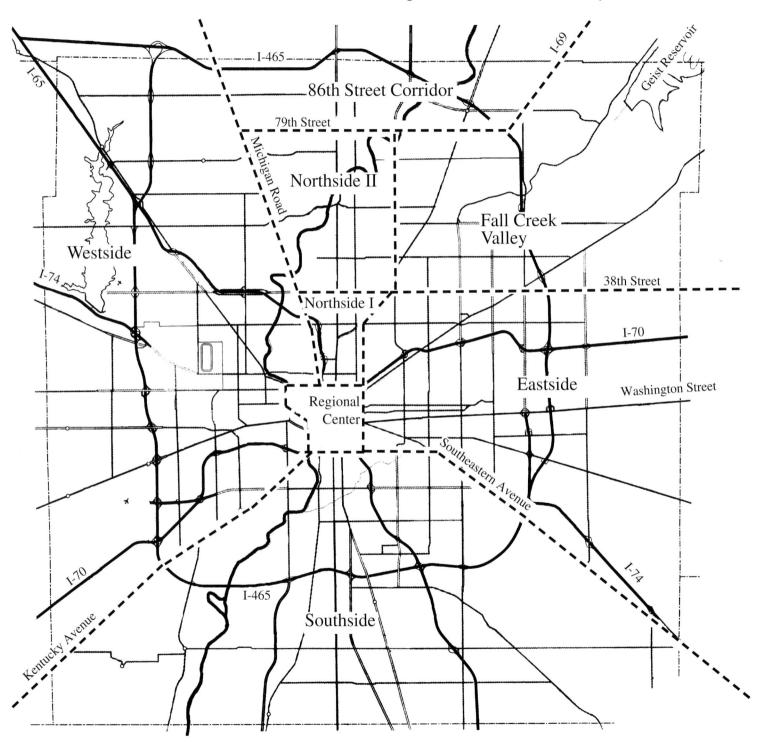

Introduction to
Featured Buildings

The county map at left outlines the nine divisions of the guidebook in which buildings are organized geographically. Directory listings appear with each of the individual maps that follow to help you locate a building. If you cannot pinpoint it on the map, check the index at the back, which will give you its page number.

Each building contains a standardized heading that includes its map and photo number, name, address, architect, contractor, and year of completion. All architectural and construction firms are local unless otherwise specified. The name of the firm is listed as it was when the building was completed, which is not necessarily its current name. (All permutations of firm names appear in the index.) Individuals in the firm such as the project architect or designer have not been listed, since most buildings result from the collaborative efforts of many individuals. For historic buildings that have undergone renovation or restoration, the name of the original architect and date of construction are included within the text when known.

Because of the length and complexity of headings, we have not included individual listings of clients and owners. Granted, all the architecture in this guidebook was built for their use, paid for with their money, and wherein it is successful, was challenged by their dreams and needs. The "owner" of a building is sometimes easy to identify, as for example the person for whom a home is built. In other projects, the owner or client is a very complex and seemingly disparate set of people. For example, the clients for the Circle Theatre were the Indianapolis Power and Light Company, the City of Indianapolis, and the Indianapolis Symphony Orchestra. In a very real sense, the client must also include the users—in this case, the music-loving public. In order to provide more descriptive information about the building, listings of owners and clients were omitted.

Similarly the developer was not individually cited, since this is not standard information for all headings. During the 1970s and 1980s, there were dramatic changes in the way projects could be financed. The speculative developer took on a greatly expanded role, conceptualizing projects and marshaling capital, tax credits, and investors to make these projects happen. Developers who were key pioneers in the revitalization of downtown Indianapolis by bringing "impossible" projects into being may not be specifically cited, but their contributions are nonetheless appreciated. Many of Indianapolis' dramatic changes are due to their creative vision in using economic forces of the period.

As a criterion for inclusion in the guidebook, all buildings that have won awards for excellence in architectural design from the Indianapolis chapter of the American Institute of Architects (now AIA/Indianapolis), or from the biennial competition of the Indiana Society of Architects (now AIA/Indiana), were automatically included. These awards are listed underneath the text blocks as are the individual winners of the city's annual Monumental Awards and design awards of national scope.

While there have been many significant architectural projects focusing only on the interiors of buildings, these were excluded from the book if these interiors do not allow public access. For those who may use the guidebook in future years and wonder why a certain building constructed in 1993 was not included, it was necessary to establish a cutoff date of June 30, 1993. Therefore, only buildings substantially completed by that date were included.

Architecture cannot be experienced from a single photo and brief description. Therefore, we encourage you to go see these buildings in person and make your own observations. Happy touring!

Mile Square

Monument Circle
01. Monument Restoration
02. Circle Theatre
03. Test Building
04. Associated Group Headquarters

05. Bank One Center Tower
06. Market Tower
07. Illinois Building
08. 101 West Ohio
09. Capital Center
10. American United Life Building
11. Emelie Building
12. 300 North Meridian
13. INB Tower Renovation
14. First Indiana Plaza
15. City Market
16. Marion County Jail
17. Claypool/Embassy Suites Hotel
18. Indiana Repertory Theatre
19. Indiana Roof Ballroom
20. Merchants Plaza
21. Convention Center Expansion
22. Hoosier Dome
23. Pan American Building and Plaza
24. Westin Hotel
25. Eiteljorg Museum
26. AT&T Building
27. Pennsylvania Center
28. Lockerbie Marketplace
29. 225 North New Jersey Street
30. Farm Bureau Insurance Headquarters

Indiana Government Center
31. Indiana State Capitol
32. Indiana Government Center South
33. Indiana Government Center North
34. Government Center Parking Facility

The Canal
35. Fire Station 13
36. Canal Square Apartments
37. Canal Overlook Apartments
38. American College Sports Medicine
39. Historic Landmarks Headquarters
40. 500 Place
41. West Walnut Street Bridge
42. Technology Transfer Center

Wholesale District
43. Union Station
44. Holiday Inn Union Station
45. Omni Severin
46. Canterbury Hotel
47. Harness Factory Lofts
48. Morrison Opera Place
49. Omega Communications
50. Century Building
51. Majestic Building

Massachusetts Avenue
52. Hammond Block
53. Stout's Gray Building
54. Marott Center
55. Oxford Building

Mile Square

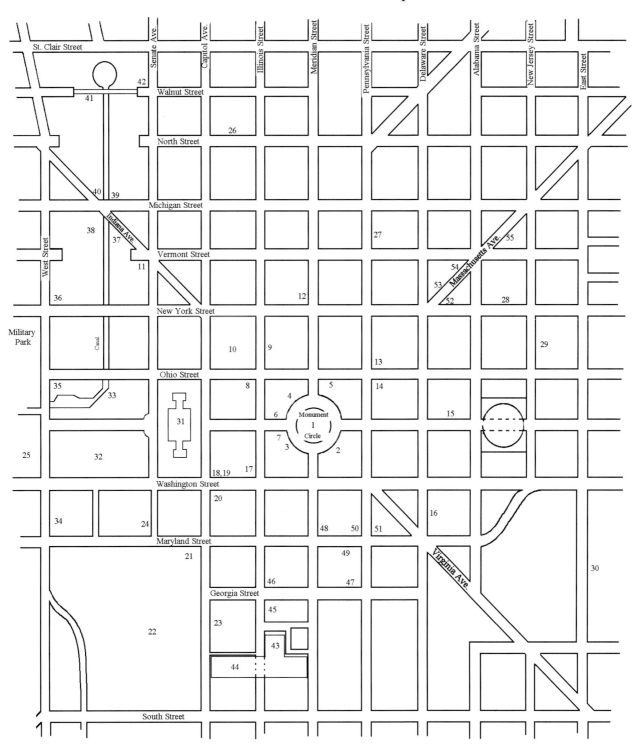

1. The Soldiers and Sailors Monument Restoration

1. The Soldiers and Sailors Monument Restoration
Monument Circle
Architect: Schmidt Associates Architects, Inc.
Contractor: Geupel DeMars Inc., 1987
Jungclaus-Campbell Co., Inc., 1990

A historian of American city planning called this monument a "visual exclamation point marking the center of the city and, very nearly, the center of the state itself." Built on the site originally reserved in the 1821 plan for the governor's residence, its role as the symbol and focal point of Indianapolis cannot be overstated. The 284-foot-tall monument was constructed in 1888-1902 primarily to commemorate the state's veterans of the Civil War. Architects from around the world submitted designs to a competition that resulted in Bruno Schmitz of Berlin being named architect with Rudolph Schwarz as principal sculptor. By the 1980s time had taken its toll on the monument. Many original elements—such as candelabrum light fixtures, bronze and limestone sculptural elements, decorative railings, and parts of the statuary figures—had disappeared. The east and west basins of the cascade fountains leaked badly; structural anchors were severely deteriorated due to years of Christmas lighting; and the limestone was stained a greenish color from the bronze work.

The exterior restoration completed in 1987 addressed a comprehensive replacement of all missing elements. The bronze astragals (the collar-like projections that gird the monument's shaft) and the four bronze terrace candelabra were completely disassembled, cleaned, and repatinated. All exterior limestone was cleaned chemically. The most prominent and debated part of the exterior restoration was the creation of a new observation level enclosure. Originally the observation level was an outdoor platform, open to the sky, but in 1936 it was enclosed, resulting in the removal of the cornice and turret at the base of the Miss Victory statue. The deteriorated condition of the 1930s work prompted a new enclosure with an aluminum glazing system, designed to be as transparent as possible, and reconstruction of the capping cornice. The second phase of work focused on the reconstruction and restoration of the interior, including the original brick vaults and arches that support the terrace and stone steps, and the correction of major structural problems.

1988 Indiana Society of Architects, Merit Award
1990 Monumental Award

2. Circle Theatre

2. Circle Theatre

2. Circle Theatre
45 Monument Circle
Architect: Archonics Design Partnership in joint venture
        with Dalton, van Dijk, Johnson & Partners,
        Cleveland, Ohio
Construction Manager: Geupel DeMars Inc.
1984

The Circle Theatre was the first building constructed in Indianapolis expressly for the presentation of feature-length motion pictures; indeed, it was one of the first such movie palaces in the Midwest. The 3,100-seat theater, built at a staggering cost of over $500,000, opened on August 30, 1916. The architectural team of Rubush & Hunter took design inspiration from current trends in Neoclassical Revival architecture. What makes the building unique is its expression of a style promulgated by late-18th-century British architects Robert Adam and his brothers. Exterior elements such as the classical Greek figures in the terra-cotta facade's frieze and tympanum, and interior features like the richly detailed, bas-relief proscenium frieze and the plethora of intricate plaster moldings throughout the house, are characteristic of the style. Films were shown in the Circle Theatre for a period of 65 years interspersed with plays, stage shows, musical performances, and a variety of other forms of entertainment. Following the movie theater's closure in 1981 and a brief period of vacancy, the building began a new lease on life in 1984 as the concert hall of the Indianapolis Symphony Orchestra.

The $6.1-million renovation adapted the old theater to orchestra performance requirements: the proscenium was enlarged, the stage area was expanded with a 14-foot addition into the back alley, and the lobby was enlarged by the removal of rear seating and the addition of a new dividing wall closer to the stage. Highlights of the restoration included the reconstruction of the original box-seat balconies with their mirrored backdrop and restoration of the terra-cotta facade with its mural painting and copper marquee. In order to improve the acoustics of the theater, numerous electronic enhancements were subtly incorporated into the restoration.

1984 Monumental Award
1985 Indianapolis Chapter, American Institute of
Architects, Honor Award
1986 Indiana Society of Architects, Citation Award

4. Associated Group Headquarters

4. Associated Group Headquarters
120 Monument Circle
Architect: Ratio Architects, Inc.
Contractor: F. A. Wilhelm Construction Co., Inc.
1991

In 1950 native son Nathaniel Owings of Skidmore, Owings and Merrill designed a new building for J. C. Penney's on the site of the 19th-century English Theatre and Hotel. In 1982 the McGuire & Shook Corporation renovated the structure into office space for Blue Cross/Blue Shield and replaced the stone facade with a controversial black mirror-glass rendition. The new corporate headquarters of the Associated Group represents a second dramatic transformation of the 1950 building. In an effort to reflect the historic urban context of the Circle, a new facade of gray granite veneer accented by red details was designed over the existing exterior stud wall, attached to a new steel structural frame behind. A new recessed fourth floor was added over the central section; its resemblance to an attic story and the simulated pilasters of the second and third floors are classical in character. The building's corners are emphasized by copper pyramidal roofs, while the central entry is denoted by a large two-story window flanked by two stainless steel columns. On the roof four large pyramidal skylights mark the new four-story atrium inside, which was cut out of the existing concrete structure.

1992 Indiana Society of Architects, Citation Award
1992 Monumental Award

3. Test Building
54 Monument Circle
Architect: Browning Day Mullins Dierdorf Inc.
Contractor: Stenz Construction Corporation
1982

Although the nine-story Test Building appears to be a conventional office building of its period with shops at street level, it is notable as one of Indianapolis' earliest large parking structures. The parking function on portions of floors one through six, combined with ground-floor commercial spaces and offices above, was an example of mixed use that was progressive for its year of construction, 1925. The local architectural firm of Bass, Knowlton and Company devised a design that responded to numerous architectural and engineering problems. During the 1982 exterior restoration, the storefronts along the Circle facade were returned to their original configuration, based on a few that had survived on Market Street. Special attention was paid to the 13 scrolled panels of carved stone at the third-floor level created by sculptor Alexander Sangernebo, which depict scenes of technology of the 1920s as well as local scenes. The building's main entrance lobby, notable for walls of Tennessee marble and an ornamental plaster cornice, was returned to its original condition.

3. Test Building

5. Bank One Center Tower

5. Bank One Center Tower

5. Bank One Center Tower
111 Monument Circle
Architect: The Stubbins Associates, Inc., Cambridge,
        Massachusetts
Construction Manager: Huber Hunt & Nichols Inc.
1990

In a city like Chicago or New York, a 51-story building is only average in height among other high rises, but in downtown Indianapolis, the Bank One Center Tower— with nearly one million square feet of office space—is a colossus. It towers above the skyline and can be seen clearly from 10 miles away. Although it has a Monument Circle address, the building fronts on Ohio Street and is sited on axis with the World War Memorial Plaza to the north. Land acquisition for the building began in the early 1970s when five historic buildings stood in the way; demolition work began in January 1980 with the Hume-Mansur Building, and for many years, the site was an empty, grassy plot. The architect, who is best known for the Citicorp Building in midtown Manhattan, chose a gray granite for the exterior that was quarried in Spain and

Sweden, cut in Italy, and assembled into panels in Cleveland. The building's statistics are mind-boggling: it contains over 12,000 tons of steel; its metal decking could cover about 20 football fields; 18,000 cubic yards of concrete were poured; and its 21 passenger elevators daily convey nearly 5,000 office workers, more than the population of many small towns in Indiana.

Most architectural assessments of the building acknowledge that the tower pays deference to the city's urban traditions by referencing one of our most distinctive monuments, the World War Memorial, in its stepped, pyramidal "hat," and by respecting the city's grid. The three-story lobby along Ohio Street is generously sized and impressive with its Italian white marble floor and articulated glass curtain wall. At both the Pennsylvania and Meridian street entrances, skylit lobbies are flanked by wood-paneled bays for retail space, somewhat reminiscent of shopping arcades of 1920s buildings. Overall the tower's conservatism is in tune with the image of a banking institution—the building does not dazzle, it does not overwhelm.

6. Market Tower

6. Market Tower

10 West Market Street
Architect: Lohan Associates, Inc., Dallas/Chicago
Associate Architect: Ratio Architects, Inc.
Contractor: Huber Hunt & Nichols Inc.
1988

The design of the 32-story Market Tower successfully incorporates a number of references to neighboring downtown buildings. The choice of contrasting granites for the exterior reflects the city's masonry tradition; the upper floors step back in a manner reminiscent of the Circle Tower Building; the hipped, copper roof recalls traditional buildings of the 1920s like the Columbia Club; and the four-story entry arches on Market and Illinois repeat a common design theme of the grand Roman entry arches found in the nearby Guaranty, Test, and Illinois buildings. Around the small lobby's first three floors, retail space accessible by escalators expands the traditional ground-floor commercial use, which is so important to the quality of street life in the downtown. A fountain between the escalators enlivens the space, while the entry arch's form is continued in the lobby's coffered ceiling.

6. Market Tower

7. Illinois Building

17 West Market Street
Architect: HDG Architects, Inc.
Contractor: MacDougall & Pierce Construction, Inc.
1988

When the 10-story Illinois Building designed by Rubush and Hunter was built in 1925, it was one of the premier office buildings in downtown Indianapolis. By the 1960s and 1970s, when its lower floor housed a G. C. Murphy variety store, it had fallen to second-class status. In 1982 the development of a food court on the first floor and mezzanine level revived its street-level activity. During construction of the new Market Tower across the street, Mansur Development Corporation began a $16-million renovation of the lobby and upper floors. The most noteworthy change was the construction of a four-story atrium, complete with waterfall and sheer glass walls, in the building's old light court, which formerly extended up from the third floor. The new atrium starts on the seventh floor, enabling the conversion of the lower three levels to greater floor area. On the atrium's south side, an all-glass wall was built with the expectation that there would be a good view of the Circle Centre mall.

7. Illinois Building

8. 101 West Ohio Street

9. Capital Center

201 & 251 North Illinois Street
Architect: Browning Day Mullins Dierdorf Inc.
Contractor: Browning Construction, Inc.
1986 and 1988

Capital Center consists of two office towers—one to the north of 17 stories, one to the south of 22—built over a three-level parking garage. The primary exterior material, a reddish gray polished granite, has become the principal design signature of the commercial development of R. V. Welch and its successor Browning Investments. Fenestration consists of uniform ribbon bands except at the central sections of the towers. The angularity of the massing produces those highly leasable spaces: the corner offices. (See Landmark Center, which it closely resembles, designed at approximately the same time by the same firm.) On the west side of the two towers paralleling Illinois Street, a glass galleria provides an interior street for ground-floor commercial spaces and the branch bank. At sidewalk level, the towers are adjoined by a plaza with a rare example of public sculpture incorporated into a 1980s high-rise office development. The larger-than-life-size bronze figures by Philadelphia sculptor Zenos Frudakis continue to raise eyebrows.

8. 101 West Ohio Street

Architect: Browning Day Mullins Dierdorf Inc.
Construction Manager: Huber Hunt & Nichols Inc.
1987

The confines of a relatively small site produced a 22-story tower that takes full advantage of its urban location at the southwest corner of Ohio and Illinois streets. Above the sixth floor on the south and west sides, the structure was cantilevered 10 feet to capitalize on available air rights. The building is covered with insulated steel panels, painted silver, which alternate and contrast with the bands of windows of blue glass. In a downtown dominated by masonry structures, 101 West Ohio is the only slick-skin, high-rise building. Pointing upward from the roof parapet is a 55-foot-tall tower housing a Xenon light stick, which distinctively identifies the building on the city's skyline. (The image seems to evoke a cigarette extruded from its pack.) At street level, two large glass areas visually open the granite-finished lobby to the busy corner.

9. Capital Center

9. Capital Center

10. American United Life Insurance Company Building
1 American Square
Architect: Skidmore, Owings & Merrill, Chicago
Contractor: Huber Hunt & Nichols Inc.
1982

At 38 stories, the AUL Building surpassed the INB Tower and became the tallest building in Indiana until it too was superseded 10 years later by the Bank One Tower. Designed by the architects of Chicago's ultra-high-rise buildings, the Sears Tower and the John Hancock Center, the AUL Building is clad in traditional Indiana limestone and faces toward Monument Circle. The main tower takes the plan of an elongated hexagon from which two wings of eight lower floors extend in a stair-stepped, buttressing effect. Extending to the southeast corner, the main entry is located within a three-story glass-covered atrium with a floor of Brazilian granite and walls of Italian marble. The ground floor was designed around an open interior courtyard landscaped like a garden. Public use of the adjacent cafeteria makes the courtyard more of a public space than the average interior court. The building is one of the most energy-efficient high rises in the country. Groundwater is used for a heat exchanger system to heat and cool the building, thereby reducing its energy costs by 60 percent. Encircling and enhancing the site are brick sidewalks and rows of linden trees. The building's siting has been criticized for closing off the first block of Indiana Avenue and blocking the view down the original diagonal street.

10. American United Life Building

11. Emelie Building
334 North Senate Avenue
Architect: Browning Day Mullins Dierdorf Inc.
Contractor: Stenz Construction Corporation
1987

Originally built in 1902 as an apartment building with ground-floor commercial space, this three-story brick building was transformed into an architectural firm's offices, saving it from the demolition experienced by nearly all of the buildings that once surrounded it. At the turn of the century, the building's owner, German immigrant Frederick Schmid, was the largest manufacturer of finished lumber in the city. (The building was named in honor of his wife.) Although the architect remains unknown, its builder was the Brandt Brothers firm. The limestone decorative detailing of the facade was restored in this certified renovation, and a major addition was added to the rear to provide adequate space for the firm's operations. Conference rooms and the reception area are housed on the first floor, while design studios and offices are located on the second and third levels. A three-story atrium was created at the center of the building.

11. Emelie Building

12. 300 North Meridian Street

Architect: Haldeman Miller Bregman Hamann, Dallas
Construction Manager: Browning Construction, Inc.
1989

At the northwest corner of Meridian and New York streets on a site that historically has seen a succession of structures, most recently a parking garage, the new 300 North Meridian tower rises to 28 stories with a style and elegance that immediately made it a popular favorite among local fans of architecture. While the choice of an unconventional reddish granite from South Dakota combined with black glass windows makes a darker statement than most downtown buildings, the high rise does take cues from surrounding buildings, most obviously the Gothic-inspired Chamber of Commerce building next door. Its exterior appearance is all the more remarkable for the fact that the first nine floors are devoted to 335 parking spaces comprising more than one-third of the tower's square footage. The building's vertical characteristics, emphasized by pointed projections of contrasting granite and setback corners, draw the eye upward to a low, copper-colored dome that crowns the structure. The row of glass dormers at the top floor illuminate a two-story library of the building's prime tenant, a large law firm.

12. 300 North Meridian

12. 300 North Meridian

13. INB Tower Renovation

1 Indiana Square
Architect: Lamson & Condon, Inc.
Contractor: F. A. Wilhelm Construction Co., Inc.
1992

When built in 1970 to the design of Dallas architect Thomas E. Stanley, the 36-story Indiana National Bank Tower was the tallest building in the state. After 22 years of exposure to the elements, the marble panels on the upper 31 stories had cracked and were replaced with aluminum panels. At a cost of $10 million, this "re-skinning" represented half the cost of the original construction. The top floors of the plain modernist box were redesigned with horizontal banding, giving the effect of a cornice in an attempt to bring the building in style with 1980s high rises. As part of the project, the 10-foot-tall letters that spelled out the name of the bank were taken down and replaced by a new lighting scheme featuring a solid blue band and vertical stripes on the east and west facades. Chicago architect Christopher Rudolph and Houston lighting designer Richard Jeter share credit for the "recladding with light," which has changed the city's nighttime skyline but has not received rave reviews.

13. INB Tower Renovation

14. First Indiana Plaza

14. First Indiana Plaza
135 North Pennsylvania Street
Architect: CSO/Architects, Inc.
          3D/International, Houston
Contractor: Duke Associates
1988

Built on the site of the Denison parking garage, the 29-story First Indiana office tower was one of eight high-rise buildings constructed downtown during the 1980s that dramatically changed the skyline of the city. The checkerboard applied to its facade, where red polished granite and precast concrete form a grid around reflective glass of red and gray, is its most distinctive feature. The first three floors step out from the tower, creating a solid base and reinforcing the urban corner of Ohio and Pennsylvania ttreets. Not apparent from the exterior is the parking located on the second through sixth floors (in addition to one level below grade). The lobby's use of contrasting colors of polished granite creates an opulent effect. An architectural critic summed up the building by calling it "a restrained and civilized building with simple but handsome details and a tight logical plan." First Indiana Plaza, occupied principally by a banking institution, is one of several buildings that have transformed Ohio Street into downtown's new financial district.

15. City Market Restoration and New Wings
222 East Market Street
Architect: Perry Associates, Architects;
          James Associates, Architects
Contractor: Geupel DeMars Inc.
1977

The old city market building with its new wings is one of the busiest lunchtime gathering places downtown. The market is filled with many small specialty food shops, and a portion of the original hall still functions as a fruit and vegetable market. While the site was designated for the city market with the city's first plan in 1821, this building designed by architect D. A. Bohlen dates to 1886. It is notable for its elegant cast-iron columns and roof trusses fabricated locally by Hetherington and Berner. The construction of a mezzanine balcony was part of the renovation work. The new wings on either side have triangular footprints that form open plazas, leaving the restored market facades visible. Two-story glass walls on the south side allow sunlight into the wings, provide continuous views of the old market, and visually connect the interiors with the plazas. On the west plaza, one of the entrances to Tomlinson Hall, constructed in 1885 and destroyed by fire in 1958, was preserved as an architectural fragment. On the east plaza, a Howard clock located for 50 years at a watchmaker's shop on Indiana Avenue was relocated and restored. Most recently Ratio Architects, Inc. undertook a renovation of the market interior, which is now highlighted by a brighter, more lively color scheme.

15. City Market Restoration

15. City Market Restoration and New Wings

16. Marion County Jail

17. Claypool Court/Embassy Suites Hotel
110 West Washington Street
Architect: CSO/Architects, Inc.
           with D. I. Design, Baltimore
Contractor: Geupel DeMars Inc.
1985

This mixed use development was built by Melvin Simon and Associates on the site of the Claypool Hotel, a landmark of the early 20th century demolished in 1969. The lower three floors of the building house 70,000 square feet of street-level retail shops arranged around a mall-like central court. The 360 suites of the hotel are stacked around a 12-story atrium illuminated by a massive sky roof. On the exterior the shopping function is denoted by the green glass projections while the hotel is expressed by bands of windows. The white precast concrete panels and the rooftop's architectural gymnastics inspired by Post Modernism have led some critics to label the building "glitzy" and soon to be outdated. Others have decried the southeast facade's diagonal orientation; however, it may yet relate to the Circle Centre mall's design.

1985 Monumental Award

16. Marion County Jail
40 South Alabama Street
Architect: The McGuire & Shook Corporation;
Associate Architect: Phillips Swager Associates, Peoria
Contractor: Tousley-Bixler Construction Co. Inc.
1986

This $18-million project involved a maximum security addition to the existing jail, constructed in 1965 by the same architectural firm. Visiting rooms, indoor and outdoor recreational facilities, health clinics, sheriff's office, and dayrooms were part of the program in addition to over 300 new single cells. The main facade seen here fronts Alabama Street, which is seldom appreciated due to traffic patterns. Stripes of tan-colored, ground-faced concrete block and scored block alternate at all five stories. Vertical window slits mandated by security concerns appear in a random pattern. A three-story central section is cut back deeply from the plane of the facade to provide a triangular, sheltered entry court. At roof level a steel space frame adds a high-tech touch. This subdued yet attractive building demonstrates the architect's interest in going beyond simple necessity in designing an urban correctional facility.

17. Claypool Court

17. Claypool Court/Embassy Suites Hotel

18. Indiana Theatre

18. Indiana Theatre
134 West Washington Street
Architect: Woollen Associates, Architects
Contractors: Glenroy Construction Co. Inc.;
　　　　　　Kenneth Smock Associates, Inc.
1980-1982, 1985

Once doomed for demolition, this 1927 theater has become a staple for theatergoers in Indianapolis. As originally designed by the architectural firm of Rubush and Hunter, the motion picture palace held 3,200 seats. In the building's conversion to the home for the Indiana Repertory Theatre, the interior—which had undergone a series of alterations since its construction—was completely reconfigured for more intimate dramatic performances: the main stage now accommodates 500 while the upper stage seats 250. Only the two-story lobby's original polychromed wood carvings, exuberantly modeled on Spanish Baroque designs, were restored. On the street, a restaurant and bar were created to make the theater an active part of Washington Street. Merchants Plaza across the street provides an open plaza from which one can truly appreciate the rich Churrigueresque detailing of the six-story, white terra-cotta facade, which was restored down to the marquee and box office. In the 1985 phase the building was linked to the adjacent commercial buildings, the state capitol, and the state offices via a system of tunnels. Located in the space of a former bowling alley, the tunnel to the shops at Claypool is worthy of a visit for its diverse lighting and series of ramps, steps, and upbeat colors.

1982 Indiana Society of Architects Honor Award
1986 Indianapolis Chapter, American Institute of Architects, Citation Award

19. Indiana Roof Ballroom
140 West Washington Street
Architect: CSO/Architects, Inc.
Associated Architect: HDG Architects, Inc.
Contractor: Geupel DeMars Inc.
1986

Few buildings in Indianapolis recall as many memories as the Indiana Roof Ballroom, which opened in September 1927. Located on the sixth level of the theater building, the large, two-story space features a replica of a Spanish village designed around an oval maple dance floor. The two-story Mediterranean-style houses, with their stucco walls, loggias, balconies, tile roofs, wrought-iron work, and towers, provide a romantic setting for the dancers. Nestled into the village at the north end of its courtyard is the stage where some of the country's most famous big bands played during the roof's heyday. Rising over the entire village scene is an elliptically domed ceiling of midnight blue plaster with twinkling electric stars. Before Melvin Simon & Associates undertook the refurbishment of the Indiana Roof, it had fallen into shabby condition after closing in 1971. While changes were necessary to upgrade the facility, the impact of changes on the historic design were minimized. Plaster motifs were carefully restored and hand-stenciled ceiling painting was reproduced.

1987 Indianapolis Chapter, American Institute of Architects, Citation Award

19. Indiana Roof Ballroom

20. Merchants Plaza

20. Merchants Plaza

20. Merchants Plaza
115 West Washington Street
Architect: JV III Architects, Houston (Caudill, Rowlett,
        Scott; Koetter, Tharp & Cowell; Neuhaus &
        Taylor)
Local Architect: Browning Day Pollak Associates Inc.
Construction Manager: Geupel DeMars Inc. in joint venture
        with Turner Construction Company, Cincinnati
1977

Located on the site of the Lincoln Hotel that was demolished in 1973, the Merchants Plaza complex was built over the vacated right-of-way of Kentucky Avenue at the southwest diagonal street's intersection with Washington Street. At the time the largest single privately developed project in the history of the state of Indiana, the square-block complex consists of twin 15-story office towers, trapezoidal in plan, the 535-room Hyatt Regency Hotel, underground parking, and restaurants and shops on the first three levels. Ground breaking occurred in November 1974, and construction was completed in early 1977. At the time it was built, the atrium—the 19-story-tall inner lobby that is a Hyatt trademark, connected with the areas flanked by the east and south towers—was one of the largest enclosed spaces in the country. Through the use of angular exterior walls and entrances positioned on the diagonal, the project reflects the diagonal flow of traffic that once traveled over this block. At the midblock Washington Street entrance, there is a triangular landscaped plaza. The hotel wing's facades are distinguished by windows set at an angle in triangular bays that project from the brick walls. The 20th floor's revolving, circular restaurant affords one of the city's few public places to enjoy great views of the downtown.

21. Convention Center Expansion

100 South Capitol Avenue
Architect: HOK, St. Louis
Associated Architect: Plus 4 Architects, P. C.
Construction Manager: F. A. Wilhelm Construction Co., Inc.
1993

With the convention center operating at its capacity and attracting nearly two million people a year, work began on a $43-million expansion to capitalize on the continuing growth of the convention market and keep pace with new centers in the Midwest. Most people regard the original convention center, constructed in 1972 to the designs of architects Lennox, James & Loebl, as an austere building. The original *Indianapolis Architecture* book called it "nothing more than a beautifully detailed factory" with "a series of dull gargantuan rooms offering volume and little else." With these type of criticisms in mind, the architects strove to create a new face for Maryland Street with a brick and limestone facade that reflects the materials of nearby Pan Am Plaza and St. John's Catholic Church. Two glass-enclosed skywalks at the second-floor level connect the convention center with the Westin and Hyatt Regency hotels. The highlight of the interior is a second-floor ballroom the size of a football field that can accommodate up to 4,000 people. Abundant windows take full advantage of views of the Statehouse across Capitol Commons.

21. Convention Center Expansion

22. Hoosier Dome

100 South Capitol Avenue
Architect: HNTB in joint venture with
        Browning Day Pollak Mullins Dierdorf Inc.
Construction Manager: Huber Hunt & Nichols Inc.
1984

The 61,000-seat Hoosier Dome, home of the Indianapolis Colts, dramatically changed the skyline of Indianapolis when its roof was inflated in one day in August 1984. Rather than finding a suburban site as is typical in many cities, a decision was made to support downtown revitalization with an urban location. The restricted site led to some interesting solutions, such as the main entry's diagonal siting at the northeast corner, facing Capitol's one-way, southbound traffic. As a component of Indianapolis' desire to be the "amateur sports capital of the world," the dome annually hosts the Indiana State High School Basketball Championship, which draws thousands of spectators, as well as other events. The Hoosier Dome also doubles as a major addition to the Convention Center when its stadium floor is used for exhibit space. The translucent fabric of the roof, which totals over seven square acres, is made of two layers of teflon-coated fiberglass one-sixteenth of an inch thick, supported by air pressure created by 20 high-volume fans. Geiger-Berger of New York served as structural engineers.

22. Hoosier Dome

1984 Indianapolis Chapter, American Institute of Architects, Citation Award

24. Westin Hotel

24. Westin Hotel
50 South Capitol Avenue
Design Architect: HNTB Architects Engineers Planners
Project Architect: Lamson & Condon, Inc.
Contractor: F. A. Wilhelm Construction Co. Inc.
1987

Located on the vacated right-of-way of Senate Avenue between Washington and Maryland streets, this new 15-story hotel takes full advantage of its "front yard," Capitol Commons. The main entry drive, accessible from both the north and the south, leads to a porte cochere located at the base of a cascading glass wall that marks the entry lobby. The two floors of "function block"—restaurants, bar, ballroom, meeting rooms, retail shops, etc.—are defined by large rectangular windows, while the floors above share an unrelieved uniformity of smaller rectangular windows. The fan parapet centered over the 12-story vertical element is the facade's only ornament. While the main elevation has been criticized for its lack of three-dimensional qualities, the north and south ends curve on a tight radius and then step back, providing an interesting contrast to the planar front facade when viewed from the east/west streets.

23. Pan American Plaza and Office Tower
201 South Capitol Avenue
Architect: Browning Day Mullins Dierdorf Inc.
Construction Manager: Browning Construction, Inc.
1987

Planned to commemorate the Pan American Games held in Indianapolis in the summer of 1987, this development consists of a two-acre public plaza, a mid-rise office building, two indoor ice-skating rinks that frame the plaza's north and west sides, and a 1,100-car underground parking garage. Bounded by Capitol Avenue and Georgia, Illinois, and Louisiana streets, the ceremonial plaza serves to link Union Station, the Hoosier Dome, and the convention center. The nonprofit Indiana Sports Corporation undertook the development to provide revenue for its activities, foremost of which is promoting amateur sports events in the city. Commercial tenants for the 12-story office building help to subsidize the headquarters of a number of sports organizations lured from other cities. The diamond paving patterns of the plaza, which is fairly successful as an urban development, provide more architectural interest than the tower with its uniform facades of brick banding and grid of precast concrete.

1987 Monumental Award

23. Pan American Plaza and Office Tower

25. Eiteljorg Museum of American Indian and Western Art

25. Eiteljorg Museum of
American Indian and Western Art

25. Eiteljorg Museum of American Indian and Western Art

500 West Washington Street
Architect: Browning Day Mullins Dierdorf Inc.
Construction Manager: F. A. Wilhelm Construction Co., Inc.
1989

To find an appropriate architectural expression to house an outstanding collection of Native American and Western art, the architects sought inspiration in the architecture of the American Southwest. While the museum's color and certain architectural features are reminiscent of pueblo architecture, an 80,000-square-foot building necessarily results in far more monumental scale and massing. The steel frame structure is clad with two-by-four-foot blocks of desert-hued dolomite (from Minnesota). Subtle horizontal banding is created by the slight projection of selected courses. The two-story building rests on a 10-foot-high circular wall with a base of rough-textured red sandstone (imported from Germany). An *Architectural Record* writer thought it recalls the stone walls of ceremonial kivas. Closer to pueblo architecture is the long entry canopy resting on columns of Western red cedar trunks, which is reminiscent of a pueblo arcade without literal rendition of posts and vigas.

The museum includes permanent galleries for the extensive collection of paintings and artifacts, a sculpture court, a gallery for traveling exhibits, collection storage and support areas, administrative offices, and a large gift shop. At the center of the floor plan is a two-story vaulted stair hall, which provides access to the upper galleries. Throughout the interior the architects used rich woodwork—teak screens and trim and mahogany counters and cabinets—to accent the monochromatic surfaces. The Eiteljorg Museum is among the most popular of Indianapolis' new buildings. It has also been called by *Record* "an unlikely addition to downtown Indianapolis" which "plays by its own rules."

1989 Monumental Award
1990 Indiana Society of Architects, Merit Award
1991 Indianapolis Chapter, American Institute of Architects, Merit Award

26. AT&T Service Network Center

112 West North Street
Architect: Odle/Burke Architects
Contractor: F. A. Wilhelm Construction Co., Inc.
1986

This three-level building houses AT&T administrative offices, test facilities, and equipment for long-distance switching. The building's monolithic form is complemented by the choice of its main material: jumbo utility brick with matching mortar. The use of specially molded, curved brick at the rounded corners and the four-foot diameter brick piers transforms what would otherwise be a utilitarian design into a sophisticated one. An architectural critic felt that "the short, squat columns emphasize the weight of the masonry above and contribute to the overall solidity of the structure." Indiana limestone trim, an aluminum fascia, and an effectively presented logo are the sole decorative elements. Despite the semi-industrial function, the building makes an attempt to relate to its urban context through its entry and orientation to the sidewalk.

26. AT&T Service Network Center

27. Pennsylvania Center

27. Pennsylvania Center

429 North Pennsylvania Street
Architect: CSO/Architects, Inc.
           with Slade Associates
Contractor: Stenz & Associates, Inc.
1987

There is no difficulty discerning the old from the new in this nighttime view that dramatically underscores the contrasting components of the Pennsylvania Center. On the right (south) is the four-story, 1925 Reserve Loan Life Insurance Company Building designed by the well-known architectural firm of Rubush and Hunter and constructed by the William P. Jungclaus Company. Where a parking lot had existed to the north, a major new addition with marble and mirror glass facade was constructed in 1987. The two sides now function as one building. As part of the old building's renovation, a new atrium, open from basement level to the skylight, was created. The new addition is respectfully set back from the front line of the original building. In its mirror glass facade is reflected the World War Memorial Building.

1988 Indianapolis Chapter, American Institute of Architects, Merit Award

28. Lockerbie Marketplace

28. Lockerbie Marketplace

28. Lockerbie Marketplace

New York and Alabama streets
Architect: Gordon Clark Associates, Inc.;
        HDG Architects, Inc.
Contractor: F. A. Wilhelm Construction Co., Inc.;
        Shiel-Sexton Company
1987

Based on the premise that downtown residential development is sustained by available services such as a grocery store, dry cleaners, and drug store, the Mansur Development Company developed the square block bounded by Vermont, New Jersey, New York, and Alabama streets as a mixed use community center. Four buildings combine to form the Lockerbie Marketplace development: 303 North Alabama Street, the old Sears Roebuck & Co. Building of 1929; 333 North Alabama Street, the Vienna Building with its major new addition to the north; 324 East New York Street, the old "M.W.A." Building; and 350 East New York Street, an all-new building combining office and retail space. This aerial photo demonstrates the relationship of the four buildings to the abundant parking provided. With the continuous facades of Vermont Street (most

of which have undergone renovation) and the great focal point of St. Mary's Church enclosing the northeast corner of the block, the parking lot has become the *piazza* of the development. The ground floor restaurant of 333 North Alabama overlooks a landscaped courtyard with fountain. The special importance of the project is its proximity to numerous downtown residential areas, whose residents can walk to shopping, making the Marketplace unique to Indianapolis.

The Sears Building underwent a remarkable transformation when the turquoise aluminum panels added in the 1950s were pulled off and the true architectural character of the building was once again revealed. Originally designed by Nimmons, Carr & Wright, with the local firm of Pierre & Wright consulting on the project, the Sears Building needed extensive rehabilitation in its conversion to new office space and ground-floor grocery store. New windows were installed, substantial amounts of brick were replaced, and limestone detailing around the front entry and tower was restored. In addition to the surface parking lot, there is parking under the building.

29. 225 North New Jersey Street
Architect: HNTB Architects Engineers Planners
Contractor: Webb/Henne—Target Constructors
1986

The architect completely transformed the six-story Printcraft Building, a 1923 industrial structure, into a contemporary office building and headquarters for its firm. Because of the structural capacity of the old building's concrete frame, which was designed with Foster Engineering Company's patented unit slab system, it was feasible to clad the building in "granitized" precast concrete panels. The color banding of the panels is particularly effective when combined with the mirror glass at the curved corner over the entrance. Stainless steel details accent the first floor. A penthouse addition integral to the exterior's design masks the rooftop mechanical equipment.

29. 225 North New Jersey

30. Farm Bureau Insurance Headquarters (before)

30. Farm Bureau Insurance Headquarters
225 South East Street
Architect: Ratio Architects, Inc.
Contractor: F. A. Wilhelm Construction Co., Inc.
1992

No transformation of an Indianapolis industrial building has been more complete than this metamorphosis of an abandoned, 80-year-old tire and rubber factory into an office building for 800 white-collar workers. As the first development of the Quadrant Four Corporate and Science Campus, a downtown alternative to the suburbs, the project involved the major demolition and environmental cleanup of 38 structures and a smokestack on 10 acres. After the primary building was stripped down to its reinforced concrete shell, a new exterior wall was built of glazed curtain wall sections, traditional red brick, and precast concrete panels. Only the original bay divisions remain. A new two-story entry lobby was created on the west side of the building by cutting away the existing concrete structure. Two new floors, an elevator core, and a massive, two-level parking structure to the west were added. Regrettably the tower seen in the "before" shot was also lost in the process; now there is a landscaped roof garden for employees to enjoy on their lunch hour.

30. Farm Bureau Insurance Headquarters (after)

31. Indiana State Capitol Restoration

31. Indiana State Capitol Restoration

31. State Capitol Restoration

31. Indiana State Capitol Restoration
100 North Senate Avenue
Architect: The Cooler Group, Inc.
Contractors: Summit Construction Company, Inc.;
                Glenroy Construction Company, Inc.
1988

In celebration of the centennial anniversary of the state-house's completion, a restoration of its exterior and its interior public spaces was undertaken. When architect Edwin May designed the building in 1878, it was one of the largest and most ambitious capitols in the United States. Its construction spanned 10 years during which time architect Adolph Scherrer overtook the project after May's death. During a century of use and abuse, the building had withstood numerous alterations and renovations: all entrances had been replaced with aluminum storefronts with the loss of the monumental white oak doors on the north and east; all of the original lighting fixtures except those on the fourth floor had been removed in the 1960s and replaced by modern fixtures of inappropriate scale; the atria were cluttered with large wood shacks containing temporary offices and media facilities; the interior public spaces had not been painted since 1958; and all of the interior woodwork had been badly neglected. Clearly the building had become an embarrassment to the state and was due for a comprehensive treatment of its ills.

Highlights of the restoration included the discovery of the original decorative paint scheme of the plaster walls. More than four acres of plaster were hand-stenciled, re-creating the Victorian-era designs. Using the surviving chandeliers and a single sconce as patterns, 131 lighting fixtures were replicated or restored. The large colored glass dome of the 235-foot-high rotunda, which had been leaking and threatened with removal, was restored. In the corridors, the woodwork around the entrances to office suites was reinstated. One of the most dramatic exterior improvements was simply the cleaning of the limestone.

1988 Indianapolis Chapter, American Institute of Architects, Citation Award
1988 Monumental Award

32. Indiana Government Center South

32. Indiana Government Center South

32. Indiana Government Center South
402 West Washington Street
Architect: HNTB Architects Engineers Planners
Associated Architects: Edmund Hafer Architect;
                              Blackburn Associates Architects, Inc.
Contractor: Huber Hunt & Nichols Inc.
1990

The Indiana Government Center South creates a unified presence for the government of the State of Indiana, extends the urban massing and detailing of the Indiana State Capitol Building, and reestablishes the continuity of West Washington Street from downtown to the newly formed White River State Park. With over a million square feet of new office space, this new public building possesses as much presence and creates more urban space than any new project built in Indianapolis during the past 25 years. The entire complex, Indiana Government Centers North and South, provides Indianapolis with a truly monumental civic space rarely built in American cities today. The pedestrian loggias along the two principal east/west streets—Washington and Market streets—are important elements of this civic image (besides providing the practical effect of protecting people from the elements). The new center is appropriately clad in Indiana limestone. The entrances are marked by towers roofed in copper that are reminiscent of the State Capitol Building to the east. On the interior, the five-story barrel-vaulted atrium that provides access to the legislative conference center is the most monumental space of the entire complex. Its design inspiration was the skylit gallery spaces of the 1888 statehouse. Bi-level public courtyards to the east and west of the conference center, which were designed to allow light into the offices, feature grand staircases and sculptural elements.

1992 Indiana Society of Architects, Merit Award
1993 Indianapolis Chapter, American Institute of Architects, Civic Improvement Award

33. Indiana Government Center North

33. Indiana Government Center North

33. Indiana Government Center North

100 North Senate Avenue
Architect: CSO/Architects, Inc.
Associated Architects: 3D/International, Houston
Contractor: Huber Hunt & Nichols Inc.
1993

The original 1960 State Office Building by Graham, Anderson, Probst, and White of Chicago was one of the more aesthetically pure modernist buildings in Indianapolis. As part of the overall redevelopment of the Indiana Government Center, the 14-story structure was renovated to improve energy conservation and replace the inefficient mechanical systems. The skin of the original building (glass and limestone panels) was replaced with a new granite, limestone, and glass curtain wall that appears much more massive and brings the building into the context of the new building adjacent to it. An additional 100,000 square feet of office space was constructed as part of the project. The building serves as a northern boundary for the public space bordered by the Indiana Government Center South, as well as a termination to the north/south axis of the canal. The loggia is based upon the precedent of the southern loggia but is sprinkled with subtle detailing differences. One of the most delightful aspects of the Indiana Government Center North is the new terrace and outdoor spaces on the northwest corner of the building where the canal turns at the employee dining room.

1993 Indianapolis Chapter, American Institute of Architects, Civic Improvement Award

34. Indiana Government Center Parking Facility

34. Indiana Government Center Parking Facility

34. Indiana Government Center Parking Facility
401 West Washington Street
Architect: Kennedy Brown McQuiston Architects
Construction Manager: F. A. Wilhelm Construction Co., Inc.
1988

Located across the street from the Indiana Government Center South, this parking garage was the first building of the new government complex to be constructed, alleviating a critical shortage of parking space. When the state charged the architects with designing a building that would not look like a parking garage, the architects responded with a structure that "broke the mold" for urban concrete parking garages. The forms are responses to the basic functions of the building: stair "towers" on the corners, a mass of horizontal floors in the center, and an automobile entrance at the east end. These masses are articulated by a variety of materials and patterns. The first floor is sheathed with Indiana limestone, creating a base, while the upper floors are of brick, punctuated with various openings or windows and accented by courses of darker brick. Shades of blue highlight handrails, windows, and the massive air shafts.

The most prominent feature of the 3,000-car garage is the octagonal tower on the northeast corner of the building. The interior of this stair tower has been treated more like a building lobby than what is generally found in parking garages; beneath the concrete ceiling's exposed geometric structure are brick walls, stainless steel doors, and tile floors. The underground tunnel connection to the state government complex verges on the opulent, with marble dadoes and custom-patterned carpeting. The garage is set back from Washington Street by 100 feet of lawn, which lends a greater degree of architectural presence. The Indiana Government Center Parking Facility contributes significantly to the state's remaking of West Washington Street.

1989 Indianapolis Chapter, American Institute of Architects, Honor Award

35. Fire Station 13
429 West Ohio Street
Architect: Browning Day Mullins Dierdorf Inc.
Contractor: F. A. Wilhelm Construction Co., Inc.
1987

35. Fire Station 13

Fire Station 13, the first building to be built within the Lower Canal Improvement Area, was intended to serve as a prototype of the design guidelines for new construction along the canal. The basic idea was to introduce low-rise development along the waterway to offset the high-rise skyline to the east. Due to the triangular site imposed by the canal and the programmatic requirement for a five-bay station with a 60-foot-long apron in front, the building acquired an interesting sawtooth plan along its canal facade that reduces the scale of the large building. The steel frame structure is faced with alternating courses of split-faced and a lighter color ground-faced concrete block creating a solid striped effect at the first-floor level. Warm stucco covers the second and third floors, highlighting the recessed, square windows. Color is important to the design, from the teal green hipped roofs of standing-seam terne, to the green glazed aluminum frame overhead doors of the fire truck bays, to the red steel lattice work calling attention to the front entry. Hidden somewhere deep within the design of the fire station is the idea that the building could be a marina and dock for a fanaticized fleet of gondolas floating along the canal. A judge of the 1987 awards program assessed the overall design with the comment: "it would be good in any city under any context."

1987 Indianapolis Chapter, American Institute of Architects, Honor Award
1988 Indiana Society of Architects, Citation Award

35. Fire Station 13

36. Canal Square Apartments
402 West New York Street; 403 West Vermont Street
Architect: Sherman-Carter-Barnhart, PSC, Lexington
Contractor: Arbor Contractors
1990

Covering a city block bounded by New York, West, and Vermont streets and the canal, this large development of 275 apartments includes retail space at canal level and a 500-vehicle parking garage. To avoid perception as a four-story monolithic structure, the facade was divided into smaller elements by projecting and recessing the exterior walls of adjacent apartments and giving each projection its individual gable roof. While the main exterior material is brick, large areas of synthetic stucco provide contrast and color. On the canal side seen here, the wings of the building that extend eastward are raised on loggias to adhere to canal design guidelines. By keeping the parking structure largely concealed within the perimeter of the complex, the building projects a residential image on all sides without the visual impact of a large multistory parking garage facing the streets. Also included is an inner courtyard with swimming pool and sun deck.

36. Canal Square Apartments

37. Canal Overlook Apartments

37. Canal Overlook Apartments
430 Indiana Avenue
Architect: Kennedy Brown McQuiston Architects
Contractor: Charles C. Brandt and Company, Inc.
1988

Located on a triangular site between Indiana Avenue, Vermont Street, and the east side of the canal, this development of 124 apartments stylistically appears to reflect design traditions of a waterfront building, from its porthole references to its rooftop widow's walk. Its colors—two shades of gray with white trim—recall seaside buildings. The irregularity of the site proved to be one of the most difficult problems to solve, since the building stretches to the limits of its property line. The wings of the building extend to the edge of the canal and are raised on loggias to allow pedestrian circulation along the waterway. By keeping the parking concealed underneath the complex, the building avoids the visual impact of a large parking garage. Office space is incorporated on the lower levels of both the Indiana Avenue and canal sides. One of the most pleasant aspects of the building is its canal walk, which includes a small fountain just south of the Michigan Street bridge.

38. American College of Sports Medicine Headquarters
401 West Michigan Street
Architect: Peckham Guyton Albers & Viets, Inc., St.
            Louis, Missouri
Contractor: Charles C. Brandt Company, Inc.
1984

The most interesting aspect of this building's exterior—the undulating brick wall along its east elevation—was a direct response to the site, the original address of the Kuhn House (see Historic Landmarks Foundation Headquarters). Located along the historic canal, the wall recalls wave patterns evoked by the waterway. The building's sign leaves no question as to the identity of this structure. The American College of Sports Medicine is a professional association of team physicians, trainers, coaches, physiologists, and other experts in sports medicine and related specialties. The organization's headquarters include private offices, multipurpose rooms, a library, a lounge, and various support facilities. Interiors feature use of glass block windows and partitions.

38. College of Sports Medicine

38. American College of Sports Medicine

39. Historic Landmarks Foundation of Indiana Headquarters

340 West Michigan Street
Architect: Ratio Architects, Inc.
Contractor: Shiel-Sexton Co., Inc.
1991

In 1984 when the Charles Kuhn House was threatened with demolition, the 400-ton structure was moved to its present site along the canal, where it remained vacant and awaiting a use for six years. Historic Landmarks Foundation of Indiana then chose it as the site of its new state headquarters. The architect's challenge was to design a major addition to the 1879 Italianate house without compromising the building's historic significance. A new three-story glass atrium joins the brick addition to the old house, physically indicating the division between the old and new. Ceiling and floor levels were aligned with the old building for functionality of plan and to create a unified exterior design. The original building had no basement, but the new site offered the opportunity to incorporate canal-level commercial spaces fronting a raised terrace. One of the more successful examples of the old building's influence on the new addition's design is the new third-floor balcony railing, which reinterprets the house's bracketed cornice.

39. Historic Landmarks Foundation of Indiana Headquarters

40. 500 Place

40. 500 Place

500 Indiana Avenue
Architect: Blackburn Associates Architects, Inc.
Contractor: Oscar Robertson Associates;
            Shiel-Sexton Co., Inc.
1992

Keeping with the tradition of "flatiron" buildings on Indiana Avenue, 500 Place takes its form from its triangular site. Located at the intersection of the canal and Indiana Avenue (where a tower rises to celebrate the juncture), this building was designed to contribute to the redevelopment of the historic area while taking design cues from neighboring buildings. For example, the general size and rhythm of the windows was derived from local historic buildings as was the choice for a traditional brick facade. Along the lower level of the three-story canal facade, there is an open loggia that responds to pedestrian circulation along the waterway. Because of the unusual triangular form, two skylit atrium wells provide natural light to the core of the building.

42. Technology Transfer Center
714 North Capitol Avenue
Architect: Everett I. Brown Company
Contractor: Browning Construction, Inc.
1991

As the first building of a Science and Technology Park, co-developed by the Near North Development Corporation and Browning Investments, the goal of this center is to attract high-tech companies to an eight-block area parallel to the historic canal. The Electronics Manufacturing Productivity Facility, a joint venture between the Navy and private industry, is the anchor tenant, occupying the first two floors of the building. The canal level, with exposed ceiling structure up to 14 feet high, reflects the special requirements of the manufacturing area. Both the canal side and north elevations feature a three-story glazed window wall with pedimented top, which is repeated in a two-story version at the south elevation. Color plays an important role in the building's architectural expression: buff brick on the upper two floors contrasts with the ground floor red brick, and green window lintels and panels at the pediments add interest.

42. Technology Transfer Center

41. Walnut Street Pedestrian Bridge
West Walnut Street and the Indianapolis Canal
Architect: Ratio Architects, Inc.
Contractor: E. H. Hughes
1991

The Walnut Street pedestrian bridge is a part of the Walnut Street Basin of the Indianapolis Canal Walk, the city's long-term project to turn a historic water transportation corridor into a linear park. The city's goal is to use the park as a catalyst to spur residential and commercial development in the canal district, which until recently was primarily industrial. The bridge consists of massive limestone abutments, a framework of mechanically fastened, lightweight steel members, and a wooden walkway. The lively design contains references to Indianapolis' past bridges. Although an architectural project, the design benefits from the contribution of the project's structural engineer, Wetzel Engineers.

41. Walnut Street Pedestrian Bridge

43. Union Station Restoration

43. Union Station Restoration

43. Union Station Restoration

39 Jackson Place
Architect: Browning Day Mullins Dierdorf Inc.
　　　　　Woollen, Molzan and Partners
Construction Manager: F. A. Wilhelm Construction Co., Inc.
1986

The country's first "union station"—that is, a centralized station for the common use of passengers of many independent rail lines—was constructed adjacent to this site in 1853. The building featured in these photos, designed by architect and engineer Thomas Rodd of Pittsburgh, was built as a replacement in 1887-88. It is one of the finest examples of the Romanesque Revival style in the Midwest and one of the city's most historically and architecturally significant buildings. The three-story-high, barrel-vaulted, skylit waiting room has been likened to a cathedral and is one of the most outstanding public spaces in the state of Indiana. Major alterations and additions to the station, designed by the local firm of D. A. Bohlen and Son in 1912-13, resulted in such features as the waiting room's stained-glass wheel windows and the immigrant waiting room. The 14 elevated tracks, train shed, and pedestrian concourse, which replaced the 1880s cast-iron train shed, date to a 1916-22 expansion project designed by architects Price and McLanahan of Philadelphia. Recognized for its major achievements in traffic engineering, the seven-acre train shed complex is among less than a dozen that survive in the United States today.

For all of its glory, Union Station went through a slow deterioration. From the 200 passenger trains that passed through daily at the turn of the century, traffic had almost ceased by 1970 when the Penn Central fell into bankruptcy. Several attempts were made to stabilize the building in the late 1970s, but it took the comprehensive approach of developer Robert Borns to save the station as a festival marketplace. Preserving the most significant architectural elements, the $30-million restoration focused on retaining the experience of a station in its conversion to over 100 restaurants and shops. As an example of the extensive work necessary in the two-year project, nearly 90 percent of the ornate plaster in the head house (1880s building) had to be replaced because of destructive water damage. The development of the trackside market retained the open structural supports of the train shed, incorporating skylights above and references to the rails in the new floor.

1986 Indiana Society of Architects, Citation Award
1986 Indianapolis Chapter, American Institute of Architects, Merit Award
1986 Monumental Award

44. Holiday Inn at Union Station
123 West Louisiana Street
Architect: Browning Day Mullins Dierdorf Inc.
Construction Manager: F. A. Wilhelm Construction Co., Inc.
1986

Here's a Holiday Inn that doesn't look like all the others you've seen. The allure of staying overnight in a railroad car, even for those who never traveled in a train before, was a powerful influence in the transformation of the west section of Union Station's elevated train shed and concourse. While the highlight to guests may be the 13 Pullman train cars remodeled into suites at track side, the architectural significance of the 275-room hotel lies in the way new construction was fit into the existing building, accentuating the station's original structural steel system. The new umbrella-like, glass-roofed canopy at the entrance distinguishes the hotel function from the restaurants to the east.

44. Holiday Inn at Union Station

44. Holiday Inn at Union Station

45. Omni Severin Hotel

45. Omni Severin Hotel
40 West Jackson Place
Architect: Ratio Architects, Inc.
Contractor: F. A. Wilhelm Construction Co., Inc.
1989

The Severin Hotel (later known as the Atkinson Hotel) was constructed in 1912-13 to the design of local architects Vonnegut and Bohn. In 1989 the 12-story building simultaneously underwent a major renovation and transforming expansion. This photo focuses on the Jackson Street side of the addition made to the south of the old hotel, directly across from Union Station. The Illinois Street elevation continues the brick facade, limestone trim, rectangular window pattern, and ground-floor rustication of the original building. However, the south side's twin towers with glass curtain walls give the hotel an entirely new image. The number of guest rooms was expanded from 333 to 423, including 27 suites, 11 two-story penthouses, and nine penthouse rooms with walkout balconies. Interior restoration work focused on the historic lobby with its grand marble staircase and moulded plaster detailing. The monumental, two-story-tall, arched windows that had been blocked in the late 1960s were opened, once again bathing the original lobby with natural light.

46. Canterbury Hotel

47. Harness Factory Lofts
30 East Georgia Street
Architect: Ratio Architects, Inc.
Contractor: McCarthy Brothers, St. Louis
1986

Originally constructed as the John W. Murphy Building in 1910-11, this structure was named for one of the wholesale district's leading wholesale dry goods merchants. The Murphy Building was unique in that it housed small wholesale and manufacturing operations in office suites more on the pattern of an office building than a warehouse. In the early 1980s it mistakenly acquired the popular name "harness factory" from an adjacent building. Among the first generation of concrete frame buildings in the city, its open column grid and expansive windows made it well suited for conversion to 101 loft apartments. Exposed ceilings with generous floor-to-floor heights allowed open and airy interiors.

46. Canterbury Hotel
123 South Illinois Street
Architect: Browning Day Mullins Dierdorf Inc.
Program Manager: Toth-Ervin Inc.
1984

Constructed in 1928-29 as the Hotel Lockerbie but known from the 1930s on as the Warren Hotel, this 12-story building was designed by architect Bennett Kay of Indianapolis. As one of several hotels in the vicinity of Union Station, it catered to travelers. As passenger trains declined in number, the clientele of the Warren likewise decreased, forcing the hotel to close in the mid-1970s. It remained vacant for a decade until its rebirth as the Canterbury Hotel, which offers upscale lodgings modeled on a small, elegant European hotel. By reducing the number of rooms from the original 200 sleeping rooms to 100, larger accommodations were made possible. Suites on the third through eleventh floors have varied room arrangements, many with formal sitting areas and separate adjoining parlors. The top floor is devoted to penthouse suites with loft bedrooms illuminated by skylights. As part of the hotel's exterior restoration, an elegant new entrance with marquee was installed. The first floor enjoys open reception areas where existing architectural elements were restored.

1985 Indianapolis Chapter, American Institute of Architects, Citation Award

47. Harness Factory Lofts

48. Morrison Opera Place

47 South Meridian Street
Architect: Archonics Design Partnership
Contractor: Charles C. Brandt and Company, Inc.
1979

When an initial feasibility study concluded that this building should be torn down, it was covered in 1950s porcelain panels and all of its windows were bricked in. An about-face approach saved it and made it a demonstration project for the potential of rehabilitating historic commercial structures south of Washington Street. The new name, Morrison Opera Place, refers to an earlier building on this site that was destroyed by fire. This building, constructed in 1871, is now the only surviving building in the wholesale district to exhibit three floors of the arcade motif in which the round-arched windows' hood molds are connected by an impost course. During the 1979 architectural work, the bracketed Italianate cornice was reproduced based on the original, and a new simplified storefront was added along both the Meridian Street and part of the Maryland Street facades. Typical of projects of this era, the interior was refinished to expose brick walls and wood structural members; original elements such as pressed metal ceilings, decorative cast-iron columns, and a curving oak stairway were retained.

48. Morrison Opera Place

49. Omega Communications Building

49. Omega Communications Building

29 East Maryland Street
Architect: Archonics Design Partnership
Contractor: Stenz Construction Corporation
1982

For many years known as the Hatfield Paint Building, this commercial building is the lone surviving unit of a larger structure constructed in 1867-68 as the Holland and Ostermeyer Block. Somewhat akin to the speculative commercial strip of our time, the "block"—a building type composed of modular units—was important to the development of the mid-19th-century wholesale district. In the architectural work undertaken in 1982, the intent was to marry both historic and contemporary styles in lieu of a strict restoration. Replacement of missing elements that had disappeared over time relied on simple, straightforward new forms that retained the character and proportion of the original building. The new cornice of sheet metal and satin finish aluminum is an example of the blending of old and new elements. In like manner the new storefront features simplified and abstracted components. On the interior, the mezzanine space was opened up to reveal original cast-iron columns with ornate capitals and a wood coffered ceiling. A new bridge connects the mezzanine with a staircase, providing access to the second floor.

1982 Indiana Society of Architects, Citation Award

50. The Century Building

51. Majestic Building

47 South Pennsylvania Street
Architect: Woollen, Molzan and Partners
Contractor: MacDougall & Pierce Construction, Inc.
1983

In 1895-96 the prosperous Indianapolis Gas Company erected its new 10-story Majestic Building designed by the firm D. A. Bohlen & Son. It was the first "skyscraper" in Indianapolis and indeed one of the first in the Midwest outside Chicago. A large ground-floor space was reserved for the company's public lobby, where gas customers paid their bills and did business in surroundings that vied with the poshest bank lobbies of the era. Some 85 years later, this space had experienced a sad metamorphosis through a lowered ceiling, partitioning and cubicles, blocked windows, and other insensitive alterations made during a succession of makeshift modernizations. When an extensive program of restoration and renovation was undertaken throughout the building in the early 1980s, many of the original architectural features of the ground-floor space were discovered to have survived intact. The potential of adaptively reusing it as a restaurant was realized, capitalizing on features such as the 18-foot ceilings, marble-sheathed Corinthian columns, leaded-glass transoms, ceramic tile floor, and mezzanine level.

50. The Century Building

36 South Pennsylvania Street
Architect: HDG Architects, Inc.
Contractor: Shiel-Sexton Co., Inc.
1983

In 1901 Samuel H. Brubaker and Company of St. Louis designed this seven-story brick building for the printing industry. The only major exterior alteration that occurred over the next 80 years was the removal of the projecting bracketed cornice, which was restored during the course of the 1983 renovation. Ground-floor storefronts and double-hung windows were replaced or restored to their original proportions. Most of the work focused on the interior of the building, where a former light court was enclosed by a gently vaulted skylight to form a 50-foot-square, 100-foot-high atrium. The black-and-green Italian marble floor of this space represents one of the major investments in materials, made with the desire to create a Class A office building. Along the atrium's west side, where a parking garage was added, a 40-foot-long waterfall cascades down against a black marble wall.

1984 Indiana Society of Architects, Honor Award

51. Majestic Building

53. Stout's Gray Building

53. Stout's Gray Building
314 Massachusetts Avenue
Architect: Schmidt Associates Architects, Inc.
Contractor: Shiel-Sexton Co., Inc.
1983

Known as Stout's Gray Building for the color of its brick facade, this narrow, three-story building (only 16 feet wide) was constructed in the 1870s for commercial use. By the time of its 1983 conversion into an art gallery and residence for the gallery owner, the original ground-floor facade had been nearly obliterated. Exterior restoration focused on rebuilding the tall storefront configuration, which amply lights the first-floor gallery, and replacing missing architectural elements. The upper floors work like a townhouse with bedrooms on the third floor and entertainment and living spaces on the second. To provide an open and light-filled space, no full-height partition walls were used in the new plan, and a light shaft was constructed to bring in additional natural light.

1983 Indianapolis Chapter, American Institute of Architects, Honor Award
1984 Indiana Society of Architects, Citation Award

52. Hammond Block
301 Massachusetts Avenue
Architect: Schmidt-Claffey Architects, Inc.
Contractor: MacDougall & Pierce Construction, Inc.
1980

Known as the Budnick Building from 1945 to 1980, by which time the building had become an eyesore, this 1874 flatiron building underwent a dramatic transformation in its conversion from a fishing supply store to professional offices. Rehabilitation of the Hammond Block created a downtown landmark that inspired similar projects along Massachusetts Avenue. Most of the inappropriate changes that had occurred to the building over the years took place at the ground floor, due to its having been lowered to sidewalk level. The original raised first floor was restored and made accessible by new cast-iron steps. Following federal preservation guidelines, the exterior was cleaned chemically, and architectural features such as the window caps and cornice were painted to match stone elements. Bricked-up windows were opened, and a new identifying parapet tablet resembling the original was installed. This project opened the eyes of many Indianapolis citizens to the possibilities of historic preservation.

1981 Indianapolis Chapter, American Institute of Architects, Merit Award

52. Hammond Block

54. Marott Center
342 Massachusetts Avenue
Architect: Kennedy Brown McQuiston Architects
Contractor: Stenz Construction Corporation
1986

Built in 1906 as a department store by developer George Marott, this building was designed by the locally prominent firm of Rubush and Hunter. It exhibits one of the city's most representative facades of the Chicago School of architecture as characterized by the wide bays and three-part windows. During the exterior restoration, the cornice was reconstructed and the transom was repaired based on photo research. However, the story of the building's transformation into law offices focused on the interior rather than the exterior. A new four-story, skylit atrium was created above the first-floor commercial space by opening up the grand staircase. The woodwork of the stairs, with original balusters and railings, richly counterpoints the modern qualities of the atrium, such as its pentagonal form and whitewashed walls.

54. Marott Center

55. Oxford Building

55. Oxford Building
316 East Vermont Street
Architect: Ratio Architects, Inc.
Contractor: Shiel-Sexton Co., Inc.
1990

As with many buildings on the diagonal Massachusetts Avenue, this building dating from the 1890s has two facades: one on Massachusetts and one on Vermont Street. The building's unique shape, consisting of two trapezoids connected at an angle, provided a structural challenge in opening up the building for use as a studio for an advertising agency. The most dramatic change was in converting an existing light well into a three-story atrium capped with an octagonal glass belvedere at roof level. Structural steel is used as a decorative element throughout the building in steel railings, steel grated bridges that span the atrium, cantilevered spiral stairs to the belvedere, and contrasting blue canopies at the first-floor level. (Don't expect to stay dry when you stand under the canopies in the rain!)

1993 Indianapolis Chapter, American Institute of Architects, Citation Award

Regional Center

Regional Center directory

61. St. Phillip's Church
62. Goodwin Plaza Housing
82. Ferger Building
83. Sigma Theta Tau Building
84. Walker Theatre
85. Lockefield Garden Apartments
86. IU Natatorium
87. Indianapolis Sports Center
88. National Institute of Fitness & Sports
89. IU Track & Field Stadium

90. IUPUI Library
91. University Place Hotel
92. University Place Conference Center
93. IU Medical Research & Library Bldg.
94. Riley Hospital for Children
95. Ronald McDonald House
96. Whale & Dolphin Pavilion
97. Waters Building.
98. River Promenade
99. Water Company Pumping Station

Regional Center

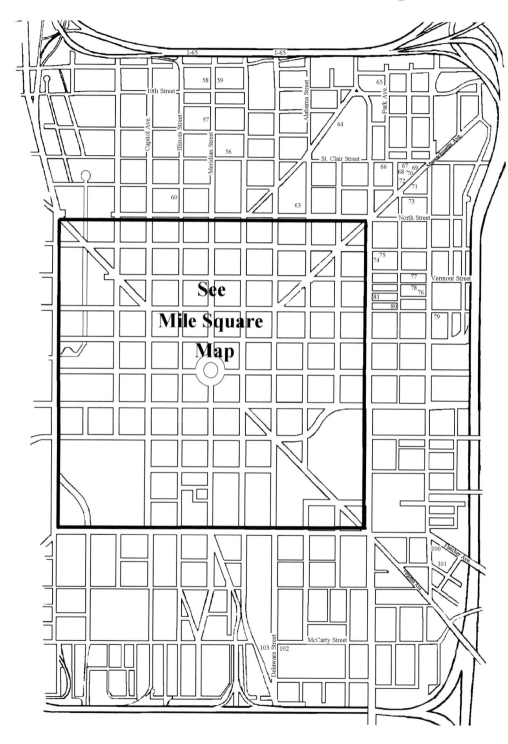

56. Central Library
57. Turnverein Apartments
58. WTHR Studios
59. Landmark Center
60. Design Printing Company
63. Riley Tower Renovations
64. Renaissance Place
65. Chatham Park
66. Jones-Atkinson House
67. Phoenix Theatre
68. Cordell Residence
69. Old Fire Station 2
70. Chatham Block
71. Three-S Reproductions
72. Argyle Block
73. Real Silk Lofts
74. Lockerbie Town Homes
75. Lockerbie Glove Factory
76. Sutphin Residence
77. La Rosa Residence
78. Lockerbie Flats
79. Rowland Associates Building
80. Carriage houses
81. Binford House
100. Fletcher Place Methodist Church
101. Union Laundry Lofts
102. Eli Lilly & Company Headquarters
103. Eli Lilly & Company Garage

57. Turnverein Apartments

57. Turnverein Apartments
902 North Meridian Street
Architect: Browning Day Mullins Dierdorf Inc.
Construction Manager: Stenz Construction Corporation
1985

Constructed in 1914 for the Independent Turnverein, a German social and athletic association, this building was designed by architect Adolf Scherrer in a distinctive local variation of the Prairie style. Long having lost its original function (serving in interim years as a classroom building for IUPUI), in the early 1980s the opportunity arose to save the building through conversion to luxury apartments. High points of restoration work included restoring the lower and upper level windows, all of which had been bricked in, and returning the main lobby, with its grand stairway of marble and walnut, to its original glory. To utilize the many and varied spaces of the building, 51 unique floor plans were developed, many with two levels and private entrances or terraces. At the northeast corner of the site, between the original building and a 1954 addition, a new addition was built for townhouse-style apartments. This infill portion has been praised for being compatible in scale, materials, and architectural detail with the original building, although it could have been set back in deference to the historic structure's four-square massing.

1985 Indianapolis Chapter, American Institute of Architects, Merit Award

56. Central Library Interior Restoration
40 East St. Clair Street
Architect: James Associates, Inc.
          with H. Roll McLaughlin, FAIA
Contractor: Alte Bauart, Inc.
1985

Constructed in 1913-16 to the design of eminent French-born architect Paul Philippe Cret, with Zantzinger, Borie & Medary as associate architects, this limestone, Doric-inspired library has been called "the best classic building in America." Its 100-foot-long, 43-foot-high main reading room, with its ceiling decoratively painted in Pompeian style to reflect the history of Indiana, is one of the grandest interior spaces of the city. Nearly 70 years' accumulation of airborne pollution had taken its toll on the ceiling, which is covered with linen originally hand-painted and stenciled in a Philadelphia studio. Restoration was complicated by a misguided cleaning effort in 1939 that removed a protective layer of varnish. In the six-week restoration undertaken on scaffolding à la Michelangelo, 147 colors and glazes were matched and approximately 20 percent of the ceiling was overpainted. Measures were undertaken to preserve all underlying original artwork. The 12-foot-diameter circular lighting fixtures of solid bronze were taken down and redecorated with the same rich colors found throughout the room. In addition to the restoration of interior plaster, marble, stone, and oak woodwork, cove lighting in the east and west reading rooms was reinstated and new cork flooring was installed throughout.

56. Central Library Interior

58. WTHR Channel 13 Studios
1000 North Meridian Street
Architect: Browning Day Pollak Mullins Dierdorf Inc.
Contractor: Geupel DeMars Inc.
1983

The offices and studios of television station WTHR are located within this 40,000-square-foot facility constructed of Indiana limestone and reflective glass. The sleek, curving lines of the low-scale building, emphasized by the continuous bands of windows at each story, are unlike anything else constructed on Meridian Street. This has led some critics to praise the building while others criticize its lack of relationship to the street. The site accommodates parking for employees, visitors, and mobile broadcasting vehicles, a 200-foot broadcast tower, and a helicopter landing pad. The site's landscaping was among the first to include seasonal displays of flowers, which in turn inspired other such plantings in the downtown area. Within the building the circulation pattern allows visitors to observe television broadcasting and production without disrupting activities.

58. WTHR Channel 13 Studios

59. Landmark Center

59. Landmark Center
1099 North Meridian Street
Architect: Browning Day Mullins Dierdorf Inc.
Contractor: Browning Construction Inc.
1984

Located just south of the interstate at the northeast corner of 10th and Meridian streets, this 12-story office building has been likened to a medieval sentry tower at the walled entrance to a city. The architect's desire for a highly visible building for this location, and Browning Investments' need for a maximum of corner offices, resulted in the unusual 12-sided plan. The structure is the first of this developer's downtown speculative office buildings to utilize an assembly of a precast concrete frame with a panelized, polished granite skin. At the four major pedimented elevations, a projecting triangular bay of darkly tinted glass rises from the third through 12th floors, adding to the overall angular effect. Although originally sited to be square with the corner site, the building was shifted 45 degrees off axis resulting in a greater play of its diagonals.

60. Design Printing Company Addition
626 North Illinois Street
Architect: Robert H. Hindman and Associates, Inc.
Contractor: Challenger Construction Inc.
1985

In making a major addition to this three-story building from the 1920s that has always served the printing industry, the architect picked up a number of design cues from the original building without making a literal copy of it. The success of the project derives from several factors: its siting, respectfully stepped back from the main structure; its basic form, with the new gable end emphatically echoing the original; and its materials, from the dark brick and suggestions of half-timbering to the perfectly matched, glazed green tile roof. An architectural critic summed it up: "What makes this a sensitive addition is that it uses just enough form from the original structure to assure context and harmony."

60. Design Printing Building

61. St Phillip's Church

61. St. Phillip's Episcopal Church
720 North Martin Luther King, Jr. Drive
Architect: Woollen, Molzan and Partners
Contractor: DBD Construction Co.
1986

The arches of the Church of Santa Chiara in Assisi, Italy, whose buttresses span across an adjacent street, inspired the form of this new church. The shifting of planes on the front elevation of the church reflects the differing functions as they are organized in plan. Behind the southern half of the facade, the side with the large half-arch window, is the choir loft of the sanctuary. A freestanding wall above the flat roof of the north side completes the facade's dynamic symmetry and lends a greater sense of presence to the building. The sanctuary is infused with direct and indirect light through a variety of windows, while the altar is softly lit by vertical windows on the north side.

63. Riley Towers Renovation
600 North Alabama Street
Architect: Ratio Architects, Inc.
Contractor: Sexton Companies
1989

Riley Towers, a pair of 30-story high-rise buildings with a mid-rise one between, was constructed in 1963 to the designs of architects Perkins and Will of Chicago. It was to have been part of a much larger development on the model of Chicago's Sandburg Village. Renovations in 1989 created a new image for Indianapolis' tallest residential buildings and dealt with the practical aspects of upgrading 500 apartments nearly 30 years old. A new exterior color scheme of burgundy spandrel panels and green vertical mullions greatly adds to the towers' presence. Atop each building, clusters of flagpoles and horizontal metal banding lend a new identity on the skyline while screening mechanical units and visually balancing the cantilevered balconies. An economy of means gave Riley Towers a more vertical thrust and a new look somewhat reminiscent of Russian Constructivist architectural work of the early 20th century.

63. Riley Towers Renovation

62. Goodwin Plaza Housing
601 West St. Clair Street
Architect: Blackburn Associates Architects, Inc.
Construction Manager: Cloverleaf Properties, Inc.
1984

As the first new housing project built in an inner-city black neighborhood in 10 years, Goodwin Plaza was intended to help preserve the residential character of the area while restoring the feeling of community that had been undermined by blight. The three-story building incorporates 100 one-bedroom apartments that radiate in four directions from a central entrance and community room, the social center of the building. A courtyard off the parlor to the rear of the building provides a garden setting for gatherings removed from the street. The combination of painted wood siding and brick ground-floor and center sections, detailed with courses of darker brown jumbo brick, gives the building a residential character so often missing in institutional housing projects.

62. Goodwin Plaza Housing

64. Renaissance Place Residences
Walnut, St. Clair, and Arch streets
Architect: Browning Day Pollak Mullins Inc.
Contractor: Borns Construction Co.
1982

For years the city waited for a developer to come forward to construct housing on lots across the street from Riley Towers, cleared for grand-scale urban renewal. When Borns Management Corporation submitted a proposal to build suburban-style condominiums on the land, it was accepted. The 30 frame buildings, each containing four units, enjoy front or backyards, individual driveways, and garages. While some critics have dubbed the project "Nora comes downtown" for its low-density solution to an urban site, the condos proved to be very popular, selling out within a few days of their completion.

64. Renaissance Place Residences

65. Chatham Park

65. Chatham Park
930-940 North Park Avenue
Architect: Mozingo Associates, Inc.
Contractor: RDC, Inc.
1987

This residential condominium development of six units is a modern variant of traditional side-by-side doubles, which from this view appear to form a line of row houses. Called "Neo-Victorian" in style, the buildings are distinguished by a mix of siding materials—lap siding, wood shingles, and decorative panels. The repetition of bay windows and entry porches creates a rhythm along the street facade. At the corner of Park and 10th, the mass of the building is stepped back to provide an interesting north elevation. Highlighting the exterior design is a varied paint scheme in which the trim boards are accentuated by their whiteness.

66. Jones-Atkinson Residence
515 East St. Clair Street
Architect: Mozingo Associates, Inc.
Contractor: R. Thomas Jones
1989

This new house draws its design inspiration from the John Owen Residence, an 1867 Italianate farmhouse in Johnson County. Without attempting a direct copy, the architect followed the general proportions and materials of the traditional "I" house type. Variations such as the overscaled cornice brackets and the limestone details distinguish it as a modern building. (The three-car garage attached at the rear is also a dead giveaway!) The brickwork of the chimneys, the blind arches of the end walls, and the paneled wood reveals at the front entrance are notable. On the interior, the typical pattern of self-contained rooms was opened up to accommodate a modern, informal life-style. Cherry and painted woodwork was modeled on the Colonial Revival style.

66. Jones-Atkinson Residence

67. Phoenix Theatre

67. Phoenix Theatre
749 North Park Street
Architect: James E. Lingenfelter, AIA;
　　　　　Urban Amenities/Architecture
1989

Originally built in 1907 as the First United Brethren Church, this building was designed by the prominent local architectural firm of Rubush and Hunter. It served a number of successive denominations after the original congregation moved to a larger church at 704 North Park. By the early 1980s it was in a state of great disrepair and had lost most of the original stained glass in its Gothic-style windows. In 1988 a new adaptive use as a community theater saved the building. As part of its transformation, many of its stylistic details were restored, from the crenellations at the north entrance to the careful repair of all windows, keeping the wood tracery in place. The interior includes a steeply raked, 150-seat house with a box office and lobby on the main floor; classrooms and a rehearsal space on the lower level; and administrative offices in the former choir loft.

69. Old Fire Station 2 and Livery Stable

748 Massachusetts Avenue
Architect: Schmidt Associates Architects, Inc.
Contractors: Jungclaus-Campbell Co., Inc.;
        S. C. Nestel, Inc.
1985-90

Built in 1871, this building is now the oldest remaining fire station in Indianapolis. It was in continuous use until the early 1930s when a new station on East 11th Street replaced it. Over subsequent decades it was used as a garage and underwent many unfortunate alterations including the construction of a one-story addition built along the street line in the late 1940s, which obscured the building. One of the first steps in its conversion into the headquarters for the Indianapolis Professional Firefighters Union was the demolition of this addition. The union also purchased the adjacent building at 750 Massachusetts Avenue, originally built in 1894 as a livery stable. Utilizing the undeveloped space between the buildings for all vertical circulation, the two structures were developed in concert for varied uses: a museum will occupy the station's original apparatus room with overflow space in the old stable; union offices are on the station's second floor; and the Survive Alive program, a fire safety program for schoolchildren, occupies the second floor of the livery. Highlights of the thorough exterior restoration include the reconstruction of the third stage of the bell tower, which had disappeared over the years, and the replacement of inappropriate doors and windows with units matching the originals.

69. Old Fire Station 2 and Livery Stable

68. James and Elizabeth Cordell Residence

68. James and Elizabeth Cordell Residence

729 North Park Avenue
Architect: Heartland Design/Architects
Contractor: Meyer & Najem Corporation
1988

The Italianate style of architecture popular in the 1870s influenced the design of this new house in Chatham Arch. Features common to the historic style include the tall proportions, hipped roof, cornice brackets, and side porch. The projecting wood frame bay, the dominant element of the main facade, is patterned from 1890s urban home designs by Frank Lloyd Wright. This residence was among the first of the new arrivals in this neighborhood, which has recently experienced a significant revitalization.

70. Chatham Place Block

700 Massachusetts Avenue
Architect: Mozingo Williamson Architects, Inc.
Contractor: RGK Real Estate Development
1992

Occupying a prominent site along Massachusetts Avenue at Chatham Square, the Chatham Place Block's unusual form was dictated by the bounds of the parcel of land upon which it was built in 1875. Its most distinctive feature is the arcade of cast-iron columns and stone arches. The original storefronts of this Italianate building were never altered, a testimony to its fine design. The building has been redeveloped to combine first-floor commercial use with two-story residential units on the second and third floors. This development retained historic features such as the original open walnut staircase, which has become the focal point of one of the five residential units.

70. Chatham Place Block

71. Three-S Reproductions Building

71. Three-S Reproductions Building

643 Massachusetts Avenue
Architect: Charles A. Totten, Jr.
Contractor: Meyer & Najem Corporation
1992

The construction of the new headquarters for Three-S Reproductions is significant as the first new building in the Massachusetts Avenue historic district in over 30 years. Responding to the scale of late-19th-century commercial buildings along the avenue, this brick building takes its place as a background infill structure. The arched windows on the second floor and the large glass areas at street level recall commercial buildings of the late 1800s. The prominent carved limestone sign at the entrance reflects a pride of ownership that has been lost in this day of speculative office buildings.

73. Real Silk Lofts

73. Real Silk Lofts
611 North Park Avenue
Architect: Mozingo Associates, Inc.
Contractor: Van Rooy Development
1988

Seventy condominiums transformed three buildings of the former Real Silk Hosiery Mills into one of the largest-scale adaptive reuse projects of its type in the city. The main building—a five-story, reinforced concrete structure that expanded the plant's production capacity by 50 percent—was originally built by the Ferro Concrete Company in 1929. The condominiums take advantage of large industrial sash windows that offer abundant natural light, views of downtown, and greenhouse-like balconies. The 14-foot ceilings add to the spaciousness of one- and two-bedroom units that average over 1,200 square feet each. A new entry to the building was created at the site of the adjacent 1924 power plant, which retains its tall stack as a reminder of its industrial heritage.

72. The Argyle Building
600-614 Massachusetts Avenue
Architect: Bradbury Associates Inc.
Contractor: William S. Connor & Company
1987

When constructed by the John S. Spann Company in 1911, this large flatiron building contained 90 sleeping rooms and 10 commercial establishments in the storefronts along Massachusetts Avenue and East Street. During the building's conversion to 46 HUD-sponsored apartments in 1974-75, the storefronts were removed, their openings were boarded and stuccoed, and small new aluminum windows to illuminate ground-floor apartments were installed. The 1987 architectural work re-created the storefronts' large expanses of glass, transoms, and low paneled bases, particularly important at the building's point with its distinctive bowed projection. The exterior materials of brown, salt-glazed brick, and terra-cotta trim were in excellent condition, requiring only a minor amount of cleaning where the 1970s supergraphics had extended. The Argyle is another example of how architectural treatments of some of our older buildings have come full circle in the relatively short period of time between the mid 1970s and the present.

72. The Argyle Building

74. Lockerbie Town Homes
North and South Lockerbie Circle
Architect: Archonics Design Partnership
Contractor: Sweet & Co.
1982

Developed in concert with the conversion of the Indianapolis Glove Company building to housing, these 54 new town houses and the factory condominiums nearly doubled the population of the Lockerbie Square historic district. The town houses have been described as a good example of new housing of contemporary design that responds well to the nearby historic buildings. The two-and-a-half-story units reflect late-19th-century design with their tall proportions, narrow windows, gabled roofs, and arched entries. The encircling historic brick wall of the 1878 Little Sisters of the Poor Home for the Aged, which was located on this site until its demolition in 1968, was retained but punctured with openings for streets, drive-ways, and sidewalks.

1984 Indianapolis Chapter, American Institute of Architects, Citation Award

74. Lockerbie Town Homes

75. Lockerbie Glove Company Condominiums

75. Lockerbie Glove Company Condominiums
430 North Park Street
Architect: Archonics Design Partnership
Contractor: Stenz Construction Corporation
1982

While the conversion of industrial buildings to residential use had been common in urban centers across the United States for more than a dozen years, the transformation of the Lockerbie Glove Company's manufacturing building to housing was the first project of its type in Indianapolis. Located at the southwest corner of Michigan and Park streets, the six-story factory was originally constructed between 1908 and 1916. The conversion to 60 condominiums capitalized on the interior's 12-foot ceilings, exposed brick walls and heavy timbers, and the large original windows. Because the project followed federal restoration guidelines, only minor modifications were made to the exterior. This view from the west shows the new glass-enclosed entry from North Lockerbie Circle and the surrounding Lockerbie Town Homes. At the Park Street side, the elegant bronze entry marquee was retained.

76. Samuel B. and Kerry Sutphin Residence

76. Samuel B. and Kerry Sutphin Residence
422 North College Avenue
Architect: Barry Smith
Contractor: Hank Gunn, Whitestown
1986

This rear view of the Sutphin Residence, with its lap pool in the foreground, demonstrates the possibilities for the residential development of vacant lots in historic districts. The main elevation facing College Avenue is reflective of historic homes along the street, especially in its materials (wood lap siding, trim boards, and detailing). The steeply pitched, hipped, pyramidal roof is reminiscent of a popular roof form in Indianapolis during the 1890s. The front window wall, however, helps to distinguish this house as a modern building. The private rear elevation exhibits greater design freedom, as shown by the large window openings and the balconies with pipe railings at the second- and third-floor levels.

77. Joseph and Delores La Rosa Residence
627 East Vermont Street
Architect: Bentley La Rosa Salasky Design, New York
Contractor: Libra Construction
1988

For over 60 years the site of this house was a vacant lot until the new owners saw the potential for building on a narrow, 34-foot-wide lot. They turned to family member and Indianapolis native Salvatore La Rosa, whose architectural practice runs the gamut from shopping malls in Japan to homes for movie producers. Conscious of the design guidelines for historic districts, he made use of a traditional L plan, wherein the mass and width of the new building is visually reduced by setting the west wing back behind the front porch. While constructed of traditional materials, the two-and-a-half-story house is updated by color and pattern, most notably with terra-cotta color horizontal stripes and the whimsical diamond shapes that accent the yellow brick. Many consider this house the most distinctive in Lockerbie.

77. Joseph and Delores La Rosa Residence

79. Rowland Associates Building

79. Rowland Associates Building
701 East New York Street
Architect: WareAssociates, Chicago
Contractor: F. A. Wilhelm Construction Co., Inc.
1992

Located in the secondary area of Lockerbie's historic preservation district between industrial buildings and Victorian homes, this former television repair facility was imaginatively transformed into a new studio for interior designers. The original concrete block structure was virtually windowless. The client's desire for views toward downtown led to the addition of a new second story, oriented to the west. Because the new studios required large amounts of natural light, a glass atrium space was created at the core of the building, where client consultation areas, the library, and displays are located. Large, brightly colored interior pylons in this space are artfully lit, making them prominent from I-65 at night. Two courtyards enclosed by textured brick walls were designed for the north side, one of which is located at the hidden entry underneath the trellis.

78. Lockerbie Flats
621 East Vermont Place
Architect: Powers Kappes Architecture
Contractor: Stenz Construction Corporation
1985

This industrial building in the heart of Lockerbie Square was known for many years as the Peak Nut Building, a warehouse for a nut-packing business. The fact that it was tightly bounded by four alleys and had no available parking hampered its adaptive reuse until the architects incorporated parking within the structure. Today it houses 15 apartments with a common roof deck affording views to the downtown. Retaining existing openings, industrial window sash, and doors maintains the warehouse character while new additions such as the attractive front entry signal the new use.

78. Lockerbie Flats

80. Lockerbie Carriage Houses
302 North Park Street; 536 East New York Street
Architects: Perry Associates, Architects; James Kienle, AIA
1985; 1987

The construction of "carriage houses," a euphemism for garages, is reestablishing the former density patterns in many of Indianapolis' historic districts. These two in Lockerbie both incorporate apartments on their upper levels. At left, the carriage house for the Governor James B. Ray Residence needed to pay deference to the 1830s Greek Revival house, moved to this site in 1977 from 902 St. Peter Street. Although a sizable structure, the new building remains subsidiary to the main one and incorporates trim boards at the gables and corners reflective of the Greek Revival style. The carriage house for 536 East New York Street at right employs a mixture of siding styles that add interest and scale to the building.

80. Lockerbie Carriage Houses

81. Thomas and Kai Binford Residence

81. Thomas and Kai Binford Residence
501 Lockerbie Street
Architect: Perry Associates, Architects
1978

As one of the first new houses in Lockerbie Square, this building's prominent site at the corner of busy East Street made it a visible sign of the historic district's resurgence. Until the early 1970s, a grocery store had been located on this site. The general form and proportions of the new two-story brick home reflect the massing of neighboring historic houses, making it an early local example of contextualism. Design elements common to 1870s Italianate homes, such as the projecting front bay and cornice-level eyebrow windows, are rendered anew in a simple, straightforward manner. On the interior, first-floor rooms are 14 feet tall while those on the second floor are 12 feet; these ceiling heights are an important factor in conveying the scale of historic houses in the district. The new carriage house was diminished in scale, and roof forms were bridged downward in deference to the small 19th-century residence across the alley.

83. Sigma Theta Tau International Center

83. Sigma Theta Tau International Center
550 West North Street
Architect: HNTB Architects Engineers Planners
Contractor: Glenroy Construction Co., Inc.
1989

The offices of an international nursing society and the Center for Nursing Scholarship with its library are housed in this three-story building at the intersection of West Street and Indiana Avenue. Criticized for turning its back on the neighborhood, the building entry and its two-story reception lobby fronts west toward its parking lot. The architects maintain that while the building does not face Indiana Avenue, it still reinforces the street by its continuation of the urban wall. The highlight of the building is the semicircular plaza with its colonnade of paired columns, which faces south. The plaza provides a formal outdoor space that brings natural light into the building. Its classical inspiration, from railings to attic, is obvious. The uncommon choice for buff-colored and tan brick in a variegated pattern blends well with the Walker Building across the street; the brick is accented by cast stone banding.

82. Ferger Building/McGinnis Residence
500, 502 Indiana Avenue
Architect: Mozingo Associates, Inc.
Contractor: Stenz Construction Corporation
1991

Originally built around the turn of the century as two commercial buildings, these structures faced demolition by neglect until they were redeveloped as a residential *pied-à-terre* for the owner with commercial lease space on the ground floor. The exterior was restored to its historic appearance with two significant additions: a roof deck with a pyramidal roofed pavilion (intended to function as the "backyard gazebo") and a garage door that is disguised by a *trompe l'oeil* mural of the old Ferger drugstore. Passersby do a double take when the storefront rises to allow a car to enter. From the roof deck the owner enjoys a spectacular view of the downtown skyline.

82. Ferger Building/McGinnis Residence

84. Walker Building

84. Walker Building

84. Walker Building
617 Indiana Avenue
Architect: Wright/Porteous & Lowe, Inc.;
        Robert L. LaRue & Associates Inc.
Contractor: Stenz Construction Corporation;
        J. Beard Construction Management
1980-88

One of only six National Historic Landmarks in Indianapolis (the federal government's highest designation for historic buildings), the Walker Building is the premier cultural landmark of the city's African-American community. The fortune of Madam C. J. Walker (1867-1919), whose thriving cosmetics firm and beauty school made her one of the country's first black millionaires, was the driving force behind the structure. Built in 1927 at a cost of more than $1 million, it was designed by the firm of Rubush and Hunter, architects of the Circle and Indiana theaters, and constructed by the William C. Jungclaus firm.

The building originally housed an interesting combination of functions: a 1,300-seat theater, a fourth-floor ballroom, a cosmetics factory, and commercial space. The Walker was the first black-owned and operated theater in the country.

The 1980s architectural work focused on returning the four-story building to its original grandeur when it was a venue for the top black jazz musicians of the 1920s and 1930s. Following initial emergency repairs such as a new roof, the ballroom and exterior were refurbished. The colorful terra-cotta trim was repaired, new entry canopies were built, and the roof sign was restored. A decision was then made to preserve the original theater space, and its ornate wood carvings and exotically painted trim, reflecting African, Moorish, and Egyptian motifs, were retained. As a consequence of widening Martin Luther King Jr. Drive, the underground cafe called the Coffee Pot unfortunately was lost.

85. Lockefield Gardens
960 Locke Street
Architect: HDG Architects, Inc.
Contractor: Sexton Companies
1987

The original Lockefield Garden Apartments, constructed in 1935-37 to the design of local architects William Russ and Merritt Harrison, are significant as one of the nation's first group of federally planned housing projects of the Public Works Administration. Their innovative design and 25-acre site plan—consisting of an interior tree-lined mall with chevron-shaped buildings aligned in rows on either side—strongly reflects European prototypes of large-scale housing and urban design projects of the International Style. They were of unparalleled importance as a source of pride to the local African-American community. When abandoned in 1974, the 748-unit complex quickly deteriorated and became endangered. In 1983 the City of Indianapolis demolished 17 structures. A solution was then found to save and renovate the remaining seven buildings along Blake Street and redevelop the site with 294 new apartment units. The original commercial retail space at the corner of Indiana Avenue was included in the project. The new three-story units seen at left reflect the materials used in the original buildings: brown and tan brick with modest trim of brown brick and limestone. While the loss of two-thirds of the original complex was controversial to the city's preservation community, the revitalized Lockefield Apartments have been quite successful, particularly among IUPUI students and staff of the nearby medical complex.

85. Lockefield Gardens

86. IU Natatorium and School of Physical Education
IUPUI Campus
Architect: Edward Larrabee Barnes Associates, New York
Project architect: Browning Day Pollak Mullins Dierdorf Inc.
Construction manager: Tousley-Bixler Construction Co.
1982

Two large facilities—a natatorium with three pools and a physical education building with gymnasia, courts, and offices—are housed in this $21.5-million building, which was completed for the 1982 National Sports Festival. This was one of the first projects undertaken in the city's plan to become "the amateur sports capital of the world." Its short design and construction schedule (22 months from start to finish) affected some of the architect's basic decisions, such as constructing the entire structure of cast-in-place concrete. The focus of the building is the 50-meter competition pool and adjacent diving pool, which athletes from around the world compliment. It is flanked by 5,000 bleacher-style seats for special events. (At the first-floor level, a wide concourse that laterally bisects the building provides the vantage point for this photo.) Here diffused natural light from a monitor atop the three-hinged roof truss illuminates a white tile interior with striking red accents. The thrust of the trusses is taken to the exterior of the building by monolithic flying buttresses that add power to the east and west facades. In 1991 a four-level parking garage was constructed at the northeast corner of the building; it was apparently planned from the beginning, yet its design has little relationship to the original structure.

86. I U Natatorium and School of Physical Education

87. Indianapolis Sports Center
815 West New York Street
Architect: Browning Day Pollak Mullins
Construction Manager: Geupel DeMars Inc.
1979

Located on a 13-acre urban site adjacent to the IUPUI campus and Military Park, this center provides recreational facilities for both the city and the university. Tennis is the name of the game here, with 18 hard courts, four clay courts, and six indoor courts. It was the first new sports venue built in downtown Indianapolis in the wave of facilities designed to attract major sporting events. The 10,000-seat stadium is the home of the annual U.S. Men's Hard Court Championships. A steel truss roof deck protects the spectators in the southern section of seats. A private Champions Club and a pressroom are also incorporated into the facility.

87. Indianapolis Sports Center

88. National Institute for Fitness & Sport

88. National Institute for Fitness & Sport
250 North University Boulevard
Architect: Browning Day Mullins Dierdorf Inc.
Construction Manager: Huber Hunt & Nichols Inc.
1987

Most people are familiar with only one component of this immense 120,000-square-foot facility, namely the fitness center with its 200-meter indoor running track, weight rooms, and aerobic areas. However, NIFS also houses a testing and research center with examination facilities and laboratories plus a public education area with a 120-seat auditorium and resource library. The low-slung building is sheathed in white precast concrete panels with a connecting red metal band that accents its horizontal spread. The curved glass block exterior wall corresponds to the indoor walkway that provides an observation area above the track and exercise area. From the hydraulically adjustable curves of the track (the only one like it in the U.S.) to the oak lockers and tile floors of the locker rooms, NIFS is one of the most well-appointed facilities of its kind in the country.

88. National Institute for Fitness & Sport

90. IUPUI University Library

90. IUPUI University Library
755 West Michigan Street
Architect: Edward Larrabee Barnes/John M. Y. Lee & Partners, New York
Associate Architect: HNTB Architects Engineers Planners
Contractor: Reinke Construction Corporation
1993

The new main academic library for the IUPUI campus replaces an inadequate facility that long ago had ceased to meet the needs of the university's growing student body. This library will house one million books and will be linked to all libraries in the Indiana University system by a state-of-the-art computer network. Sited with a diagonal orientation between New York and Michigan streets, this building is an exception to the orthogonal layout of the campus' academic structures. Because the library is so large, there are two entrances: one at grade from the campus, and one on the second level that is linked to nearby academic buildings. This view is from the northeast in a quadrangle formed by the new Science, Engineering and Technology buildings. Although the four-story library is clad in Indiana limestone, the large amount of glass used— from the gabled skylight that runs down the spine illuminating the core to the curtain walls of the cantilevered third and fourth floors—gives it a hybrid, high-tech look.

89. IU Track and Field Stadium
New York and Agnes streets
Architect: Browning Day Mullins Dierdorf Inc.
Construction Manager: Geupel DeMars Inc.
1982

As a venue for the National Sports Festival, the Pan American Games, the U.S. Olympic trials, and many other top competitions, this track has become known as one of the fastest in the country. The very form of the 13,500-seat stadium, which was designed to align as many seats as possible with the start/finish line, appears to be streamlined for speed. The backdrop walls of the bleachers gracefully rise to a large, bunker-like press box at the top. The nine lanes plus inside jogging lane of the 400-meter oval track are composed of a rubberized surface. Field events take place on the grass infield.

89. I U Track and Field Stadium

91. University Place Hotel

850 West Michigan Street
Architect: Ellerbe Associates, Minneapolis
Contractor: Huber Hunt & Nichols Inc.
1987

With the growth of IUPUI and the IU Medical Center, the need arose for a hotel on campus to host conferences and conventions. The large amount of square footage devoted to the ballroom and to flexible meeting room space can accommodate a broad range of functions. The 270-room University Place is clad in brick, stone, and concrete to compliment the existing and familiar character of surrounding academic buildings. The top three floors of the 10-story building are highlighted by concrete panels that introduce a geometric pattern of color to the brick masonry. Along the base of the hotel, broad segmental arches extend to identify the entry and south courtyard as special areas. "Prefunction" areas for both the ballroom and meeting rooms overlook the landscaped garden court, which is shared by the conference center.

91. University Place Hotel

92. University Place Conference Center

92. University Place Conference Center

850 West Michigan Street
Architect: Edward Larrabee Barnes Associates, New York
Associate Architect: HNTB Architects Engineers Planners
Construction Manager: Geupel DeMars, Inc.
1987

University Place Hotel and this two-story conference center are unified by massing and detailing of brick construction, most importantly the broad segmental arches executed in soldier brick. Together the two structures enclose a courtyard open to the south side; with its trees and flowers integrated with seating areas, it is one of the most pleasant outdoor spaces in the city. In addition to their common hallway link on the north side, the two buildings are connected by a wide pergola on brick piers that extends across the courtyard. The main feature of the conference center is a two-level auditorium with 338 seats. The facility also includes a fully equipped computer lab, advanced fiberoptic telecommunications, and a studio for video teleconferencing and worldwide satellite hookup. A 385-car underground parking garage is located below the courtyard.

94. Riley Hospital for Children Expansion

94. Riley Hospital for Children Expansion
Indiana University Medical Center
Planners: Ellerbe Becket, Minneapolis
Architect: Boyd/Sobieray Associates, Inc.
Contractor: Kettlehut Construction, Inc., Lafayette
1986

In 1978 planning began for this major expansion of Riley Hospital, which dates back to 1924. The square footage of this specialty referral center for young patients from throughout the Midwest was nearly doubled in the new "wing." The five-story atrium is the most interesting interior space because of the manner in which the facade of the original hospital was incorporated into the west wall. Picking up on the building's brick facade, limestone trim, boldly punched windows, and gabled roof, the new four-story building revives these architectural elements with creative massing. This view from the southeast shows the courtyard off the stepped-back corner where the first floor's dining area and radiology suite are located. Here architectural features of hearth and home, most prominent among them the corbeled chimney, are found in a patio and garden setting.

93. Medical Research and Library Building
Indiana University School of Medicine
Architect: Ellerbe Becket, Minneapolis
Associate Architect: Boyd/Sobieray Associates, Inc.
Contractor: Geupel DeMars, Inc.
1989

The programmatic combination of medical laboratories and a library takes interesting form in this building that serves as a focus for all clinical research at the Indiana University School of Medicine. The postdoctoral research facilities are located in the five-story brick wings, which intersect at a perpendicular angle to frame the cascading glass towers of the library's reading areas. The series of glazed pyramids is meant to act as a symbolic gateway to the medical campus and is most effective illuminated at night. Materials were chosen based on other buildings on campus. The canted stone spandrels below the recessed laboratory windows, which contribute to the facade's visual interest, echo those of Riley Hospital. On the interior, conference rooms and lounges enjoy views of the light-filled atrium.

1990 Indiana Society of Architects, Citation Award

93. Medical Research and Library Building

95. Ronald McDonald House, Limestone Court facade

95. Ronald McDonald House, Michigan Avenue facade

95. Ronald McDonald House

Indiana University Medical Center
Architects: Archonics Design Partnership;
    HNTB Architects Engineers Planners
Contractors: Brandt Construction Inc.;
    Kettlehut Construction, Inc., Lafayette
1982; 1989

Designed to house the families of critically ill children who are receiving care at Riley Hospital, this building was intended to provide a comfortable, homelike setting to encourage support among parents. The construction is a combination of heavy timber and wood frame with a brick veneer and limestone trim. The gabled forms make a contemporary statement of "home" while providing a compatible neighbor to the medical school's campus. In addition to the bedrooms, kitchens, laundries, and recreation rooms, the focal point is a two-story great room with a central fireplace that rises the full height of the space. In 1989 the Ronald McDonald House was more than doubled in size for additional guest rooms, apartments for transplant recovery patients, and administrative areas. As part of the expansion, a new entry with porte cochere was developed on Limestone Court, the side street off busy Michigan Street. A courtyard between the original and new sections offers a pleasant play area for children.

1992 Indiana Society of Architects, Citation Award (Expansion)

97. The Waters Building

97. The Waters Building

Indianapolis Zoo
Architect: James Architects & Engineers, Inc.
  with Jerry Johnson Associates, Boston
Construction Manager: Geupel DeMars Inc.
1988

In recent years aquariums have played a role in the revitalization of some cities, having been received enthusiastically by residents and tourists alike. The Waters Building—which contains almost half a million gallons of water and is home to approximately 150 species of aquatic life—is the first large-scale aquarium in Indiana. Following the zoo's natural biome philosophy, this structure blends into the site, allowing one to wander through the waters of the world in a subdued architectural environment. The fan-shaped Waters Building is experienced as a building without a major facade. The landscaping around the building creates a feeling of descension, as one would descend into the depths of the oceans. Once inside the structure, the spaces are simple and mostly defined by walls of water. The exhibits create the space and overtake the "architecture."

96. Whale and Dolphin Pavilion

Indianapolis Zoo
Architect: James Architects & Engineers, Inc.
Construction Manager: Geupel DeMars Inc.
1989

The Whale and Dolphin Pavilion is one of the world's largest, fully enclosed facilities of its kind, holding 2.3 million gallons of salt water and seating 1,500 persons. The scale of the building is not immediately apparent from the exterior, largely due to its surrounding landscape. The exterior material is concrete block with very little pattern or detail. The monitor roof captures the high south light and spreads it evenly throughout the interior, providing a comfortably bright space for watching the marine mammal performances. The interior architecture continues the simplicity of materials and forms with perforated, acoustical concrete block walls, plain concrete floors, metal bleachers, and steel roof trusses. A ground-level gallery, which doubles as a dining area for special events, provides a panoramic underwater view of the animals between shows.

96. Whale and Dolphin Pavilion

99. Water Company Pumping Station

99. Water Company Pumping Station

801 West Washington Street
Architect: James Associates
Contractor: Ripberger Construction Co.
1981

An abandoned pumping station, which began operation in 1871 to provide the first public water service for the city, was converted to new use in 1981 as the headquarters for the White River State Park Development Commission. (This project should be acknowledged as a forerunner of adaptive reuse projects in Indianapolis.) Despite a tornado in the 1930s, which eliminated a wing of the structure and damaged a cupola, the solid brick building with its hipped, slate roof had survived in relatively good condition after a decade of vacancy. The architectural elegance of the building, which camouflaged its industrial use, most likely contributed to its survival. The 18-foot-tall cupola was reconstructed as part of the exterior restoration. Depending on the future of the 250-acre park, the building eventually could be adapted for another use.

98. River Promenade

White River Park
Architect: Danadjieva & Koenig Associates, Tiburon,
        California
Contractor: Contractors United, Inc.
1988

Stretching a half mile along the west bank of the White River behind the Indianapolis Zoo, this pleasant walkway is one of the few plans for White River Park realized by 1993. Over 1,200 enormous limestone blocks, donated as discards from three of Indiana's largest quarries, are piled into 15-foot-tall walls that line the path. This effectively masks both the zoo's mechanical units and the river's floodwall. On 16 of the blocks, inscriptions and reliefs have been carved to celebrate the history of the state's limestone industry in an outdoor gallery. Three bas-reliefs depict celebrated buildings constructed of Indiana limestone: the Empire State Building, the National Cathedral, and the Indiana Statehouse. A Gothic-inspired rose window is seen in this view looking toward the downtown skyline. Until White River Park is more fully developed, this trail regrettably will continue to be a little known feature of the city.

1992 American Society of Landscape Architects, Honor Award

98. River Promenade

100. Fletcher Place United Methodist Church

501 Fletcher Avenue
Architect: David B. Duvall
Contractor: F. A. Wilhelm Construction Co., Inc.
1988

As the premier landmark of the Fletcher Place historic district, this church has deep historical associations. In 1872 members of the pioneer Fletcher family donated the site, which was once part of the Fletcher farm, Wood Lawn. The pastor at that time, Charles Tinsley, is credited with its design, but his more famous father, William Tinsley, architect of Christ Church Cathedral and numerous mid-19th-century midwestern buildings, may have had a strong hand. When the Methodist Church vacated this structure in the early 1980s and a temporary use as a community center failed, the building was threatened with demolition. The Fountain Square & Fletcher Place Investment Corporation then stepped in and undertook an exterior restoration that dramatically changed the building's appearance. Peeling layers of gray paint were stripped; stained-glass windows were restored and protected, including the replacement of the entire wood tracery of the rose window; and the abundant sheet-metal (not stone) trim around gables and Gothic arches was refurbished. Many masonry and metal-work contractors donated their time on the project. While the former church is now vacant and awaiting a reuse, the building has regained its stature as a landmark of the near south side.

100. Fletcher Place United Methodist Church

101. Union Laundry Lofts

101. Union Laundry Lofts

735 Lexington Avenue
Architect: American Consulting Engineers, Inc.
Construction Manager: Geupel DeMars Inc.
1990

Built in 1911 for the Union Co-operative Laundry Company and later known as Mechanics Laundry, this industrial building exhibits the fine detailing more common to school buildings of its era. Its architectural qualities made it attractive for development into housing. Ranging from studio apartments to a three-bedroom unit, the old laundry now houses 27 luxury condominiums. One of the more interesting uses of the existing structure was the conversion of an old smokestack into circular bathrooms and storage space in a three-level condominium.

102. Eli Lilly and Company Corporate Headquarters

Delaware and McCarty streets
Architect: Browning Day Mullins Dierdorf Inc.
Interior Design Architect: Lohan Associates, Chicago
Construction Manager: Geupel DeMars Inc.
1992

The renovation and expansion of the Lilly Corporate Headquarters was the culmination of a planned transition that began in the early 1980s to create a cohesive research center and corporate campus. New lobby and office spaces flank the renovated administrative office tower, which stair steps down to the west to form an entry court off Delaware Street and to the south to frame a landscaped garden. The stepped-down wings visually lower the height of the high-rise office tower, bringing it more into scale with other campus buildings. The development of a new pedestrian entrance, vehicular drop-off, and three-story lobby were important elements of the design solution. Automobile circulation is organized around a large circular fountain of Swedish red granite that is the focus of the entry plaza. The new construction and the renovated office tower were blended by recladding the exterior in warm-colored granite and Indiana limestone, materials chosen for visual continuity with surrounding brick and limestone buildings. The corporate headquarters building now provides a place at which corporate functions, access by visitors, and the public countenance of the corporation come together.

102. Eli Lilly and Company Corporate Headquarters

103. Eli Lilly and Company Parking Garage

103. Eli Lilly and Company Parking Garage

Delaware and McCarty streets
Architect: CUH2A, Princeton, New Jersey
Construction Manager: Geupel DeMars Inc.
1989

This parking garage at the McCarty Street campus of Eli Lilly and Company illustrates how a utilitarian feature such as employee parking can enhance an architectural setting. The concrete-framed buildings are clad with a combination of limestone and brick. Openings in the exterior walls of the garage, required for ventilation, are given proportions similar to those of windows in adjacent buildings. Grilles needed for the security of employees are functional but also decorative, similar in design to grilles of older Lilly buildings nearby. Although the garage's location is in the foreground of public view, it is a low-key, background building, reserving prominence for research and office buildings on campus.

Northside I

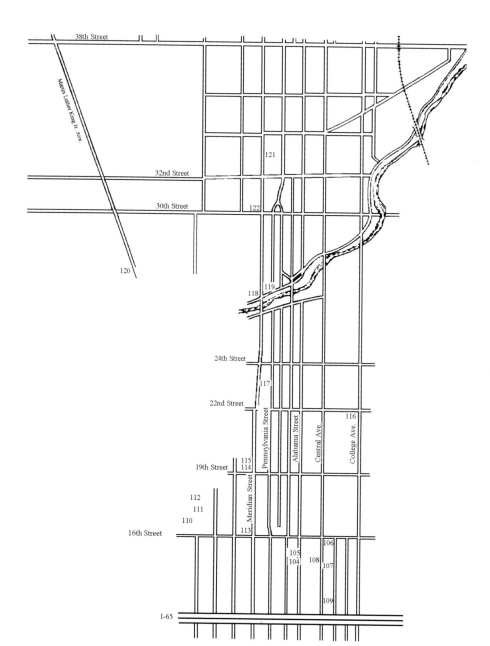

The Old Northside

104. Shawn Grove Park Pavilion
105. Lucas-Bussard Residence
106. All Saints Parish Hall
107. Tech Houses
108. Double Residence
109. Carriage House

Methodist Hospital

110. Methodist Hospital West Building
111. Methodist Hospital Facilities Center
112. Ruth Lilly Health Center

16th to 38th Street

113. Indiana Energy Headquarters
114. Boy Scout Service Center
115. MIBOR Headquarters
116. Grace Apostolic Church
117. Meridian Foot & Ankle Clinic
118. Technology Center, Ivy Tech
119. Marott Hotel
120. Cleo Blackburn Health Center
121. St. Richard's School
122. Children's Museum Additions

104. Shawn Grove Memorial Park Pavilion
1401 North Alabama Street
Architect: Restoration•Preservation•Architecture, Inc.
Contractor: Restoration•Preservation•Architecture, Inc.
1981

There had been no park in the Old Northside district until the tragic death of a resident prompted a fitting memorial to her memory. With two lots donated by a resident and a third purchased by the neighborhood association, a site on the east side of Alabama was developed for a variety of recreational uses, from passive seating areas and children's play structures to a volleyball court. This L-plan pavilion, which recalls traditional park shelters, reflects some of the design vocabulary found in nearby residences: a steeply pitched roof with ridge cresting, columns and brackets similar to those found on porches, and a pyramidal roof above the open tower.

104. Shawn Grove Memorial Park Pavilion

105. Lucas-Bussard Residence

105. Lucas-Bussard Residence
1428 North Alabama Street
Architect: Woollen, Molzan and Partners
Contractor: Libra Construction
1991

This new single-family residence references the surrounding historic neighborhood in many ways while ultimately deriving its form from interior functions and the Lucas' desire for natural light in all spaces. The tower on the corner, porches on both floors and in the front and rear of the house, and a mixture of historic wood-siding patterns all reflect the influences of the adjacent homes. The form—a triple gable along the south elevation—allows natural light into all of the major spaces of the home. The location of the house on the northern edge of the site allows still more light to enter the windows and creates an open space to the south for gardens and yard.

107. Tech Houses

107. Tech Houses

1501-1527 North Central Avenue
Architect: Perry Associates, Architects
Contractor: Career Education Center with the architect
1982-88

The clearance of a contiguous series of lots on the east side of Central Avenue left a major void in the Old Northside historic district for many years. In the 1980s the lots were developed for six small houses identified as a "micro neighborhood" by the commemorative sidewalk plaque at the corner of Central Avenue and 15th Street. The unique factor about these houses is that they were all built by students of the Indianapolis Career Education Center in a cooperative program between the Chamber of Commerce and Arsenal Technical High School. Each frame house is unique, varying in number of stories, roof form, or color, but all share design themes common to the more modest of 19th-century houses to be found in the district. The houses are sited on a northeast diagonal line stepping back from the corner of 15th, which defers to and maximizes the presence of All Saints Church at the end of the block. Although criticized for their low scale in relation to surrounding homes, collectively these houses contribute to reestablishing the historic density of the neighborhood.

106. All Saints Church Parish Hall

1553 North Central Avenue
Architect: Bradbury Associates Architects
Contractor: K. P. Meiring Construction
1988

The original church was built in 1909 as the Cathedral of the Episcopal Church in Indianapolis. The congregation's commitment to the homeless prompted them to convert their existing parish hall to the south of the sanctuary into the Dayspring Center, a shelter for homeless families. The north addition, a new parish hall, responds to the design guidelines of the historic district by locating the new facade just forward of the transept to permit the full exposure of the side chapel entrance and the stained-glass windows of the nave. The Gothic limestone arch at the front entry and the covered connecting walkway are reflective of the lancet windows and doorways of this historic church. The simplified limestone and brick details of the new portion recall the more elaborate details of the old church.

106. All Saints Church Parish Hall

109. Carriage House

109. Carriage House
1321 North Central Avenue
Architect: Able Ringham Architects;
                   Anna Waggoner, AIA
Contractor: Clay Hargitt
1989

This new building contains an apartment on its upper level and a garage for 16 classic cars on stackers on the ground floor. Despite its sizable program, the building's massing and Victorian-inspired design allow it to fit well into the historic district. The exterior's bright yellow fishscale shingles and orange clapboard siding are combined creatively, particularly at the south facade seen here. Large square windows trimmed in teal blue parallel the west gable line and divide the two colors. Other distinctive features include the foundation's flared base, the Stick-style brackets that support the eaves, and the oversized dormer windows that illuminate the apartment's cathedral ceiling.

108. Double Residence
1468 North Central Avenue
Architect: Mozingo Associates, Inc.
Contractor: Charles Blunck
1988

Designed to appear as a large-scale, single-family residence similar to its Old Northside neighbors, this new residential building actually houses two units. Built on a corner lot, it fronts both Central Avenue and the side street with separate entrances for each residence. While its scale, massing, and materials are consistent with surrounding historic buildings, design details—such as the wide, horizontal stripes, overscaled circular vents in the gable ends of porches and bays, and the windows—all mark it as a contemporary design. The blue/green and cream paint scheme, which is particularly detailed at the windows, works well to highlight architectural features.

108. Double Residence

110. Methodist Hospital West Building

1701 North Senate Boulevard
Architect: Smith, Hinchman & Grylls Associates, Inc., Detroit
Contractor: Geupel DeMars Inc.
1986

When the urban street grid surrounding Indiana's largest hospital constricted physical changes, Senate Avenue was rerouted to the west to create a new suburban setting for a major eight-story addition. Designed to change the hospital's public image by creating a new approach and front yard, the addition consolidated outpatient access and replaced about half the total bed space as well as all major diagnostic and therapeutic services. While a complex program, the project managed to draw together the existing facilities while making an architectural statement of its own. On axis with the older building to the east and slightly forward of the matching new Professional Office Building to the north, the gently curved west facade dominates the other parts of the complex. Interestingly the bulge grew out of a functional reason: the additional space required by the central nursing units. (Some feel the building line responds to the curve of I-65 which it faces.) Horizontal banding, echoing the ground floor's limestone base, demarcates the upper floors. The placement of two 800-car parking decks helps to enclose the new circular entry drive and frame the building. On the interior, a generous pedestrian "street" connects the old and new facilities and interior courtyards in a hotel-like atmosphere. Patient and visitor traffic is segregated to ensure the patients' well-being in transport. The prominent solarium on the seventh floor is part of an oncology/hospice unit.

1986 Detroit Chapter, American Institute of Architects, Honor Award

110. Methodist Hospital West Building

111. Methodist Hospital Facilities Center

111. Methodist Hospital Facilities Center

1800 North Capitol Avenue
Architect: Schmidt, Garden & Erikson, Inc., Chicago
Contractor: Tousley-Bixler Construction Company, Inc.
1982

With the construction of the Facilities Center, Methodist Hospital achieved a necessary first step in renovating and expanding the hospital complex. Replacing a powerhouse built in 1928, this three-story building provides all electrical and mechanical support for the 1,100-bed hospital. The structure is composed of two basic parts: the "machine" portion, housing boilers and heat distribution equipment, expressed by exposed boiler stacks and strong structural massing, and the "services" portion, which includes laundry, loading dock, administrative offices, and an employee cafeteria with a dining terrace. At the east side along Capitol, the services portion acknowledges pedestrian scale primarily through the use of reduced massing of the street facade. Here the structure's support system is exposed, giving a sense of lightness. White metal panels above a concrete base accentuate the machine aspect while achieving energy efficiency. One AIA juror felt that the Facilities Center demonstrated that a building in which all the "back lot" services were placed could be an asset to the community.

1986 American Institute of Architects, Modern Healthcare Facilities Design Award

113. Indiana Energy Headquarters
1630 North Meridian Street
Architect: Ratio Architects, Inc.
Construction Manager: Coghill and Associates, Inc.
1988

New additions to the offices of Indiana Energy nearly tripled the size of the facility. To respect and compliment the original building, sited close to the right-of-way line of North Meridian Street, the large mass of the four-story addition and parking garage was kept back from the street. Pavilions of glass curtain wall, capped by low copper-clad arches, rise at the north and south ends of the new addition. The limestone of the existing Meridian Street facade was continued in the new portions. Illustrated in this photo is the curved wall of the new corner entry, which is in tune with the restrained Art Deco style of the old building. Intimate outdoor spaces, such as this small plaza with sculpture, were incorporated into the urban setting. The design anticipates a future addition to the north.

113. Indiana Energy Headquarters

112. Ruth Lilly Center for Health Education
2055 North Senate Avenue
Architect: James Architects & Engineers, Inc.
Contractor: Brandt Construction Co.
1989

Located at the north end of the Methodist Hospital campus, this facility houses one of the country's premier educational programs focusing upon healthy life-styles. The building is organized around a 300-foot-long spine that extends to form a north canopy where school buses arrive and a south canopy where they depart. The brick facade consists of a light tan field accented by seven narrow stripes of white glazed brick, which emphasize the linear form and circulation pattern of the building. The steel structure, painted a light powder blue, is exposed at the entries and the west elevation, where it reveals the curved wall of the main theater. Seven teaching theaters are equipped with the latest interactive technology.

112. Ruth Lilly Center for Health Education

114, 115. Boy Scouts Service Center and Metropolitan Indianapolis Board of Realtors Headquarters

114. Boy Scouts Service Center
1900 North Meridian Street
Architect: The InterDesign Group
Contractor: Summit Construction Co.
1989

To provide a greatly enhanced visibility for scouting, the Crossroads of America Council of the Boy Scouts of America purchased the 30-year-old NCR Building and undertook an extensive renovation that completely transformed the structure. The new facilities, twice as large as the old quarters in the English Foundation Building, contain a "trading post" on the main floor for retail purchase of scouting paraphernalia and offices for administration and field service representatives on the second floor. The brick building was covered in white enameled aluminum panels. Influenced by its neighbor to the north, it has a front drive to a diagonally projecting porte cochere adjoining its lobby. The two buildings appear to share a forecourt and are now experienced as an ensemble piece.

115. Metropolitan Indianapolis Board of Realtors Headquarters
1912 North Meridian Street
Architect: CSO/Architects, Inc.
Contractor: Carlstedt Dickman Inc.
1988

The new two-story headquarters of the Board of Realtors houses a 250-seat training center, a resource library for a community of over 3,000 realtors, and offices for day-to-day operations like the multiple listing service. The two-story building, sheathed in precast concrete panels, features a gabled porte cochere that adjoins the central, gabled atrium. The most obvious thing about this building is the way in which it was sited at a 45-degree angle to Meridian Street. The architects explain that it was uniquely placed at this angle to give more public exposure to the main facade and to make room for a landscaped frontyard and entry drive. Critics decry its disregard for the traditional siting of buildings along one of the city's most prominent thoroughfares and point out the irony of the group that apparently overlooked the urban planning implications.

116. Grace Apostolic Church

649 East 22nd Street
Architect: Blackburn Associates Architects, Inc.
Contractor: Brandt Construction Inc.
1990

If you miss this building's exceptional spire while driving north on College, you may not recognize the building as a church. The unusual forms and its off-white color give no clue as to function. Most interesting are the brick buttresses that fan out from the eight-sided building, each with a square opening resembling a window. Housed within is a major auditorium-style sanctuary with a sweeping balcony. Seating can accommodate more than 2,100 churchgoers. (To give a sense of the sanctuary's size, Clowes Hall seats 2,200 people.) The choir is bathed in natural light by a skylight directly under the open spire that begs to become a belfry. At the back of the balcony, a line of windows provides good natural light to the upper part of the sanctuary. To distract from the metal ceiling, star-like lighting fixtures designed by the architect float across the room.

116. Grace Apostolic Church

116. Grace Apostolic Church

117. Meridian Foot & Ankle Clinic

2291 North Meridian Street
Architect: Plus 4 Architects, P. C.
Contractor: R. L. Turner Corporation
1988

This medical care clinic features seven patient exam rooms as well as x-ray and photographic rooms, a surgical suite, and a laboratory. The waiting area is surrounded by a curved glass block wall that introduces natural light while maintaining privacy and security for patients. The crisp white stucco walls and variety in massing helped it to win a "people's choice" award for commercial architecture. If it was located in a low-scale suburban office park, it would be a standout. However, because it is sited on one of Indianapolis' most important streets, it has been criticized for its presentation of a blank wall to the street..

117. Meridian Foot & Ankle Clinic

119. Marott Hotel

119. Marott Hotel
2625 North Meridian Street
Architect: Hutchcraft and Associates
Contractor: Jarvis DeLoach and Jobst Partnership
1984

Designed by W. K. Elridge and built by the prolific Indianapolis contractor Edgar G. Spink, the Marott Hotel opened in November 1926 with 234 apartments. For many years the Marott was the premier hotel for visiting statesmen and celebrities, from Winston Churchill and Herbert Hoover to Clark Gable and Marilyn Monroe. Indianapolis businessman George J. Marott (1858-1946) conceived of the building as a residence hotel, but over the years there was an increasing emphasis on transient rooms rather than apartment use. Continual subdivision ultimately led to the building's decline as an elegant residential structure. In the early 1980s new investors returned the hotel to the original number of luxury apartments. In renovating the twin towers of 10 stories, all 2,000 of its original windows were replaced; the color of the new units resulted in a well-publicized conflict with meeting the federal government's guidelines for certified restorations. The entry canopy, overscaled to shelter the building's guests, has been criticized for its lack of relation to the original marquee, which had disappeared by the early 1950s. Despite these flaws in the eyes of some, the prominently located Marott Hotel has regained its position of importance as a city landmark.

118. Technology Center
Indiana Vocational Technological College
Architect: Everett I. Brown Company
Construction Manager: Skillman Corporation
1990

Paralleling Meridian Street at its intersection with Fall Creek Parkway, this new three-story building on the Ivy Tech campus reinforces the importance of the North Meridian corridor. Its main facade of tan brick presents a great variety in fenestration, interesting detailing such as simulated quoins at the first floor, and an element of color absent from many academic structures. For a building full of classrooms to teach practical technologies, from welding and metallurgy to drafting and electronics, it contains a number of surprises. Upon entering the main entrance on the west side, one encounters a three-story rotunda lobby that is the circulation hub of the building. Directly to its east is the stairway expressed on the exterior at the first-floor level by curved glass block under a segmental arch. The octagonal tower at the southeast corner belongs to a cafeteria at the first floor, a conference room at the second, and a faculty/staff lounge at the third.

118. Technology Center

121. St. Richard's School

121. St. Richard's School
3243 North Meridian Street
Architect: Woollen, Molzan and Partners
Contractor: Summit Construction Company, Inc.
1988

Trinity Episcopal Church/St. Richard's School, designed by McGuire and Shook in the 1950s, needed to expand on its very tight site at the intersection of busy Meridian Street and 33rd Street. An older classroom wing was expanded; a new building was constructed along 33rd Street; and a new multipurpose building was located in the middle of the site to enclose a cloistered courtyard that provides light to additional classrooms. The prominence of the existing church on Meridian Street was maintained by constructing the larger buildings behind the church or east along the side street. A design goal was to provide a seamless transition between old and new. To this end, the new additions employ the same stone on the facades, including limestone arch detailing at selected openings. The new roofs are standing-seam copper, accentuating the copper detailing of the existing structures.

120. Cleo Blackburn Health Center
2800 Dr. Martin Luther King Jr. Drive
Architect: CSO/Architects, Inc.
Contractor: Wilson Blazek Corporation
1990

This Marion County public health center houses four separate functions: a medical clinic, a dental clinic, the Women, Infants, and Children program, and the office of a private physician specializing in solutions to Indianapolis' high infant mortality rate. The four functions inspired the design's incorporation of four major gables; two smaller gabled dormers relate to conference spaces within the structure. The choice of materials (red brick with stone trim) was made to complement the adjacent commercial and religious structures. The scale of the dormers and the square windows provide an appropriate scale to the predominantly residential neighborhood. The city intended that this facility be an impetus for the revitalization and development of the surrounding area. To provide an inviting atmosphere for the public and staff, the two large waiting areas feature high gabled ceilings with exposed truss work and abundant natural light.

120. Cleo Blackburn Health Center

122. The Children's Museum

122. The Children's Museum

122. The Children's Museum
3000 North Meridian Street
Architect: Woollen, Molzan and Partners
Contractor: Geupel DeMars Inc.
1989

This Children's Museum is the largest in the world, and its new addition incorporates all the colors and sparkle of a child's world. The new components make up for the original 1976 building's dour appearance and limited gathering spaces. The front elevation with its colossal arched portal and radiating sunburst window marks an entry of wonder and anticipation. Curving walls, bright colors, and terracotta ornaments contrast with and enliven the staid original brick building and its rectangular spaces. For all of the openness and light, the new spaces are subtly made for children without appearing "designed for children." The stairs are dimensioned to be comfortable for small legs with lower risers and longer treads, while the four-story atrium is full of children's artwork. Bright blue customed-designed trusses, yellow metal railings, unique columns, and a 32-foot-tall water clock help dramatize the skylit space. A key to the success of the addition was the input the groups of children had during the design process. The architects asked children to draw the types of spaces they liked best. For the 1.5 million visitors a year, the new addition has (as noted in *Architectural Record*) "transformed the duckling into a swan."

1990 Indiana Society of Architects, Merit Award
1989 Indianapolis Chapter, American Institute of Architects, Honor Award

Northside II

Northside II directory

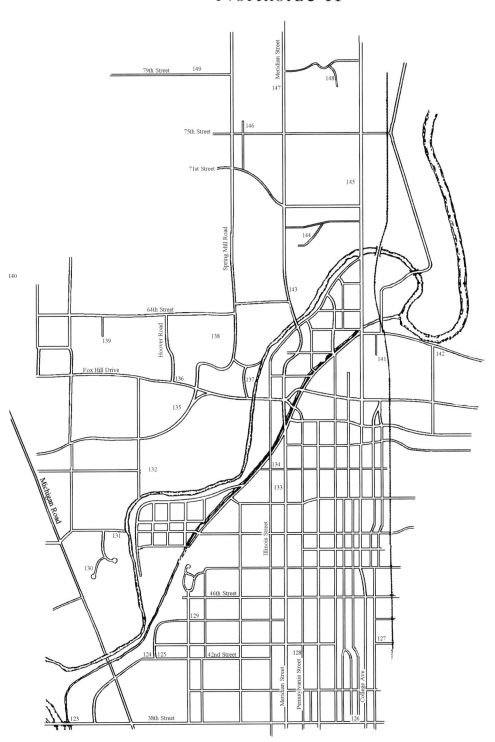

123. Hulman Pavilion, Indianapolis Museum of Art

123. Hulman Pavilion, Indianapolis Museum of Art

123. Hulman Pavilion, Indianapolis Museum of Art

1200 West 38th Street
Architect: Edward Larrabee Barnes/John M. Y. Lee
          & Partners, New York
Contractor: F. A. Wilhelm Construction Co. Inc.
1990

The four-story Hulman Pavilion, sited at the southeast of the existing Krannert Pavilion, increased the museum's exhibition area by 80 percent. It provides space for the museum's permanent collection, major traveling exhibitions, consolidated staff offices, conservation laboratories and storage, and the Eiteljorg Collection of African Art. To provide continuity with the original building, completed in 1970, the new addition is clad in Indiana limestone and has boldly expressed joints. Visitors are guided in a continuous flow of circulation through the new galleries by the use of windows and skylights, which help to relieve "museum fatigue." The traffic patterns allow for chrono-logical and cultural continuity in viewing permanent collections, so that backtracking through galleries already visited is avoided.

In conjunction with the design of the Hulman Pavilion, the existing museum—designed by Wright/Porteous & Lowe, Inc. with Richardson, Serverns, Scheeler & Associates, Inc., of Champaign, Illinois—was extensively renovated and reorganized. The gallery reorganization was designed to enable a continuity of flow with the new Hulman Pavilion's exhibition areas, permitting the new and old wings to function as a whole. The front steps and plaza level were also completely renovated and relandscaped. The Museum Cafe, which opened on the first floor of the Krannert Pavilion in 1991, is one of the highlights of the renovated museum. Plus 4 Architects, P. C. was the associated architect for the renovation work with R. L. Turner Corporation as general contractor.

124. Sweeney Chapel

124. Sweeney Chapel

124. Sweeney Chapel

124. Sweeney Chapel
Christian Theological Seminary
Architect: Edward Larrabee Barnes Associates, New York
Contractor: Geupel DeMars Inc.
1987

Sited at the edge of a wooded bluff above the canal, this chapel was constructed as the last component of the master plan for Christian Theological Seminary, which was developed 25 years earlier by the architect. Matching the low-scale classroom buildings to which it is linked, the chapel is sheathed in the same colored aggregate precast panels and is ornamented only by a large Greek cross in relief. Its forms are very simple; the main part is a cube to which the tall rectilinear bell tower and a high hipped section at the rear have been added. While the interior can accommodate up to 500 people, chapel seating is arranged in sections—main floor, balcony, and peripheral—so that small groups can use one section comfortably. The interior's simplicity is intended to foster spirituality. The oak pews, burnished stainless steel cross, and circular steel chandeliers—all designed by Barnes—stand out against the spare white plaster walls and limestone floors. Perhaps the most interesting features of the chapel are the glass grids by New York designer James Carpenter at the two west windows. The horizontal members of the grids are of a special dichroic glass that projects diagonal patterns of color-separated light against the walls. In assessing the chapel's interior, most critics feel that Barnes was successful in achieving his goal of creating "both clarity and mystery."

125. Seminary Student Apartments

Christian Theological Seminary
Architect: Edward Larrabee Barnes Associates, New York
Contractor: Geupel DeMars Inc.
1986

Across Haughey Road from the main campus of the seminary, these 36 apartments break from the mold of the academic buildings and chapel. Simple two-story, red brick buildings with gabled roofs are laid out in three stepped-back rows forming two walled courtyards on the site. Breezeways connect the individual buildings, with taller end units turned at a 90-degree angle. This plan of connected individual units lends a more traditional residential massing to the complex than the average institutional housing project. The upper-story apartments have recessed balconies with white walls that overlook the central court, while the ground-floor apartments face in the opposite direction toward private gardens.

125. Seminary Student Apartments

126. Coburn Place

126. Coburn Place

604 East 38th Street
Architect: Heartland Design/Architects;
        Korbuly/Graf Architects, South Bend
Contractor: Jungclaus-Campbell Co. Inc.
1991

Henry P. Coburn School Number 66 is perhaps the most notable of the few remaining Indianapolis public schools designed by the firm of Rubush and Hunter. Originally constructed as a 10-room building in 1915 by the William P. Jungclaus Company, in 1929 a major addition of eight classrooms and auditorium designed by Harrison and Turnock was completed. When closed by IPS and sold as surplus in 1981, the usual questions of its survival surfaced. In 1991 it was converted to housing for low-income, elderly residents in a program called "assisted living." Classrooms were subdivided to provide rooms for a capacity of 117 people. A steel frame was constructed in the gymnasium to provide a second-level dining room.

128. Moses Residence

128. Moses Residence
4242 North Pennsylvania Street
Architect: Barry Smith
Contractor: B & S Builders
1984

The Moses Residence was built on a street lined with gracious Tudor and Georgian Revival homes dating primarily from the 1920s. Its large lot had remained undeveloped until subdivided from an even larger wooded lot. Although a one-story house, its sweeping roof, massive twin chimneys, and large windows have a scale and presence that allow the clearly contemporary house to take an equal place among it neighbors. The windows of the central monitor and the overscaled semicircular fanlight over the front door admit sunlight to a modern plan. With its allusions to Georgian detail, some architectural observers have noted its likeness to the grand country houses of Virginia such as Stratford Hall.

127. Indianapolis Police Department Quadrant I Facility
4209 North College Avenue
Architect: Everett I. Brown Company
Contractor: Wilson Blazek Corporation
1989

The importance of this modest renovation/addition project may lie in the way it has helped to stabilize its surrounding neighborhood. The original brick building was built in the early 1920s as the 42nd Street State Bank and was part of a strip of commercial buildings (including the Uptown Theater) that have disappeared over the years. This survivor was remodeled in the early 1960s as an AFNB branch bank. When the police department undertook its renovation, economic constraints made it impossible to match the height of the new addition to the existing building. Therefore the new portion was placed to the rear to avoid proportional difficulties and to minimize its street presence. Security concerns in the era of drive-by shootings forced the location of windows higher up on the facade. Similarly, in the main facade's face-lift, the storefront windows that formerly extended down to floor level were reglazed in a configuration similar to the original, but with opaque panels in place of glass at the lower level. The blue gray paint scheme has been noted for emphasizing the 1920s building's most interesting architectural feature, its limestone pilasters.

127. Indianapolis Police Department Quadrant I Facility

129. Butler University Residential College
630 West Hampton Drive
Architect: James Architects & Engineers, Inc.
Contractor: Huber Hunt & Nichols Inc.
1989

This new dormitory gestures to the collegiate nature of the older buildings on campus with a few stylistic details such as the crenelated entry parapets and rock-faced lintels and string courses. However, the limestone veneer and the bright blue metal window frames with tinted glass (the most talked-about feature of the building) clearly separate it from the original campus structures. The dormitory rooms are organized around two large interior courtyards to the east and west of the central section of the building, which contains a two-story lobby and a cafeteria. The building works best as an enclosure to the newly landscaped central mall from which this photo was taken.

129. Butler University Residential College

130. Gordon and Donna Clark Residence

130. Gordon and Donna Clark Residence
4820 Buttonwood Crescent
Architect and Construction Manager: Gordon Clark, AIA
1988

The unusual shape of the lot on which this house is built derives from the two creeks that meander along its wooded acreage. The steep site was considered "unbuildable." These factors plus the architect's desire to incorporate passive solar energy led to a house that moves down a hillside while facing its primary living spaces south to catch winter sun. Deciduous trees close to the house provide shade in summer, while fewer windows in the north facade shelter the house from the street and cold winds. Living spaces are organized around a central, multilevel garden room with a bridge connecting bedroom wings. Another bridge links a loft apartment to the main house. Interior spaces include large open areas for entertaining, an intimate library, the owner's architectural office, and a raised music studio for teaching, which becomes a stage for recitals.

132. Alig Residence

132. Alig Residence

1101 Questover Circle
Architect: Deborah Berke Architect, New York
       with Cornelius M. Alig
Contractor: E. B. Rayburn Construction Corporation
1988

Straddling a narrow bluff 70 feet above the White River, this residence defines an enclave within its wooded environment. The design is organized around a visual axis oriented toward Monument Circle; the breezeway aligns with this axis, bisecting the house and offering a framed view of downtown. The rectilinear configuration of the house creates a wall between the front and back of the site, with the entry defined by a walled courtyard. Most rooms are located against the rear elevation in order to take advantage of southern light and expansive views. The materials and details of the house are simple. Limestone for trim, stucco for the walls, and zinc for the roof were chosen for their inherent tendency to weather over time, bearing evidence of the elements and allowing the structure to become further integrated into its natural surroundings.

131. Robert and Susan Johnstone Residence

1065 West 52nd Street
Architect: Kennedy Brown McQuiston Architects
Contractor: James Taylor
1988

Extraordinary specimen trees and a view to Highland Golf Course defined the placement of this contemporary frame house for a family of four. With each face of the residence visible from a distance, all were treated with equal importance. This photo illustrates the broad, interlocking gables of the north and east elevations. The interior's open plan coupled with intimate overlooks, walkways, and a den with pocket doors give a variety of private and family spaces. Rooms feature oak floors, painted trim, and tall banks of windows.

1990 Indiana Society of Architects, Honor Award

131. Johnstone Residence

133. Meridian Street United Methodist Church
5500 North Meridian Street
Architect: James Architects & Engineers, Inc.
Contractor: MacDougall and Pierce Construction, Inc.
1988

Meridian Street United Methodist Church was designed by
William Earl Russ and Merritt Harrison and constructed in
1950. This two-story addition to its west facade provides
new day-care and administrative facilities as well as handicapped access and improved fire egress. The original exterior materials of brick, limestone, leaded copper, slate, and
wood trim were replicated, as were the window, door, and
cornice detailing of the original design, resulting in an
addition that matches the quality of the original building.
The curves of the west wall provide a new design element
that gives the addition its own identity. New entries and
stairwells that serve the west parking area are more com-
plimentary to the church's formal spaces than were the old
entries in the "basement." A small interior courtyard was
created to preserve the original windows into the parlor
and classrooms.

133. Meridian Street United Methodist Church

134. Tarkington Shoppes

134. Tarkington Shoppes
5629-31 North Illinois Street
Architect: Mack Architects, P.C.
Construction Manager: Sweet & Company, Inc.
1993

From the northeast corner of 56th and Illinois streets, a
block of one-story commercial buildings dating from the
1920s and 1930s extends north to this new building
designed to fit into its context. The architect was asked to
design a building that would express the individuality of the
products of the two tenants: an interior accessories shop and
a clothing store. Charles Mayer & Company's pedimented
facade employs rusticated limestone and tall French doors to
convey its image, while Tarkington Tweed's store combines
brick, limestone bands, and an almost Victorian corner
tower repeating the pedimented motif. Large windows in
both halves encourage window shopping from the brick-
paved sidewalks lined with period lampposts. While the
effect is more eclectic than a strict exercise in infill for a historic district, the building enhances and supports the continuing vitality of this neighborhood center of specialty shops.

135. Eiteljorg-Burris Residence
5885 Stafford Way
Architect: Blackburn Associates Architects, Inc.
Contractor: Mark Adams
1991

Located behind a stand of tall pine trees in the Crow's Nest area, this large-scale residence exhibits Post Modern variations on classically derived elements. The two-story entry portico, with its barrel vault supported by four massive columns, is the hallmark of the style. The entire exterior, including the chimneys, is clad with a stucco-like finish in neutral shades of beige and taupe. Two-story-tall arched windows with contrasting trim, oversized balusters at window balconies, engaged columns at the corners, and a colossal fanlight over the front door are all individualistic renditions of classical elements. On the interior, the main level is organized around a central living space from which various rooms radiate.

135. Eiteljorg-Burris Residence

136. Fox Hill Elementary School

136. Fox Hill Elementary School
802 Fox Hill Drive
Architect: James Architects & Engineers, Inc.
Contractor: Verkler Incorporated
1992

Seen here is the diamond-shaped enclosure of the school's main entry courtyard. This angularity is repeated in the exterior walls of the classrooms, which are clustered in groups of five around corridors leading to the two upper-level multipurpose rooms at each side of the school. The buff brick facade, detailed by soldier courses at the foundation and eave lines, is set off by the darker jumbo brick of the foundation and the green window sash. The variegated shingles of the roof subtly add texture to the building. Upon entering the school, one is met by the curving wall of the media center that defines the main corridor between the east and west wings. The exterior foundation brick is carried into the interior public spaces forming a low wainscot.

137. Spring Mill Road Stable

6053 Spring Mill Road
Architect: Gordon Clark Associates, Inc.
Contractor: Ernest Renner
1978

When this 1902 stable on the grounds of the former William H. Block estate was transformed into a single-family residence, both architect and owner strove to maintain its historic integrity and character. For example, the spatial characteristics of the old hayloft were preserved in its conversion to a large family room. The three-story tower (which originally housed a water tank) was made into a vertical master bedroom suite with a sitting room on the top floor enjoying views of the White River. Due to the stable's deteriorated condition, most of the windows were replaced, and the building was resided with new clapboards on the first floor and shingles on the second. The main entry occurs where the original stable doors were located. The 1980 design awards jury lauded the old building's sympathetic remodeling and commented: "fresh planning ideas create a house of unique spirit."

1980 Indiana Society of Architects, Honor Award
1981 Indianapolis Chapter, American Institute of Architects, Merit Award

137. Spring Mill Road Stable

138. Paul Residence

138. Paul Residence

West 62nd Street
Architect: Muller and Brown, Cincinnati
Contractor: Holzer Construction Company, Inc.
1985

A mundane suburban ranch house was transformed into a very individualistic piece of architecture through a major addition to the front of the house. The architect's embrace of ornament, color, pattern, and unusual materials is evident in this photo. A series of shingle-covered projecting and recessed elements—polygonal bays topped by conical roofs of standing-seam copper and squared, gatepost-like structures set off by roof ornaments—animate the main facade. The colorful grids of porcelain panels, which occur below windows, are reflective of the designer's reinterpretation of organic architecture. Setting itself apart from the neighborhood character, this house expresses a variety of eclectic themes.

139. Charles Kiphart Residence
1209 West 64th Street
Architect: Prince/Alexander Architects, Inc.
Contractor: Prince/Alexander Cos., Inc.
1989

Located down a private lane to a wooded site with mature oaks and beech trees, this house rises like a Mayan ruin in the jungle. The main compositional units of the house—the two slant-roofed wings and the central tower—are grouped around the main entry courtyard, which brings light into the house, yet provides a sense of privacy. As one of the first steps of the house's design, architect and owner selected the desired views from each room; for example, the living room overlooks the creek, while the dining room—the largest and most important room in the house—views the ravine. The house's facade evokes monumentality, but it was executed in economical materials: split-faced concrete block and two colors of concrete brick. The alternating bands of contrasting materials are most effective at the tower with its stepped parapet. Towerwing (as its owner calls it) is one of the more individual houses in Indianapolis.

139. Charles Kiphart Residence

140. St. Monica's Catholic Church

140. St. Monica's Catholic Church
6131 North Michigan Road
Architect: Woollen, Molzan and Partners
Construction Manager: MacDougall & Pierce
                                 Construction, Inc.
1993

The new sanctuary, narthex, reservation chapel, and daily chapel were designed to implement the liturgical changes of Vatican II. The parish desired a strong religious presence in front of the existing structure located on heavily traveled Michigan Road, hence the very large scale. The brick church forms evolved from the symbolic relationship between the Eucharist, Baptism, and procession. The spaces are organized axially, beginning with the entrance to the high space of the narthex, marked by the apsidal reservation chapel. The axis terminates at the altar. The large volume of the sanctuary was necessary to create a democratic, contemporary, fan-shaped seating arrangement in which the altar is extended toward the worshipers. The small stained-glass windows of the ambulatory are from the original sanctuary, while the sanctuary's semicircular stained-glass windows were commissioned anew.

142. Broad Ripple High School Additions
1115 Broad Ripple Avenue
Architect: Browning Day Mullins Dierdorf Inc.
Contractor: Skillman Corporation
1988

In conjunction with major new additions, all departments and circulation patterns of the high school were reorganized toward more efficient operation. The project was designed in phases to allow for continuous use of the school. The first phase included new construction for the physical education department, including a 3,000-seat gymnasium seen in the photo, as well as refurbishment of the majority of classroom space in the building. The new gym's gabled roof breaks with the flat roofs of the existing high school, but its materials and the main facade's fenestration echo those of the original school. During the second phase the remainder of the building was remodeled, and a new addition was constructed for the industrial arts department. At the heart of the school a new media computer center was created to serve as the hub of educational activity.

142. Broad Ripple High School Additions

141. School 80 Loft Apartments
920 E. 62nd Street
Architect: Prince/Alexander Architects, Inc.
Contractor: Prince/Alexander Cos., Inc.
1988

In the 1980s the Indianapolis Public School system disposed of many of its older schools, primarily due to declines in student enrollment and the desire to avoid the problems of older buildings. Frances E. Willard School 80 was constructed by J. G. Kerstedt in 1929 to the Art Deco designs of McGuire and Shook. After the school was closed in 1980 and "surplused" in 1983, its conversion to 34 apartments found an immediate market for affordably priced units in a historic building. It is the most significant new multifamily housing project in Broad Ripple in recent years. The design and layout of individual units was simplified to preserve funds for common areas.

141. School 80 Loft Apartments

144. Donald and Julie Able Residence
6951 Lancet Lane
Architect and Contractor: Donald R. Able, AIA
1983

Designed with energy conservation in mind, this house utilizes water storage trombe walls at each story and takes advantage of sun orientation and natural ventilation to effect surprising energy efficiencies. The residence meets critical passive solar requirements even though the restricted site required that all four corners touch the front and rear building setback lines. The design exhibits a European influence with its stucco and brick tile exterior. The sine-curve motif is reflected internally as the central dividing wall separating formal and informal living areas; this wall snakes through the first floor culminating in the living room fireplace. The spare interiors accentuate architectural features such as elevated ceilings, changing levels, and lofts in the children's rooms. Natural light plays an important role in the experience of each space.

144. Donald and Julie Able Residence

143. David and Donna Young Residence
6720 North Meridian Street
Architect: Prince/Alexander Architects, Inc.
Contractor: Prince/Alexander Cos., Inc.
1986

The wide overhang of the low roof, the overall proportions and simplicity, and the window grids all mark the unmistakable influence of Frank Lloyd Wright in the design of this house. Located on a rise on busy North Meridian Street, the residence overlooks a wooded ravine with a small brook. This site offered opportunities for views to the surrounding scenery while at the same time it demanded solutions to allowing privacy for its occupants. Kitchen and laundry areas are situated at the front of the main level to act as insulators against street sounds. Just inside the main entry, which occurs at the window wall at left, is a gallery that unifies the home's three levels. The concrete paving in front of the house doubles as a driveway and play area for the children, while the front entry stairs can serve as the spectators' bleachers.

143. David and Donna Young Residence

146. St. Luke's Catholic Church

146. St. Luke's Catholic Church
7575 East Holliday Drive
Architect: Pecsok, Jelliffe & Randall
Contractor: F. A. Wilhelm Construction Co. Inc.
1982

This church's distinctive exterior of rough-hewn limestone blocks, highlighted by an attenuated bell tower at the south end, contrasts quite surprisingly with the refined new sanctuary seen here. The elegant form of the arched wood trusses and wood ceiling is set off by the dramatically stark ambulatory wall, ornamented only by a ceramic mosaic. The seating for the 800 parishioners is arranged in rows that are wider than the length of the sanctuary in order to bring people closer to the altar. The stained-glass windows of the clerestory were designed by Maureen McGuire of Phoenix, Arizona, and executed by the Louisville Art Glass Company. When St. Luke's was built approximately 30 years ago, the church was "temporarily" located in what was intended to be a gymnasium for the school. To connect the new church to the existing building and create a unified structure, the architects designed a large narthex that serves as the one central entrance to the entire building, as well as the reception area and gathering space for the sanctuary. The 39-foot-high space is abundantly lit by clerestory windows and is simply finished with a flagstone floor and oak woodwork.

1985 Interfaith Forum on Religion, Art & Architecture, Citation Award

145. Park Tudor Middle School
7200 North College Avenue
Architect: Fanning/Howey Associates, Inc.
Contractor: R. L. Turner Corporation
1988

Centrally located on the Park Tudor campus, the middle school building for grades six through eight continues the campus-wide vocabulary of limestone walls and hipped roofs inspired by the 1927 Foster Hall, designed by Robert Platt Daggett and Thomas Hibben. (Eli Lilly's donation of land stipulated that the school's architecture must reflect the original building.) The middle school was part of a campus expansion program that included a new gym and a science resource center. It contains 11 classrooms, a two-story library, faculty rooms, and an administrative area. Banked into its sloping site, the school affords views of the track and field complex and neighborhoods to the south. Four shed dormers, features more common to residential buildings than to academic ones, extend from the hipped roof over the seven-bay south facade. Smooth limestone trim frames the tri-part windows, and concrete shingle roofing convincingly imitates slate.

145. Park Tudor Middle School

147. Second Presbyterian Church Additions

147. Second Presbyterian Church Additions

147. Second Presbyterian Church Additions

7700 North Meridian Street
Architect: Kennedy Brown McQuiston Architects
Construction Manager: Geupel DeMars Inc.
1989

Since its construction in 1958, Second Presbyterian Church, designed by McGuire & Shook, Compton, Richey and Associates, has been a dramatic landmark on North Meridian Street. Like the Gothic Revival church itself, the new multiuse and administration wings use vertical building lines and steeply pitched roofs as dramatic counter-points to the sweeping slope of the site. The church is now an assemblage of buildings reminiscent of the character of a rural English monastic community. Educational, administrative, and meeting room spaces, which provide room for uses such as family counseling, were placed to improve traffic patterns. Design concerns that came of age during the 1980s—such as respect for existing form and detail—are particularly evident in the care taken to match the color and finish of the limestone walls and slate roof.

1990 Indiana Society of Architects, Honor Award

148. Mernitz-Strain Residence
7775 North Ridge Road
Architects: Carolyn H. Goode, AIA, 1979, 1986
             Mozingo Associates, Inc., 1990
Contractors: Bill Fox; Donoho Construction, Inc.

Sited in a meadow bordered by Williams Creek and woods, the Mernitz-Strain house is a good example of a genre of contemporary American architecture that relates to the country's tradition of vernacular frame building. The plan of the house develops from a spatial expression of the activities of the first owners, with the form dominated by a simple and commanding gabled roof. The whole composition of three and a half stories is uniformly covered in gray-stained cedar shakes. The interior exhibits a restricted palette of finishes, which allows the volume of the spaces to dominate. A "great common space" with a 36-foot ceiling serves as the centerpiece; activity rooms are located around it with private "aerie" bedrooms perched above. Forty skylights bathe the interior with light. The screened summerhouse seen in this rear view was added in 1986. In 1990 an addition designed to blend seamlessly with the original house was added to accommodate the needs of the current owners.

148. Mernitz-Strain Residence

149. Sally Gans Residence

149. Sally Gans Residence
520 West 79th Street
Architect: James W. McQuiston
Contractor: Herb Schmidt
1981

While employing traditional building materials such as horizontal cedar siding and trim boards, the design of this house is a contemporary statement made by variations on the traditional, such as the broad bands of dark green trim and the large-scale grids of the windows and front door. The variation on the front gable, clipped at its peak and divided by the recessed window stacked over the door, is its most individual element. The interior is organized by a skylit north/south hall, with rooms radiating off this central "spine." Thus the north and south facades (front and rear) appear the most symmetrical, while the east and west elevations reflect the progression of differing spaces and functions along the spine. To promote energy efficiency, the north and south windows are deeply recessed from wind or sun respectively, and closets and built-in storage are generally placed on outside corners for insulation. At the northwest corner, the garage is tucked within the volume of the house.

1982 Indiana Society of Architects, Honor Award

Fall Creek Valley

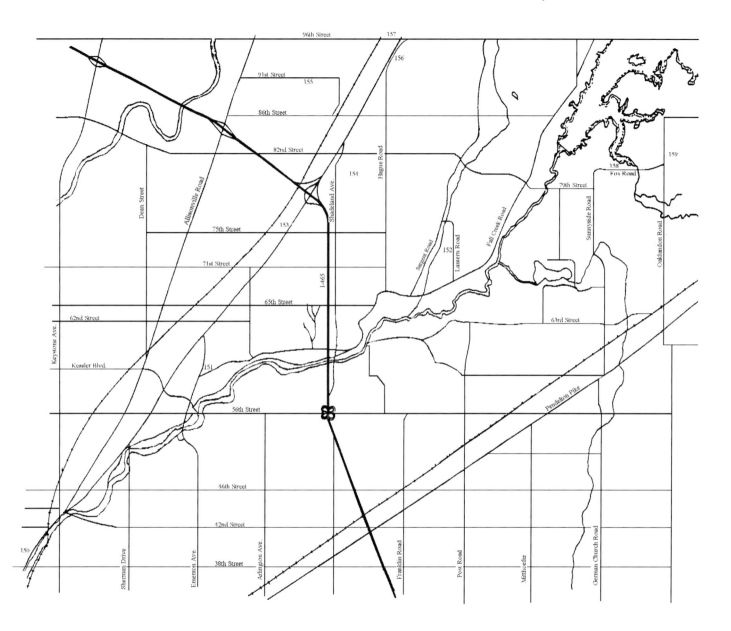

Fall Creek Valley directory

150. Fairground Entrance
151. Snyder Residence
152. Church of the Nativity
153. Metro Center
154. Community Hospital North

155. East 91st Street Christian Church
156. Boehringer Mannheim
157. Marsh Headquarters
158. Backbay at Geist
159. Holy Cross Lutheran Church

150. State Fair Gate Six Entry Plaza
Fall Creek Boulevard
Architect: Callahan Associates, Inc.
Contractor: Wilson Blazek Corporation
1989

After years of neglect, the Indiana State Fair Board is attempting to create a positive image for the future of the fairgrounds. This new vehicular and pedestrian entrance gate is one of the first manifestations of the effort. The choice of materials—common red brick with Indiana limestone detailing—relates to the majority of 1930s buildings on the fairgrounds' campus, which were built during the WPA program. The aluminum box truss that spans the piers updates the image, while the arched wood beam that carries the signage harkens back to covered bridges. A future sculpture depicting a family theme (to be chosen from a statewide competition among Indiana artists) will be located north of the entry.

150. State Fair Gate Six Entry Plaza

151. Robert and Cheryl Snyder Residence

151. Robert and Cheryl Snyder Residence
5754 East Fall Creek Road
Architect: Robert W. Snyder, AIA
Contractor: Stanley Klain
1990

Overlooking the Fall Creek Valley, this residence is located at the crest of a wooded hillside. In the main section of the house, the bold columns of random sizes reinforce the strong vertical lines of the wooded surroundings. Vertical wood siding further accentuates these lines. The elevated rooms of the main story capitalize on views to the lake, woods, and river beyond. The west portion of the house stair steps up the hill to meet the main section. On the interior, an all-white, open-laced steel staircase is a sculptural focal point connecting all three levels. From the loft overlooking the main living space, glimpses of the downtown skyline can be seen at night. The house is white, contrasting with the colors of nature, yet at all seasons fits comfortably in its natural surroundings.

152. Church of the Nativity Addition
7300 Lantern Road
Architect: Mozingo Williamson Architects, Inc.
Contractor: Brandt Construction, Inc.
1993

When the Episcopal church on this wooded, suburban site needed to double its size, a conscious decision was made to retain the simplicity and character of the existing building, a converted stone and wood stable. The new 300-seat nave was sited to the southeast, forming an L with the existing structure. Square in plan with the altar located in the southeast corner and the entrance in the northwest corner symbolically adjacent to the baptismal font, the nave's seating has a diagonal orientation. Light filters in from high clerestory windows through the soaring central space formed by barnlike wood trusses. The church's form—with its hipped clerestory stage with vertical wood siding over the limestone base—is reminiscent of medieval Russian ecclesiastical structures. The new building is in keeping with the themes of the Nativity and in harmony with the older structure while it lends a new image.

152. Church of the Nativity Addition

153. Metro Centre

153. Metro Centre
6330 East 75th Street
Architect: Simmons & Associates, Inc.
Contractor: Thomas E. Moore Construction;
        MacDougall & Pierce Construction, Inc.
1986; 1988

The site's orientation to State Route 37 allowed for the development of an office/warehouse project with retail visibility. The buildings were designed at the height of the boom in Indianapolis' speculative commercial development, when developers were competing for new tenants in any manner possible. With the goal of creating a fresh alternative to the typical warehouse design, where overhead service bay doors are often located to face the highway, the architects paid more attention to the design of the facade. The use of insulated metal panels, fluted concrete block, back-lit metal signage panels, and the incorporation of mechanical vents as a design element all gave this project a distinct, high-tech look.

155. East 91st Street Christian Church

155. East 91st Street Christian Church
6049 East 91st Street
Architect: WareAssociates, Chicago
Contractor: R. L. Turner Corporation
1991

A new 1,500-seat sanctuary, an educational facility for preschool through elementary grades, a complete music suite including rehearsal spaces, robing rooms and library, and a new administrative suite surrounding an atrium narthex were all part of the major expansion of the East 91st Street Christian Church. This view from the north shows the side view of the sanctuary and narthex. With music an important part of worship, the sanctuary's large volume of space enhances acoustics and provides an ideal environment for the 102-rank Schantz pipe organ, purported to be the largest in Indiana. Upon entering the worship space, the eye is drawn upward to natural lighting provided by semicircular dormer windows along the sides, circular windows in the gable ends, and a band of windows following the gable line above the choir. The cleanly and thoughtfully detailed building relies on simple statements of form and color to convey a strong sense of dignity.

154. Community Hospital North
7150 Clear Vista Drive
Architect: Boyd/Sobieray Associates, Inc.
Contractor: Geupel DeMars Inc.
1985

In 1982 Community Hospitals Indianapolis decided to develop a satellite facility to serve the far northeastern part of the county. The new building was sited so that it could be easily recognized from Interstate 69. The hospital consists of two components linked by an enclosed walkway: a 100-bed medical/surgical facility and a 125-bed psychiatric facility, each built to different code requirements. The nursing units utilize a triangular floor plan to reduce travel distance from the central nursing station to the patient rooms; these triangles then became a determinant of the overall plan and building footprint. The interior courtyards, also triangles, allow maximum natural light and provide recreation areas for psychiatric patients. The main entry canopies in this view repeat the triangular motif.

1985 Indianapolis Chapter, American Institute of Architects, Honor Award
1986 Indiana Society of Architects, Citation Award

154. Community Hospital North

156. Boehringer Mannheim Corporation Buildings
9115 North Hague Road
Architect: CSO/Architects, Inc.
Contractor: Shiel-Sexton Co., Inc.
1983-1990

The original buildings at this site were built in the late 1960s by the Biodynamics Corporation, which sold them to Boehringer Mannheim in 1975. Between 1983 and 1990 major additions were made to the first buildings, which more than tripled the size of the facility. Additional components included laboratories, training classrooms, offices, and a central dining room for four buildings. Two-story curvilinear atria sheathed in reflective glass occur at the point of juncture between the new and existing brick buildings. The new design projects a nonindustrial appearance more suitable to surrounding residential neighbors. With the primary facades facing I-69, the Boehringer Mannheim complex enjoys the suburban office park setting of ponds and lawns that has become ubiquitous to interstate architecture.

156. Boehringer Mannheim Corporation Buildings

157. Marsh Corporate Headquarters

157. Marsh Corporate Headquarters
9800 Crosspoint Boulevard
Architect: CSO/Architects, Inc.
Contractor: Shiel-Sexton Co., Inc.
1991

As a corporate headquarters of a large Indiana grocery chain, the building's entry facade reflects the client's desire for a conservative, solid image. A long, narrow lot and limited vehicular access created a north/south axis that orders both building and site. Beginning at the south parking area, the axis travels toward the symmetrical south facade of the five-story building and continues through two atria, terminating at a semicircular dining area at the north end. The red brickwork, accented by bands of Indiana limestone, is well detailed at the first-floor columns and pilasters. As is becoming standard with office park developments, there are two large ponds with fountains fronting the building.

157. Marsh Corporate Headquarters

159. Holy Cross Lutheran Church

159. Holy Cross Lutheran Church
8115 Oaklandon Road
Architect: Woollen, Molzan and Partners
Contractor: Brandt Construction
1990

Holy Cross Lutheran Church was founded in 1989 in Oaklandon; that year the congregation purchased 10 acres in the rapidly developing Geist area. To date the first phase of the master plan, a sanctuary and classroom/office wing, has been completed. A 200-seat traditional sanctuary is framed with laminated wood members and wrapped in a patterned brick veneer. The simplicity of the forms reflects the formerly rural nature of the site as well as traditional Scandinavian Lutheran churches. The stripes and blocks of color scale down the larger two-story mass of the sanctuary. The windows infuse a rhythm of light along the axis of the nave. The transept ends in a larger window whose mullions could be viewed to form an abstracted human figure.

1991 Indianapolis Chapter, American Institute of Architects, Honor Award

158. Backbay at Geist
11202 Backbay Lane
Architect: Archonics Design Partnership
Contractor: Herbert Lucksh
1984

This condominium development on a wooded site overlooking Geist Reservoir stands out in contrast to the single-family residential development around the reservoir. The developer's desire to create a "hillside village" led to dividing the 168 units into 42 buildings. In what appears as a single, large residence at the right, there are actually four units, a fact disguised by the building's design and variety of massing. To maximize the view of the water and wooded ravines at the inside of the site, garages and entries were located on the street side, allowing open vistas to the natural side. Floor-to-ceiling windows and two-story rooms overlooking the lake further open the units to their surroundings. To help preserve the natural setting, vegetation from the house sites was relocated after construction.

1985 Indianapolis Chapter, American Institute of Architects, Merit Award

158. Backbay at Geist

Eastside

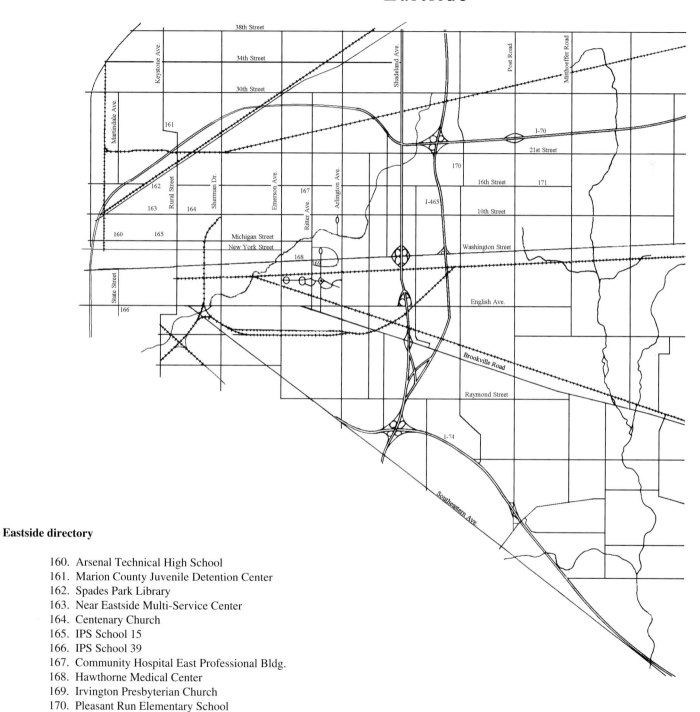

Eastside directory

160. Arsenal Technical High School
161. Marion County Juvenile Detention Center
162. Spades Park Library
163. Near Eastside Multi-Service Center
164. Centenary Church
165. IPS School 15
166. IPS School 39
167. Community Hospital East Professional Bldg.
168. Hawthorne Medical Center
169. Irvington Presbyterian Church
170. Pleasant Run Elementary School
171. Warren Performing Arts Center

160. Arsenal Technical High School

160. Arsenal Technical High School

160. Arsenal Technical High School
1500 East Michigan Street
Architect: HNTB Architects Engineers Planners
Contractor: The Skillman Corporation
1992

During the Civil War the U. S. government established a federal arsenal on 75 acres in Indianapolis that grew over the years to an extensive complex of buildings. In 1912 when the city's two high schools were overcrowded, the entire arsenal complex was converted to a high school. In 1988 HNTB completed a campus-wide master plan to study the feasibility of retaining its 16 separate structures. Infrastructure improvements, including the replacement of existing utilities, and roof repairs were the first priorities addressed. One of the initial renovation projects converted the 1869 barn to a state-of-the-art language laboratory. Its transformation from an unused storage building into viable classroom space was critical to the relocation of other departments on campus. Restoration and renovation work involving 53 separate projects are planned to extend over a 15-year period.

The Arsenal Building is one of the high school's nine buildings listed on the National Register and the most significant military structure in the city. Built between 1863 and 1865, it housed 50 soldiers and stored heavy artillery and small arms from its completion through 1903, when it was first converted to educational use. Rising three stories above a raised basement, the building is distinguished by its three-stage entrance tower with giant-order pilasters, cornice, and rusticated base of limestone. One of the interesting challenges of the arsenal's restoration involved replacement of significantly deteriorated limestone, which did not provide adequate anchorage for new stone. Sections of the cornice were removed and their original profile reconstructed with an exterior insulation finish system, which was blended to replicate limestone, down to the pseudo joints cut to simulate individual stones.

161. Marion County Juvenile Detention Center

2401 East 25th Street
Architect: HNTB Architects Engineers Planners
Contractor: Glenroy Construction Co.
1990

Located within a curve of Keystone Avenue in the midst of a residential area, the new detention center was treated in small-scaled, low-profile massing to make it as harmonious as possible with the surrounding neighborhood. At the juncture of the old, existing center and the new building, a two-story administrative and courts portion of the building serves as the public face and main entrance to the facility. Courtroom areas were designed to foster participation in the judicial process. This aerial photo clearly shows the series of individual housing pods aligned diagonally at the southeast portion of the site. The horizontal, double slot windows of the individual resident rooms are located within continuous cast-stone banding around the entire exterior, which helps reduce the overall scale. Use of contrasting buff and terra-cotta colored brick further enhances the design. Within each housing unit a large 10-foot-by-10-foot square window in a two-story dayroom allows a flood of natural light to enter from the courtyards.

161. Marion County Juvenile Detention Center

162. Spades Park Library

162. Spades Park Library

1801 Nowland Avenue
Architect: Blackburn Associates Architects, Inc.
Contractor: Wilson Blazek Corporation
1987

Located at the west end of Brookside Park, this branch library was completed in 1912 as the fourth of six branch libraries in the city built through the generosity of philanthropist Andrew Carnegie. It was designed by local architect Wilson B. Parker; George Weaver served as building contractor. By the mid 1980s the library was badly in need of repair and was threatened by replacement. As part of a major renovation that was completed in time for the building's 75th birthday, new mechanical systems and a new roof were installed, an elevator was inserted for handicapped accessibility, and the building was completely relighted and refurnished. The interior received attention uncommon to institutional rehab projects: woodwork was carefully refinished, the fireplace was put in working order, and an original oil painting was restored. Today the Spades Park Library is one of two Carnegie libraries still in operation in the city, the other being the East Washington branch, renovated in 1978.

164. Centenary Christian Church

164. Centenary Christian Church

1035 Oxford Road (Rural and 11th streets)
Architect: Woollen, Molzan and Partners
Construction Manager: Construction Planning and
                              Management
1992

A Christmas Eve fire in 1986 destroyed the original 1922 Centenary Christian Church. This new sanctuary, choir room, and support wing form an addition to the only surviving portion, the classroom structure. The design of the new addition began within the context of the existing neighborhood, composed of 1930s and 1940s bungalow-style homes. The church mass is respectfully broken into distinct functional parts to reflect this scale. The 210-seat sanctuary anchors the corner while the choir room to the south protects a new courtyard in the middle of the site. On the interior, the laminated wood structure recalls the relationship between church form and structure that one finds throughout the history of church architecture. The new stained-glass windows are made from fragments of the original church windows that were salvaged from the fire.

163. Near Eastside Multi-Service Center

2236 East 10th Street
Architect: Kennedy Brown Architects
Contractor: Gilliate General Contractors Inc.
1991

Designed by the Foster Engineering Company in 1925 as the Brookside Building, this two-story brick structure is one of the most prominent landmarks in this part of the city. It was built with Foster's unit slab system, a patented structural design in which the concrete slab acts as a cantilever. The building's renovation by Eastside Community Investments, a neighborhood-based development corporation, is the largest redevelopment project to take place on East 10th Street. Having long served as the home of the Near Eastside Multi-Service Center, the rehabilitation enabled many improvements in the center's programs, such as the consolidation of senior citizens programs on one floor behind the restored storefronts. Perhaps the highlight of the redevelopment is the new housing on the building's second floor, where 24 apartments for low-income residents are located. Unfortunately due to deterioration of the concrete floors, the original, distinctive bay windows had to be rebuilt and were simplified in the process.

163. Near Eastside Multi-Service Center

166. IPS School 39 (William McKinley)
1733 Spann Avenue
Architect: Blackburn Associates Architects, Inc.
Construction Manager: Skillman Corporation
1990

After a 10-year moratorium on new school construction in the Indianapolis Public School system, School 39 was designed to replace a 75-year-old school in bad repair. The surrounding inner-city neighborhood is one of low-to-moderate-income families with a strong sense of community, much of which is centered around the school. The building creates a citadel-like presence that enhances the importance of the school to those who enter. The repetitive use of gables echoes those of the small surrounding homes, while muted colors of brown brick and buff stone trim create a pleasant feeling. Well-landscaped play areas are given added security by being situated away from heavy traffic behind earth berms.

166. IPS School 39 (William McKinley)

165. IPS School 15 (Thomas D. Gregg)
2302 East Michigan Street
Architect: James Associates Architects
Contractor: Skillman Corporation
1987

This school replaces an architecturally significant structure originally designed by Adolph Scherrer in 1895, with a major addition by Vonnegut and Bohn in 1899. The new building is sited centrally, respecting the demolished school's remains. The two-story massing, reminiscent of many local post-World War II schools, is basic polygonal geometry except for the serrated southwest elevation. The two-tone brick exterior enlivens the facade with bay brick highlighted against brick piers. The new building contrasts with the highly articulated masonry work of the 1899 school's entries. The two surviving archways and reconstructed water table now demarcate a forecourt. The new entry is framed by cast-in-place concrete arches that mirror the historic gateways. To better understand the present generation, one sometimes must look to the ancestors with respectful interpretation.

165. IPS School 15 (Thomas D. Gregg)

167. Community Hospital East Professional Building

1400 North Ritter Avenue
Architect: BSA Design
Construction Manager: Wurster Construction Company, Inc.
1991

Located at the front door of the existing Community Hospital East, which has not changed significantly since the 1970s, this five-story building creates a new image for the hospital. Following a trend common in the 1980s, the offices of doctors in a dozen medical specialties affiliated with the hospital can be found here. The choice of a red brick facade, updated by the entry pavilion's contrasting stone panels, is reflective of the older buildings of the medical complex. Because of a limited site, a parking garage for 1,400 cars, connected to the main lobby of the building, was part of this project.

167. Community Hospital East Professional Building

168. Hawthorne Family Medicine

168. Hawthorne Family Medicine

5302 East Washington Street
Architect: Group Eleven Architecture & Planning, Ltd.
Contractor: CPM, Inc.
1992

This modest medical office building replaced an abandoned convenience store in the historic Irvington neighborhood. In order to be sympathetic with the older commercial structures along Washington Street as well as the surrounding residences, it utilizes a combination of brick and wood siding. The windows and the gables—the most prominent architectural features—are highlighted in a teal blue color. Placing the parking lot to the side of the building rather than in front of it allowed the medical office to relate to the street in a traditional manner, thereby maintaining the continuity of the historic area.

170. Pleasant Run Elementary School

170. Pleasant Run Elementary School
1800 South Franklin Road
Architect: Schmidt Associates Architects, Inc.
Contractor: Dallman Industrial Corporation
1991

When Pleasant Run Elementary School was originally built in the 1960s, it was one of six identical school buildings, all of which underwent renovation between 1988 and 1992. Imparting a measure of individuality therefore became an important design criteria. As part of this effort, bright ceramic tile appears on stucco sculptural elements leading to the entry and in the playground area. This random and lighthearted grid patterning reoccurs in the interior in terrazzo and carpeted floors and on the walls. Windows in the new classroom additions are placed low, reflecting the height of primary school students. A new media center just inside the entry now serves as the focal point of the expanded 650-student school.

169. Irvington Presbyterian Church Addition
55 South Johnson Avenue
Architect: Amt, Inc./Architects
Contractor: Brandt Construction, Inc.
1987

The desire to provide handicapped access was the immediate impetus to this addition to the Irvington Presbyterian Church, originally built in 1929 to the designs of architects Harrison & Turnock. However, as more people today enter churches from their parking lots rather than their front doors, this new addition gives prominency to that fact. A new stair tower and elevator now provide access to all three floors and basement of the church and its classroom addition. Portions of the interior, such as a relocated administrative office, were remodeled in the process. The exterior walls of the new addition are of brick, color matched to the church's limestone ashlar, while the roof over the new entry reflects the pitch of the church's tall gabled roof. The tall, narrow windows emulate the original building's Gothic proportions.

169. Irvington Presbyterian Church Addition

172. Lutheran High School of Indianapolis
5555 South Arlington Avenue
Architect: Schmidt Associates Architects, Inc.
Contractor: Glenroy Construction Co., Inc.
1991

The juxtaposition and massing of contrasting forms are the basis of Lutheran High School's architectural character. At the main entrance to the building, a gabled porch occurs between the cylindrical form of the skylit prayer chapel at the left and the tall west wall of the two-story commons—a large, flexible interior space that serves as the focal point of the school. On the interior, echoing the entry gable, is a freestanding gabled brick portal at the entrance to the commons, symbolic of home, family, and centrality. In the clerestory, small square windows and the central cruciform window provide natural lighting. With a school student body of approximately 250, Lutheran High School provides a generous floor area ratio per student.

172. Lutheran High School of Indianapolis

171. Warren Center of Performing Arts
9301 East 18th Street
Architect: Daverman Associates, Grand Rapids, Michigan
Contractor: Glenroy Construction Co., Inc.
1983

Additions to secondary schools seldom take the scale of this major addition to Warren High School, which doubles as a teaching facility and community arts center. The 1,025-seat auditorium inside, now the fourth largest in the city behind Clowes Hall, Murat Theatre, and the Circle Theatre, provides unobstructed sight lines from all seats. The house's shallow depth creates a sense of intimacy to the stage for dramatic presentations. Practice rooms, a 150-seat studio theater, music laboratories, workshops, and design studios are included in the new building. Extending from the auditorium's tri-level lobby, the curving entrance hall, lit by a band of clerestory windows and featuring towering concrete pillars, serves as a gallery for art exhibits.

171. Warren Center of Performing Arts

Southside

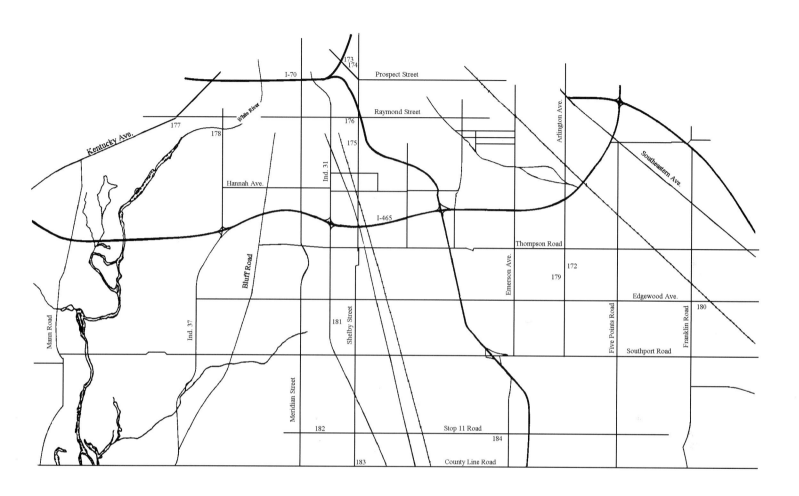

Southside directory

172. Lutheran High School
173. Woessner Building
174. Arnholter Block
175. Garfield Park Conservatory
176. Fire Station 29
177. Crossroads Greenhouses
178. Resource Recovery Plant
179. Arlington Elementary School
180. Franklin Township Middle School
181. Riviera Children's Center
182. Resurrection Lutheran Church
183. Community Hospital South
184. Mary Bryan Elementary School

173. Woessner Building

174. Arnholter Block
944-948 Virginia Avenue
Architect: David B. Duvall and Dale R. Harkins
Contractor: Miller & Sons Masonry, Inc.
1987

This double-unit commercial block was built in two stages more than a dozen years apart. Henry Arnholter built the northern half in 1886 for his harness manufacturing shop, which was located here until 1921. The southern half appears to have been built in 1900 and was first occupied by the Arnholter Brothers' grocery store. By the early 1980s corrugated aluminum panels totally obscured the original storefront design with its limestone pilasters, and windows of the upper floor were filled in with glass bricks. With technical and financial assistance from the Fountain Square & Fletcher Place Investment Corporation, a model restoration was undertaken of the main facade. Today law offices are located inside. While this is a modest project, it is reflective of the resurgence of the Fountain Square area, which is improving by small increments.

173. Woessner Building
902 Virginia Avenue
Architect: Urban Amenities/Architecture; Dale R. Harkins
Contractor: William S. Connor & Company
1985

The Woessner Building was constructed in 1915 by a prominent German-American who had operated a meat market on the site since 1877. By the early 1980s the building's storefronts were all boarded, and the second floor was being used as transient sleeping rooms. Realizing the potential for relocating a business in a near downtown commercial corridor, the owner of an insurance company purchased the building and undertook a renovation. While the exterior was returned to near its original appearance, the ground floor of the interior, which had previously been gutted, was reworked with a new plan. Directly off the corner entry, a two-story reception area was created. Surviving interior features, such as wood-work, brass hardware, and mosaic tile floors, were refurbished. Subsequent to the 1985 project, the owners refaced a nonhistoric building at 920 Virginia Avenue, borrowing themes from the Woessner Building such as the parapet with name tablet over the entry, the storefront divisions, and the general color scheme of terra cotta and dark green. The two buildings are now connected and function as one.

1985 Indianapolis Chapter, American Institute of Architects, Citation Award

174. Arnholter Block

175. Garfield Park Conservatory Renovation
2450 Shelby Street
Architect: Archonics Design Partnership
Contractor: R. L. Turner Corporation
1984

The park's conservatory built in 1954-55 was one of the earliest examples of long-span, welded aluminum structural frames in the U. S. (This building by architect David Burns replaced the rusting steel structure of Garfield's first conservatory.) By the early 1980s, the park department wished to upgrade the facility and increase public interest and usage. In conjunction with new exhibit space for seasonal, tropical, and arid plants, a new winding loop circulation system was developed to replace the center aisle circulation that originated from the building's midpoint entry. The entrance was relocated to the sympathetic new addition at the north end, which also incorporates a gift shop. The highlight of the new circulation path is the walk-through waterfall in the tropical garden area at the south. To improve energy efficiency, an insulating glass roof was retrofitted to the existing structure.

1985 Indianapolis Chapter, American Institute of Architects, Merit Award

175. Garfield Park Conservatory Renovation

176. Fire Station 29

176. Fire Station 29
602 East Pleasant Run Parkway, North Drive
Architect: Blackburn Associates Architects, Inc.
Contractor: Lee Corporation
1991

Located at the base of a hill in Garfield Park, Fire Station 29 was designed to relate to the scale and character of the neighboring homes. The building's high gabled roof peaks, red brick walls, and split-faced block foundation blend with the architectural vocabulary of its surroundings. The main level of the fire station houses the living, dining, and administrative areas as well as the four apparatus bays. On the upper level, men's and women's sleeping quarters have immediate access to the main level via the traditional drop pole. A copper-clad, barrel-vaulted entry canopy welcomes visitors.

178. Resource Recovery Facility

178. Resource Recovery Facility
2320 South Harding Street
Architect: CRS Sirrine Engineers, Inc., Raleigh
Contractor: J. A. Jones Construction Company, Charlotte,
                    North Carolina
1988

The Resource Recovery Facility, known more commonly as "the incinerator," can convert over 2,300 tons of municipal solid waste each day into steam, which is then sold to IPL to heat and cool buildings in downtown Indianapolis and on the IUPUI campus. The administration building at the left is separate from the massive waste-to-energy plant that contains a cavernous pit, three waterwall furnaces, and two overhead cranes. The architectural treatment of the two buildings works on two separate sets of scale, yet colors and materials unite the two. Technologically advanced air pollution control equipment includes dry flue gas scrubbers and fabric filter baghouses.

177. Crossroads Greenhouse
2559 Kentucky Avenue
Designer: DACE Company, Delft, The Netherlands
1989

Utilizing a free fuel source from the city's 200-acre southside landfill, Crossroads Greenhouse is an innovator in demonstrating the concept "from trash to flowers." The methane gas and carbon dioxide that result from the decomposition of organic material is piped in from the landfill and converted by generator to supply 90 percent of the greenhouse's electricity for hot water heat. The six-and-a-half-acre greenhouse was designed in the Netherlands and incorporates state-of-the-art equipment such as a recirculating ebb-and-flow irrigation system, robotic table loaders, roller conveyors, shade and energy-saving curtains, and a computer-controlled environmental system. The greenhouse has 20 bays measuring 31 by 404 feet, each containing the rolling growing tables of lightweight aluminum seen in the foreground of this photo. Crossroads was the first U.S. greenhouse to incorporate this type of easily movable growing table.

177. Crossroads Greenhouse

179. Arlington Elementary School

5814 South Arlington Avenue
Architect: The McGuire & Shook Corporation
Construction Manager: Skillman Corporation
1983

This Franklin Township school contains 15 classrooms, art and music rooms, a library, a multipurpose room, administrative offices, a resource room, and an interior courtyard that can be used as an outdoor classroom. The design challenge was to create a facility that mirrored a residential-like atmosphere throughout the building to deinstitutionalize the learning environment and integrate the facility with the community. The main facade's broad, semicircular arch and the windows flanking the doorway are divided into small, square lights by white mullions. This geometric scheme divided by brick piers is repeated without glazing in the adjacent gabled wall, which together with the entry facade, frames a front courtyard.

1984 Indiana Society of Architects, Citation Award

179. Arlington Elementary School

180. Franklin Township Middle School

180. Franklin Township Middle School

6019 South Franklin Road
Architect: Schmidt Associates Architects, Inc.
Contractor: Verkler Incorporated
1991

In designing a major addition and renovation for the existing Franklin Township Middle School (originally constructed in 1950 and expanded in the 1960s), the architect sought to transform the 1,200-student school by creating a new identity. A new curved entry portico with bold colors breaks with the nondescript rectangular portions of the old building and is the most visible and striking part of the project. Its blue tile is carried across the facade of the adjacent administrative offices in a playful, scattershot effect. Inside, the entry's curves continue in a rounded corridor space with a skylight.

181. Riviera Children's Center

6303 South East Street
Architect: US Architects, Muncie
Contractor: Wise Builders, Muncie
1992

The bright blue metal roof of this building serves as an identifying beacon for this children's center, which combines day-care facilities with a pediatric center. Reflecting sociological trends that have developed more fully since the 1970s, the Riviera Children's Center represents the higher evolution of a new building type combining educational and medical facilities. This center accommodates up to 215 children from six weeks to six years old. Approximately 25 percent of the space is devoted to a pediatric suite. (An on-site physician has proved to be a reassuring bonus to parents using the day care.) Among the variety of interesting classroom spaces, many with curved corners and child nooks, is an outdoor class area in the form of an amphitheater. Window bands focused at the entry and lobby step up to a continuous band that runs around the entire building below roof level. Another franchised facility following the same design is planned for Indianapolis' north side.

181. Riviera Children's Center

182. Resurrection Lutheran Church Sanctuary

182. Resurrection Lutheran Church Sanctuary

445 East Stop 11 Road
Architect: Brandt, Delap, & Nice, Inc.
Contractor: Booher Construction Company
1978

Characteristic of its denomination's commitment to modern church design, the exterior form of this sanctuary expresses the worship space within—not a long, narrow Gothic nave, but a community of worshipers gathered around the altar. The roof line sweeps up to opposing roof monitors, which admit light from above and serve a symbolic function. This addition to Resurrection Lutheran Church is representative of the church design vernacular of the 1970s, which sought to express space for contemporary religious use without reference to forms and details derived from history.

183. Community Hospital South

1402 East South County Line Road
Architect: Gresham, Smith and Partners, Nashville,
      Tennessee; Able Ringham Moake Park (addition)
Contractor: Geupel DeMars Inc. with Turner Construction,
      Cincinnati; Shiel-Sexton Co. Inc.
1984; 1993

The fast-growing Greenwood area encouraged construction of a new hospital at this location, just north of the county line. Built in 1984 as University Heights Hospital, Community Hospitals Indianapolis purchased it in September 1989 and renamed it. When first built as a 150-bed facility, the building was three stories tall but was planned from the outset for future expansion. Flexibility is proving to be the key to designing hospitals that are prepared to face transitions in the health-care industry. In 1993 an additional floor was added to incorporate maternity facilities called the Family Rooms. The most prominent feature of the facade, its glazed segmental arch linking the east and west sections at the fourth-floor level, changed the hospital's exterior image.

183. Community Hospital South

184. Mary Bryan Elementary School

184. Mary Bryan Elementary School

4355 East Stop 11 Road
Architect: The McGuire & Shook Corporation
Construction Manager: Skillman Corporation
1986

This Perry Township school for 600 students, kindergarten through fifth grade, was the first building in Indiana to accommodate the state's Prime Time program, which encourages reduced class size in the lower grades. Should requirements change in the future, the 32 academic classrooms were built with flexibility for reconfiguration. A domed rotunda over the entry area creates a welcoming atmosphere for students and serves as a community gathering area during events in the nearby gymnasium. The color scheme of brown brick with buff banding is reversed at the entry section to highlight this part of the building. The school's most interesting architectural feature is its playful window design in which square units step down in a triangle to ground level. In 1993 nine additional classrooms were constructed in concert with renovation of instructional space.

1988 Indianapolis Chapter, American Institute of Architects, Citation Award

Westside

Westside directory

185. IPS School 47
186. IPS School 49
187. Metro Bus Facility
188. Veterans Hospital Addition
189. Al-Fajr Mosque
190. Major Taylor Velodrome
191. St. Vincent Medical Arts Building
192. Scandinavian Health Club
193. Saturn Dealership
194. Amoco Service Station Canopy
195. Methodist Medical Plaza
196. Rehabilitation Hospital
197. Colts Training Center
198. Schwitzer Headquarters
199. Pike Township Library
200. Park 100 Innerpark
201. DowElanco Research & Development Center
202. DowElanco Employee Development Center
203. Knebel Residence
204. Rubin Residence
205. Zollman Center

Park Fletcher

206. Adams Mark Hotel
207. 1 Park Fletcher
208. Park Fletcher Post Office

The Airport

209. Airport Parking Garage
210. Eagle Air Hub

Westside

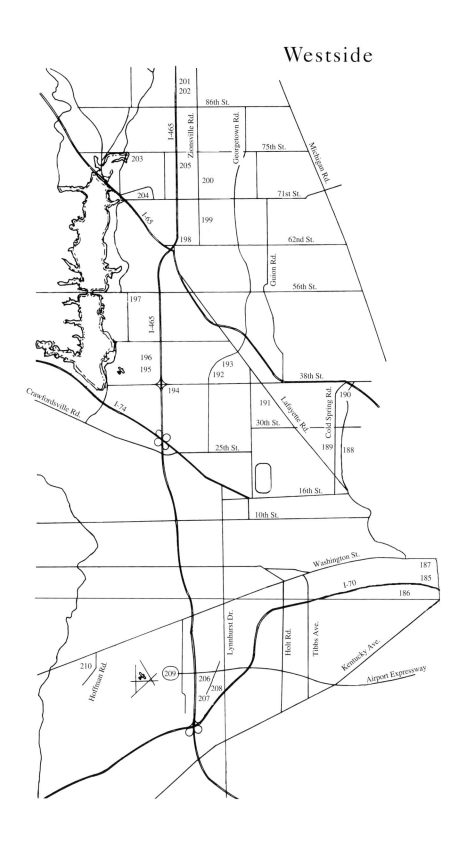

185. IPS School 47 (Thomas A. Edison)

777 South White River Parkway West Drive
Architect: Woollen Associates
Contractor: Glenroy Construction Co., Inc.
1982

This Indianapolis public school was built to house the unusual mixture of kindergarten and seventh and eighth grades. The site—in the midst of a small-scale residential neighborhood with a large manufacturing plant nearby— affords expansive views of downtown and the White River through large arched bridges. The building was broken down into distinct, smaller-scaled volumes oriented toward the river. The elevations of the building are good examples of early Postmodernism in this city and in their simplicity are reminiscent of the earlier work of Venturi and Rauch. Facade patterns refer to the arches of the bridges and childlike drawings of houses. The distinctive patterned roof is a landmark that can be seen easily from the interstate.

185. IPS 47 (Thomas A. Edison)

186. IPS School 49 (William Penn)

186. IPS School 49 (William Penn)

1720 West Wilkins Street
Architect: Kennedy Brown Architects
Construction Manager: Skillman Corporation
1992

The school's U-shaped plan is aligned with Rhodius Park and a city swimming pool to the east. The plan, massing, masonry detailing, and window fenestration are consistent with traditional designs of public schools, yet the school is reinterpreted in a modern vocabulary of utility brick, limestone, and some nontraditional forms such as the diagonal projections from first-floor classrooms. The building's uniqueness lies in the extensive use of ornamental masonry work. Cast medallions that resemble stylized compasses ornament the facade. At the east side seen in this view, the cast medallions are utilized at the crossing points of a large diaper pattern and in the frieze of soldier courses of glazed brick.

187. Metro Bus Facility

1501 West Washington Street
Architect: Archonics Design Partnership
Construction Manager: Tousley-Bixler Corporation
1985

When the Indianapolis Public Transportation Corporation had to move its bus facility from the property soon to become the new zoo, it relocated to the historic site of the manufacture of the Duesenberg automobile. The focal point of this bus maintenance and storage facility is the Duesenberg factory's machine shop, which now houses the administrative offices. (The two original plant buildings on the site were demolished.) Paralleling the old building's central light monitor, a new tall, barrel-vaulted circulation spine connects administrative, storage, and service areas and provides a visual transition between the old and the new buildings. The brick and limestone pillars that figure so prominently in this photo channel visitors into the facility and serve to screen service docks. The enormous facility of over 400,000 square feet provides storage for 350 buses and the full gamut of support services: fueling, washing, parts distribution, 37 maintenance work bays, and workshops.

1987 Indianapolis Chapter, American Institute of Architects, Citation Award

187. Metro Bus Facility

188. Veterans Hospital Addition

188. Veterans Hospital Addition

2601 Cold Spring Road
Architect: BSA Design
Construction Manager: Geupel DeMars Inc.
1993

Most of the buildings of the Cold Spring Road campus of the Richard L. Roudebush Veterans Affairs Medical Center were constructed in 1931 and reflect the profound influence of the Williamsburg phenomenon. Medical programs here focus on mental health and behavioral sciences. The purpose of the new construction was to improve patient care by consolidating outpatient psychiatric services. The major new four-story addition was inserted within existing wings of the complex, requiring the new design to respect existing form and detail. While major themes of the old buildings' Georgian Revival style are repeated—such as the hipped roof with dormers, the use of brick as the major material with limestone detailing, and the overall proportions and scale—this addition introduces new design elements that clearly mark it as a new building. Its most distinctive feature is the main facade's semicircular projection with round columns, which rests on a coursed limestone base. The addition's connections to the older buildings are expressed by glazed curtain walls.

190. Major Taylor Velodrome

190. Major Taylor Velodrome
Lake Sullivan Sports Complex
Architect: HNTB Architects Engineers Planners
Contractor: Tousley-Bixler Construction Co.
1982

With bicycle racing attracting larger numbers of competitors and increasing crowds of spectators, the city decided to augment its amateur sports center status by constructing a banked oval track specially designed for sprint races (i.e., a velodrome). The facility is named after an Indianapolis native and African-American cycling champion, Walter Marshall Taylor, known worldwide at the turn of the century. The new track brings the entire length of the race within view of a bleacher crowd of up to 3,000 while providing for high speeds through its 28-degree banking. The surface of the 333.3-meter oval is a virtually jointless concrete slab placed on compacted earth embankments. While this facility is in the forefront of U. S. tracks, there is a design innovation that distinguishes this velodrome from all others: its access tunnel enables riders and officials to move freely back and forth during races while providing the spectator with unobstructed views around the track. Carved into a hillside along I-65, the velodrome's siting provides public visibility of a lesser known sport.

189. Al-Fajr Mosque
2846 Cold Spring Road
Architect: M. Mazen Ayoubi, AIA
Contractor: DLA, Inc.
1992

On a wooded site on Cold Spring Road, this simple building is the first Islamic mosque to be built in Indianapolis, bearing witness to the growing diversity of the city's population. In 1973 the Muslim community, then comprising about a dozen families, congregated in a house near downtown; by 1990 the number of people of Islamic faith in Indianapolis had grown to about 2,000. This brick building, simple and symmetrical in form, is entered by climbing a flight of concrete stairs to an entrance porch. White metal domes sit above flat roofs to announce the building's identity as a mosque. The prayer hall (*masjid*), designed for 300 worshipers, faces Mecca.

189. Al-Fajr Mosque

191. St. Vincent Medical Arts Building

3400 Lafayette Road
Architect: Group Eleven Architecture & Planning
Construction Manager: Sweet & Co.
1989

Located near the busy retail environment of strip malls, this building's stylized design sets it apart from its neighbors and creates a highly identifiable image for the medical center. Flat planes of white stucco walls are punctuated by deeply recessed window openings that add depth and shadow to the facade. The window reveals are painted a bright yellow, providing an interesting color note. Oversized brick, relating to the residential areas to the west, steps up around the southwest corner of the building. Landscaping and a reflecting pool with fountain seek to provide a buffer from busy traffic around the perimeter of the site.

1991 Indianapolis Chapter, American Institute of Architects, Honor Award

191. St. Vincent Medical Arts Building

192. Scandinavian Health Club

192. Scandinavian Health Club

5435 Pike Plaza Road
Architect: Cedarwood Architectural Inc., Akron, Ohio
Contractor: Cedarwood Construction Co., Akron, Ohio
1989

Because this fitness center is a modified prototypical design, you'll find multiple variations of this building from Glendale, Arizona, to Columbus, Ohio. The exterior, executed in simulated stucco, relies on color rather than materials to express its message of energy: painted stripes of red, white, and teal blue divide the gray first floor from the tan second story. The bold colors are repeated in the glass canopy over the walkway that leads to the projecting entry vestibule—a sharp, triangular form glazed in both plain glass and smaller panes of reflective glass. The stair-step pattern of the vestibule's glazing is repeating on the central section of the second story. Inside are the usual features of a fitness center including a lap pool with colorfully tiled walls and a running track on the second level.

194. Amoco Service Station

194. Amoco Service Station
West 38th Street and High School Road
Architect: Acheson Thornton Doyle Architects, PC,
New York, New York
Fabricator: MERO Structures, Inc., Germantown,
Wisconsin
1993

Amoco's graceful new canopy is a definite departure from the monolithic, flat canopies that are commonplace at today's gas stations. In this first-to-be-erected prototype for the oil company, the designers sought to make the distinctive canopy form both structurally elegant and spatially light and airy. The structure over the gas pumps consists of three independent T-shaped structures, each of which is supported by double columns at the ends of the pump islands. These cantilevered and self-supporting structures do not touch but create larger arched forms when positioned side by side. The canopy's roof is made of a curved, translucent material that allows diffused natural light to illuminate the pumps by day; at night, the canopy itself glows. The station's convenience store and car wash are also prefabricated modules. In the ever-expanding role of the gas station, this one surprises with its inclusion of satellite fast-food franchises.

193. Saturn Dealership
5333 Pike Plaza Road
Architect: CRSS, Houston with
Group Eleven Architecture & Planning
Contractor: Hilliard Construction
1992

The Saturn Corporation, a division of General Motors, was created in 1985 to provide a new and unique approach to automobile retailing. In order to extend the new identity program from the manufactured cars to the buildings in which they are sold, a consistent design image was developed for Saturn dealerships nationwide. Elements such as the entry canopy, the front wall sign graphics, and the interior furnishings were created to project a high standard of contemporary design. The local architectural firm, Group Eleven, performed modifications necessary to adapt the prototype design to local conditions and budget.

193. Saturn Dealership

196. Rehabilitation Hospital of Indiana

196. Rehabilitation Hospital of Indiana
4141 Shore Drive
Architect: NBBJ, Inc., Columbus, Ohio
Associate Architect: Able Ringham Moake Park
Contractor: Carlstedt Dickman Inc.
1992

Built as a joint venture between Methodist and St. Vincent hospitals, this new 80-bed facility draws patients from throughout the Midwest who are recovering from stroke, head injury, spinal-cord trauma, or other conditions requiring general rehabilitation. A white stucco exterior creates a clean look while the space frames and entry canopies with their bright blue roofs lend a high-tech aspect. Varied ceiling heights and large windows were designed to bring the outdoors inside as part of the healing process. The central therapy courtyard provides visual and physical stimulation in a social environment. Steps at different heights and ramps at varying inclines challenge patient mobility. In addition to the center court, common areas include a gym, pool, chapel, cafeteria, and two lobbies.

195. Methodist Medical Plaza II
6820 Parkdale Place
Architect: Simmons & Associates, Inc.
Contractor: Meyer & Najem Corporation
1992

Located in the Eagle Highlands area near the juncture of West 38th Street and I-465, this satellite medical facility filled a need for health care for the rapidly growing far west side. This view of the main entrance shows one of its prime architectural features: a projecting corner of the building, supported by a single column, which serves as a porte cochere to protect patients from the elements as they are dropped off or picked up. In the background is the curving facade on columns of the outpatient facility to which it is connected. The use of soldier courses of brick in a contrasting color provides horizontal detailing.

195. Methodist Medical Plaza II

197. Colts Training Center

7001 West 56th Street
Architect: James Associates Architects
Contractor: Huber Hunt & Nichols Inc.
1987

Located just outside Interstate 465 and across from Eagle
Creek Park, the training center is less notable in the public's eye than the Hoosier Dome, but it is more vital to the
Colts' daily operations. Rendered in the football team's
colors, the building consists of a rectilinear volume that is
intersected by a lower, broad cylinder. The blue rectilinear
volume, which contains the physical conditioning spaces,
acts as a backdrop to the silver cylindrical form housing
the administrative offices and support space. The facade is
covered by vertical aluminum panels. The recessed main
entry is denoted by a large, low, arched glass transom resting on a blue glass window band.

197. Colts Training Center

198. Schwitzer Research & Development Center

198. Schwitzer Research & Development Center

6040 West 62nd Street
Architect: LZT Architects, Inc., Austin, Texas
Associate Architect: American Consulting Engineers, Inc.
Contractor: Pearson Construction Company
1990

Sited alongside I-465 and designed to be readily recognized by the interstate traveler, this building contains the
corporate offices and research and development facility of
a manufacturer of turbochargers, fan drives, vibration
dampers, and engine fans. Offices and conference rooms
are located in the one-story western section of the building,
while the industrial laboratory component is located in the
adjacent two-story portion. The exterior's horizontal
bands in shades of gray are part of an integrally colored
fiberglass, stucco-like finish system. The storm water
retention pond often serves as a mirror reflecting the
streamlined west facade to passing drivers. The addition
of solid concrete lane dividers has caused much of the
building to be lost to southbound viewers.

199. Pike Township Library
6525 Zionsville Road
Architect: The McGuire & Shook Corporation
Contractor: Construction, Inc.
1986

When the local school system sold the parcel of land for the construction of a new library to serve the residents of northwest Indianapolis, a stipulation was made that the building be designed to be compatible with an existing high school on the same site, right down to the brick color. The architects deliberately chose to keep the building profile low and in scale with surrounding residential development. A skylit foyer connects the two components of the building: the library to the south (right) and a community center at the north (left). When the library portion is closed, the public still has access to the community room and its facilities (kitchenette, lobby, restrooms, etc.). Individual reading rooms are provided for both adults and juveniles. The 1986 awards jury lauded the building for its use of structure and lighting as decorative elements.

1986 Indiana Society of Architects, Citation Award
1986 Indianapolis Chapter, American Institute of Architects, Citation Award

199. Pike Township Library

200. Buildings 110 and 111, Park 100 Innerpark

200. Buildings 110 and 111, Park 100 Innerpark
5555-5589 West 73rd Street;
7102-7196 Lakeview Parkway West Drive
Architect: Ken Carr & Associates, Inc.
Contractor: Duke Construction Management, Inc.
1986

During the 1980s, much of Indianapolis' suburban commercial development took the form of large, low-scale buildings that provided warehousing, showrooms, and offices in a complex of flexible units. These complexes proliferated in proximity to the interstate system. In the vast expanse of Park 100, called a "business park" by its developer Duke Associates, these two buildings were early examples of flexible space given a measure of architectural design. Most interesting in this development is the way the units zigzag at the corners, giving individual units more character. At alternating units, the parapets have been cut out at the corners for further accent.

201. DowElanco Employee Development Center

201. DowElanco Employee Development Center
9300 Zionsville Road
Architect: JBA Architects, P.C., Newark, Ohio
Contractor: R.L. Turner Corporation
1993

Sited centrally with a showcase atrium for visitors and exhibits, the Employee Development Center functions as a training and conference facility and includes a cafeteria, medical clinic, employee benefits office, fitness center, and central operations office. The building's center of attention is the semicircular lobby whose roof form dynamically spirals upward with skylights radiating from the circular vestibule. The north curtain wall is articulated by vertical aluminum trusses. On the south side of the center, exterior terraces for diners and conference attendees overlook a lake surrounded by prairie grasses. Enclosed walkways connect this building with the R&D Center and the new Administration Building, which will be completed in early 1994.

201. DowElanco Employee Development Center

202. DowElanco Research and Development Center
9300 Zionsville Road
Architect: JBA Architects, P.C., Newark, Ohio
Contractor: Whittenberg Engineering and Construction
             Company, Louisville, Kentucky
1992

Located on DowElanco's new 325-acre campus in the northwest corner of the county, the 15 greenhouses adjacent to the Research and Development Center are one of the most visible signs of the new company, especially when seen illuminated at night from I-465. The greenhouses' exposure to the sun was critical to the entire building's orientation. The research laboratories cover over 600,000 square feet and house over 500 scientists and support staff. The modular pods of the biology and chemistry laboratories are separated by two-story skylit atrium spaces that can readily facilitate future changes in laboratory layout and systems. The dramatic roof form seen here is repeated along the diagonal line from the center's two-story section to the beginning of its one-story area. A common palette of materials—Atlantic green granite from Quebec and reflective glass of an aluminum curtain wall—is employed for the three major buildings of DowElanco's campus.

202. DowElanco Research and Development Center

203. Donald E. Knebel Residence
7111 Andre Court
Architect: G. Joseph Ballinger, AIA
Contractor: James Taylor
1987

Located in the Normandy Farms development, this formal new home freely mixes elements of the Georgian Colonial style with contemporary architectural trends. Its most distinctive feature is the oversized, glazed entry arch within which the front door is found. The large corner columns supporting the wide overhang of the hipped roof are more for decorative purposes than structural ones. The arched dormers seem straight out of the 18th century. The house's interior was designed with the entertainment of guests a foremost consideration. To facilitate traffic flow and ease of circulation, all the public downstairs rooms have two entrances and there are wide, interconnecting hallways. The front door leads to the 27-foot-high grand foyer with silver travertine marble floor and cove lighting; this hall is flanked by steps leading to the living and dining rooms.

203. Donald E. Knebel Residence

204. George and Jan Rubin Residence

204. George and Jan Rubin Residence
6830 West 71st Street
Architect: James W. McQuiston
Contractor: Herb Schmidt
1981

Extensive renovation of a 1950s house situated high on an overlook of Trader's Point Lake used a simple, almost austere architectural design to focus attention outward to a commanding view of the lake. The owners derive great pleasure from the sense of openness and play of light within the added space. Light enters through tall windows and several skylights. The five angled planes of the ceiling reflect the natural light in constantly changing ways. Tall white walls, a glass-enclosed stairway, and natural wide-plank wood floors are simply detailed to defer to the architectural concept of light, open space.

1984 Indiana Society of Architects, Citation Award

205. Zollman Center
7439 Woodland Drive
Architect: Artekna Design
Contractor: Greenfield Builders
1992

The image created for this plastic surgery center is definitely outside the mainstream of institutional medical facilities. The angularity of its unusual massing, based on the interlocking diamonds of its plan, is emphasized by the choice of the glass skin. The gabled entry canopy leads to the central, two-story lobby over which the building's dominating gable extends. Clinical and surgical spaces are located on the first floor, while the business and personnel offices occupy the second floor. A high glass block wall on the second-floor balcony diffuses light with a prismatic effect.

205. Zollman Center

206. Adam's Mark Hotel

206. Adam's Mark Hotel
2544 Executive Drive West
Architect and Contractor: HBE Corporation, St. Louis
1978

Originally built as the 255-room Sheraton Hotel West, which held a five-year franchise, in 1983 the hotel became an Adam's Mark Hotel (one of 11 in the country). The building has undergone three expansions since its original construction, the most major of which was the west wing and ballroom in 1979. A reinforced concrete structure, this hotel—with its "egg crate" design and "heroic band" across the top—has been likened to L'Enfant Plaza in Washington, D.C., designed by architect I. M. Pei in 1966.

207. 1 Park Fletcher
5460 Southern Avenue
Architect: Hellmuth, Obata & Kassabaum, Dallas
Contractor: Henry C. Beck Company
1980

The 625-acre Park Fletcher Office Park, which first opened in 1962, benefits from its close proximity to the interstate and the airport. The 1 Park Fletcher building was sited adjacent to the airport expressway to increase its visibility. Comprised of three units that are joined in the center by a three-story landscaped atrium, the building's exterior of curving gray steel panels and reflective thermal pane window bands creates an undulating effect. Its entrance was located in front of a cluster of tall ash trees which shade the clear lobby glazing in summer and permits warming sun in winter.

207. 1 Park Fletcher

208. Park Fletcher Post Office

208. Park Fletcher Post Office
2760 Fortune Circle East
Architect: Fanning/Howey Associates, Inc.
Contractor: Lee Corporation
1992

The most striking feature of this new post office is the continuous gabled skylight that extends over the entire public service area of the building, which is brought forward from the postal support spaces devoted to mail sorting. The tall proportions, spare limestone detailing of the brick veneer, and the use of lettering as ornament give elegance to this front section. The limestone-framed entrance vestibule is pulled forward of the symmetrical main facade. The square windows at ground level are recessed to create some sense of depth for the otherwise planar facade. At the north and south ends of the service area, which are glazed as a continuation of the skylight, the mullions align with the thin limestone bands accenting the brick.

209. Airport Parking Garage

2500 South High School Road
Architect: Browning Day Mullins Dierdorf Inc.
Construction Manager: Geupel DeMars Inc.
1987

In siting a parking garage directly adjacent to an airport terminal's curbside, the architectural image of the terminal is sometimes compromised. In this case, the garage appears as an extension of the terminal, contouring in a radial plan and continuing the white concrete facade. The spiral up and down ramps of the garage create a strong architectural statement at the entrance to the airport and serve as a counterpoint to the horizontal lines of the garage. These cantilevered ramps as well as the five-story parking deck for 1,850 cars are constructed of cast-in-place concrete. Three glass-enclosed pedestrian bridges radiate from the third floor of the garage to the terminal at the departure level. On the first floor, a space frame with bubble-dome skylights extends over the entry to the ground transportation center.

1988 Indiana Society of Architects, Merit Award

209. Airport Parking Garage

210. Eagle Network Hub

210. Eagle Network Hub

2475 Hoffman Road
Architect: R. W. Armstrong & Associates
Construction Manager: Eagle Hub Builders
1993

This mammoth, utilitarian building at the fringe of the airport provides a hub for sorting the United States Postal Service's express mail. Here the connection is made between air transport and truck conveyance. The 44-acre concrete apron surrounding the T-plan building can accommodate 21 aircraft with expansion to 35 in the future. The repetitive functions contained in the program and the tight budget required design elements to be repetitive and simple. The main exterior finish of the building is a precast panel with a corrugated plastic panel used to sheathe the control tower. The tower's resemblance to a giant mailbox, complete with mail slot, works as a visual pun.

1993 Indianapolis Chapter, American Institute of Architects, Honor Award

86th Street Corridor

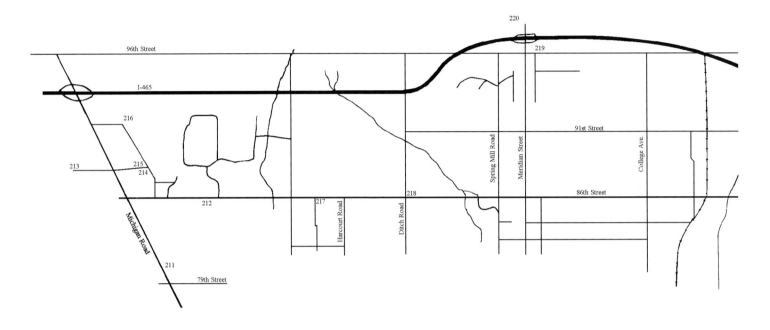

86th Street Corridor directory

211. Humane Society Building
212. Priest's Residence, Brebeuf

College Park

213. Inland Container Corporation
214. NAMIC Headquarters
215. 1 College Park
216. RCI Headquarters

217. St. Vincent's Family Life Center
218. North Willows Commons
219. Indiana Insurance
220. Meridian Tower

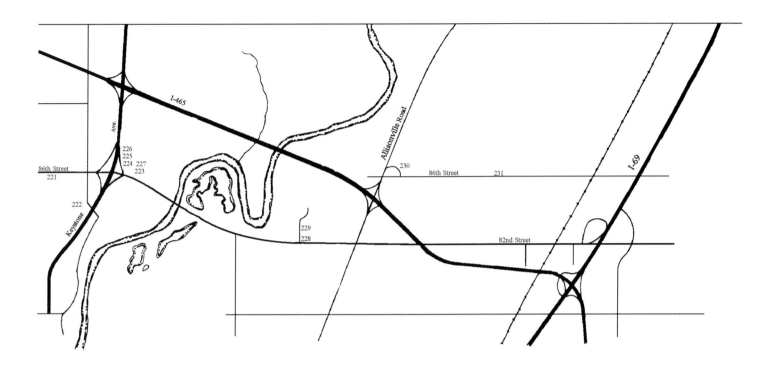

221. Hilltop School
222. Three Woodfield Crossing

Keystone at the Crossing

223. Fashion Mall Expansion
224. 8888 Keystone
225. 9100 Keystone
226. 9200 Keystone
227. Radisson Plaza Hotel

Castleton

228. Woodland Center One
229. Woodland Center Two
230. Castle Creek IV
231. Lawrence Fire Station 1

211. Humane Society Building
7929 Michigan Road
Architect: Archonics, a division of HNTB
Contractor: Carlstedt Dickman Inc.
1990

The facilities of the Humane Society of Indianapolis were sadly outmoded before this project, which was planned to improve efficiency of operations, to provide a better place to care for animals, and to enhance the society's image in the community. The building was sited parallel to Michigan Road both to afford visibility and to preserve the natural meadow below. Organized along a single corridor, the plan located spaces where people congregate—such as the lobby, the multipurpose room, and animal receiving— with a view to the meadow, while service areas were relegated to the road side. The building's size was scaled down by a series of gabled components intended to recall rural village architecture. The James and Barbara Power Residence, an Italianate house that has served as a local landmark for over a century, was preserved as administrative offices. Most of the public areas, such as the learning center seen in this view, are located near the main entrance.

211. Humane Society Building

212. Priests' Residence at Brebeuf Preparatory School

212. Priests' Residence at Brebeuf Preparatory School
2823 West 86th Street
Architect: CSO/Architects, Inc.
Contractor: Stenz Construction Corporation
1990

A master plan for the entire high school led to a number of changes and improvements on Brebeuf's campus. The construction of a new residence for the Jesuits allowed for the development of academic classrooms where the priests' apartments formerly had been located. Constructed in traditional materials, two colors of brick with limestone trim, the new residential building consists of the main two-story house with living quarters for eight priests with a connected one-story portion for future expansion. The main residence's three styles of windows, bold stringcourse, and multiple gables distinguish its design.

214. National Association of Mutual Insurance Companies Headquarters

3601 Vincennes Road
Architect: CSO/Architects, Inc.
Contractor: Brandt Construction, Inc.
1991

The offices of eight affiliated insurance organizations are consolidated in this headquarters. Completely symmetrical at each facade, the building is most interesting at its north elevation where the main entry occurs. Here the center bays step back to a pedimented, central pavilion in which the stainless steel entry doors and canopy are framed by corbelled brickwork. Window planes are recessed, thereby accentuating the pier-like divisions of the bays. Throughout the exterior, the two-color brickwork is well detailed, incorporating horizontal and vertical bands, "X" patterns, and multicolor glazed masonry units worked into recurring motifs. In the two-story lobby space, a monumental stairway leads to a continuous second-floor balcony.

214. National Association of Mutual Insurance Companies Headquarters

213. Inland Container Corporation Headquarters

4030 Vincennes Road
Architect: CSO/Architects, Inc.
Contractor: Rutherford Construction Corp.
1989

Located in the center of the Fortune Park office park, this building was initially developed on a speculative basis. However, before construction was complete, it became the headquarters of the Inland Container Corporation. The three-story building is sheathed in white architectural precast concrete with green reflective glass. The four sculptural stair towers that diagonally anchor the building are its most interesting architectural feature. A three-story atrium at the center of the building marks the main entrance. To meet the company's future growth needs, the building has been designed to allow for additions to be placed on both the east and west sides of the building.

213. Inland Container Corporation Headquarters

216. Resort Condominiums International Headquarters
3502 Woodview Trace
Architect: Cooler, Schubert, Olds & Associates Inc.
Contractor: Geupel DeMars Inc.
1981

Originally constructed as the offices of the Indiana Lumbermens Mutual Insurance Company, this building became RCI's headquarters in 1987. Its prominent siting oriented toward I-465 was important to both companies' images. The use of earth mounds and a sloping site conceal the fact that this is a four-story concrete structure of over 100,000 square feet. A four-story landscaped atrium at the juncture of the two wings marks the primary entrance. At the top floor where executive offices are located, a large walkout terrace has been enclosed in recent years.

216. Resort Condominiums International Headquarters

215. 1 College Park
8910 Purdue Road
Architect: Holabird and Root, Chicago
Contractor: Turner Construction Company, Cincinnati
1986

The bowed front form of this seven-story speculative office building makes it stand out among the buildings of College Park. The curved floor plan, designed to maximize tenants' views of the park's lake, is ideal for tenants occupying an entire floor. Color plays an important part of the all-glass curtain wall: green and oxblood red spandrels alternate with the gray window bands, all divided by gray mullions. The only relief to the glass skin occurs where the columns frame the two-story entrance lobby and adjacent lower, central sections.

215. 1 College Park

218. North Willow Commons

218. North Willow Commons

86th Street and Ditch Road
Architect: Hixson Architects/Engineers/Interiors,
  Cincinnati
Contractor: The Skinner & Broadbent Company Inc.
1989

Many features of this shopping center give it a character not usually associated with "strip malls." Designed in a style that takes cues from Georgian architecture, particularly in its arched and circular windows, the quality materials of warm brick and Indiana limestone set it apart from the average suburban development. The center is comprised of two buildings, one taking an L shape while the other importantly defines the northwest corner of Ditch Road and 86th Street. Several large, gabled pavilions give the project a scale that adds to North Willow Commons' presence.

217. St. Vincent Family Life Center

2001 West 86th Street
Architect: Archonics Design Partnership
Construction Manager: Huber Hunt & Nichols Inc.
1985

The two-story Family Life Center is a 54-bed obstetrical facility located at the northwest corner of the St. Vincent Hospital complex. The center was intentionally created as a freestanding building to depart from the institutional image and activities of the hospital, yet its proximity to the hospital required that its exterior design finishes be compatible with existing buildings. While the angularity of the facade does not evoke images of motherhood, the concept of family-centered maternity care was reinforced in the design and layout of the interior. A residential character was emphasized with the use of warm colors and natural light.

217. St. Vincent Family Life Center

219. Indiana Insurance Company Building

219. Indiana Insurance Company Building
9600 North Meridian Street
Architect: CSO/Architects, Inc.
Contractor: Duke Construction Management, Inc.
1992

Located at the Parkwood office complex at the intersection of North Meridian Street and I-465, this four-story office building is carefully sited on axis with the interstate to afford a high degree of visibility. Unlike other suburban buildings that turn their back to the highway, the Indiana Insurance Company Building's north facade is nearly as prominent as the main facade oriented to the East 96th Street entry drive. The exterior design is distinguished by precast concrete elements which frame projecting sections of the reflective glass skin in a manner somewhat reminiscent of classical colonnades and porticoes. In front of the entry a sculpture by Lyle London of Arizona is a rare bow to art in a suburban office park. The interior features a two-story lobby with a well-detailed granite floor and wood paneling.

219. Indiana Insurance Company Building

220. Meridian Tower
103 West 103rd Street
Architect: Browning Day Mullins Dierdorf Inc.
Contractor: Browning Construction, Inc.
1991

Rising at the edge of a cornfield bordering the northern loop of I-465, this elegant six-story office building appears more like a giant size piece of sculpture than a building. The bowed curtain wall facade that faces south toward the highway is composed of polished granite and reflective glass. At the main entrance on the north side, a three-level atrium lobby provides an open view for the tenants on the first three floors. The use of structural glazing affords the entry high visibility as well as natural light.

220. Meridian Tower

222. Three Woodfield Crossing

222. Three Woodfield Crossing

8425 Woodfield Crossing Boulevard
Architect: Cooper Carry and Associates, Inc., Atlanta
Contractor: Duke Construction Management, Inc.
1990

Located on the site of what was farmland until the mid-1980s, this speculative office building has been described as one of the better architectural endeavors in the Keystone Crossing area. The five-story atrium at the heart of the building, with its black-and-white marble floors and fountains, resembles a palace garden. Its arched roof truss of slender, curved girders has been likened to "a descent of Moorish courtyard into a California jet hangar—altogether a thoroughly enjoyable effect, rich, open, airy." The scored frame around the entry doors attempts to give a sense of scale to the vast atrium. Due to the building's siting, its full front may only be seen driving south on the 86th Street underpass, or from the lakeside exposure.

222. Three Woodfield Crossing

221. Hilltop School

1915 East 86th Street
Architect: The McGuire & Shook Corporation
Contractor: Geupel DeMars Inc.
1980

Designed as a center for the education of mentally retarded students ranging in age from three to 19, Hilltop School's program contained facilities beyond most schools, such as a therapy pool and vocational training rooms. Sited atop a knoll overlooking Haverstick Creek, the brick building is partially bermed and utilizes other energy-saving features. Its chief architectural statement derives from the sharp geometry provided by the dramatic diagonal rake of its roof. The building is located within the campus setting of North Central High School and the J. Everett Light Career Center.

221. Hilltop School

223. Fashion Mall Expansion
Keystone at the Crossing
Architect: CSO/Architects, Inc.
Associated Architect: RTKL, Dallas
Contractor: Duke Construction Management, Inc.
1988

Developed by Duke Associates on the site of the ill-fated Bazaar shopping center of 1974, this two-story expansion of the existing Fashion Mall followed the more successful linear arrangement of a major spine of shops leading to a large "anchor" department store. The focal point of the mall is a central skylit Palm Court of rotunda form in which 24-foot palm trees from Florida grow around the escalators. Florida appears to have provided more than the trees as the bright color scheme of white accented by pink bands would indicate. Skylights run the entire length of the mall, pleasantly illuminating both upper and lower levels of the shopping street. A second-level food court bridges over the street to the existing mall.

223. Fashion Mall Expansion

224. 8888 Keystone Crossing Plaza

224. 8888 Keystone Crossing Plaza

224. 8888 Keystone Crossing Plaza
8888 Keystone Avenue
Architect: 3D/ International, Houston
                Lamson & Condon, Inc.
Contractor: Duke Associates
1988

At 17 stories, this tower is the largest suburban office building in the state of Indiana and is larger than Towers I and II combined. Its derivation from the earlier towers' design is made obvious by the continuation of form and materials (silver reflective glass, window bands of dark grey glass, and precast concrete grid). The building's lobby, a full two stories in height, is finished in polished granite and glass. A second-story covered walkway, elevated on columns, connects the building to a parking garage, the Radisson, and the Fashion Mall.

227. Radisson Plaza Hotel

227. Radisson Plaza Hotel

8787 Keystone Crossing
Architect: Wright/Porteous & Lowe, Inc.
Associated Architect: CRSS, Houston
Contractor: Duke Construction Management, Inc.
1984; 1987

As one approaches this 400-room hotel from the entry drive at the west, the two "wings" of the building spread out in a manner likened to welcoming arms. The 12-story brick structure is perhaps the most successful architectural design present at Keystone at the Crossing from a number of standpoints: its dynamic form; its sophisticated colors and facade patterning; and its site plan for both vehicular and pedestrian access. The hotel's atrium occurs at the intersection of the two wings under a glass skyroof that slopes down from the third-floor level. In the front plaza, a covered walkway of glass pyramids over an open truss adds a dramatic amenity to the site. The window grid of the upper stories—in which white-outlined spandrels of burnt orange and terra cotta alternate, echoing the horizontal bands of contrasting brick in the building's end walls—has been called a "high-tech plaid." A major addition of 12 floors (160 suites) was added to the hotel in 1987.

227. Radisson Plaza Hotel

225. Tower II, Keystone at the Crossing

9100 Keystone Avenue
Architect: CSO/Architects Inc.
Associated Architect: 3D/International, Houston
Contractor: Duke Construction Management, Inc.
1985

226. Tower III, Keystone at the Crossing

9200 Keystone Avenue
Architect: CSO/Architects Inc.
Associated Architect: 3D/International, Houston
Contractor: Duke Construction Management, Inc.
1986

The scale of these eight-story suburban office buildings is somewhat camouflaged by the dichotomy of their forms and materials: cylindrical ends sheathed in silver mirror glass appear to be extruded from the main body of the buildings, where black glass window bands occur between the precast concrete grid. At the ground-floor levels, pedestrian plazas were created by lifting the mass of the buildings up on piers. A ring of trees helps to set the buildings off from the encircling parking lots.

225. Tower II, 9100 Keystone

228. Woodland Center One
8275 Allison Pointe Trail
Architect: The Odle McGuire & Shook Corporation
Contractor: Carlstedt Dickman Inc.
1989

This speculative office building is located at the entry to Allison Pointe office park, a development near Allisonville Road and 86th Street that was sited in a heavily wooded remnant of virgin timber. Most offices in the three-story building were oriented to maximize the view of the natural environment. Softening the angularity of the building is a gracefully curved entry pavilion with rounded piers flanking the front door. The buff-colored brick is subtly accented by terra-cotta sills below flush window bands that step down. Recessing windows at certain sections of the building provide architectural relief.

228. Woodland Center One

229. Woodland Center Two

229. Woodland Center Two
8335 Allison Pointe Trail
Architect: CSO/Architects, Inc.
Contractor: Carlstedt Dickman Inc.
1988

Spanning gullies and ravines, this new office building preserves the original topographic features of its wooded site. This view is of the interior courtyard, where wings extend from a central, two-story atrium. The upper stories of brick, with horizontal bands of contrasting molded brick and reflective glass, appear to rest on the first floor's squat columns. In the lobby one is surprised to find a bit of Pompeii in the form of a simulated wall fresco. In artist Les Seymour's San Francisco studio, he created a mural on separate pieces of canvas that were spliced together on site. Complete with missing fragments painted in to suggest an excavated piece, the wall fresco was interestingly interwoven with surrounding three-dimensional elements like the "granitized" columns.

231. Lawrence Fire Station 1

231. Lawrence Fire Station 1
6260 East 86th Street
Architect: Longardner & Associates, Inc.
Contractor: Batts Construction, Inc.
1989

Lawrence Fire Station 1 was designed to continue the idea of the vernacular firehouse as exhibited by the township's two previous fire stations (2 and 3). In addition to the five-bay fire station and the fire department's administrative headquarters, community meeting spaces are located in the building. To keep this large building's volume and foot-print as compact as possible, a one-and-a-half-story design was employed with the fire fighters' quarters located above the apparatus bays. Projecting gabled forms and dormer windows break up the mass of the building and separate the emergency rescue and fire-fighting functions. Adding interest to the red brick exterior are stripes of black brick; a band of gray brick serves as a stringcourse. Split-faced concrete block was used to emulate limestone at the window lintels and water table.

230. Castle Creek IV
5875 Castle Creek Parkway North
Architect: Archonics, a division of HNTB
Contractor: Sheil-Sexton Co., Inc.
1985

Located in the Castle Creek Corporate Park north of Castleton Square Mall, this building was sited to take advantage of the natural amenities of its wooded site. Care was taken during construction to preserve as many trees as possible. It was one of the first speculative office build-ings in Indianapolis to include a multistory glass atrium. The four-story building uses traditional materials such as brick and limestone in combination with reflective glass to create a contemporary image. The atrium, which is located at the entry, steps back at each level.

1986 Indianapolis Chapter, American Institute of Architects, Merit Award
1986 Indiana Society of Architects, Citation Award

230. Castle Creek IV

For those buildings illustrated in the essay but not included
in the section on featured buldings, here follows information on address,
archtect, contractor, and year of construction.

page 32
Meadows Executive Plaza and Shopping Center
Architect: Wolner Associates
mid-1960s to mid-1970s

page 32
USA Funds Building
11100 USA Parkway, Fishers
Architect: Everett I. Brown Company
Construction Manager: Toth-Ervin Inc.
General Contractor: Guepel DeMars Inc.
1991

page 33
Black-eyed Pea Restaurant
3916 East 82nd Street
Architect: Merriman Associates Architects, Inc., Dallas
Contractor: Telic Construction, Inc.
1992

page 33
China Coast Restaurant
5090 West 38th Street
Architect: The Vincent Association, Dallas
Contractor: Bostleman Corporation
1993

page 34
McDonald's Restaurant
Intersection of I-65 and East Main Street, Greenwood
Architect: Brandt Associates, Inc.
Contractor: Shiel-Sexton Co., Inc.
1990

page 35
Steak 'n Shake Restaurant
1501 East 86th Street
Architect: Shropshire and Ellis
Contractor: George Clark
1982 (remodeling)

page 35
Deer Creek Music Center
12880 E. 146th Street, Noblesville
Architect: Simmons & Associates, Inc.
Contractor: Shiel-Sexton Co., Inc.

1989
page 36
Carmel Civic Square
Carmel, Indiana
Architect: HNTB Architects Engineers Planners
Contractor: J.C. Ripberger and Sons
1990

page 36
Sunny Heights Elementary School
11149 Stony Brook Drive
Architect: SchenkelSchultz Architecture Engineering
Construction Managers: Ziolkowski Construction, Inc.
1993

page 37
One Parkwood Crossing
250 East 96th Street
Architect: Cooper Carry and Associates; Atlanta, Georgia
Construction Manager: Duke Associates
1990

page 38
Meridian Mark I and II
11611 and 11711 North Meridian Street
Architect: Browning Day Pollak Mullins Dierdorf Inc.
Contractor: Browning Construction, Inc.
1982; 1983

page 38
"New Tudor" Style Residence
Greenwood, Indiana

page 38
Geist Reservoir Residence
Brigantine Drive

page 39
Woodmont Condominiums
6451 Meridian Parkway
Architect: Cast Design Group
Contractor: Woodmont, Inc.
1990

page 39
Island Club Apartments
7938 Island Club Drive
Architect: Gary Weaver, Inc.
Construction Manager: J.C. Hart Company
1990

Photography Credits

All photography by David Kadlec except the following:

Introductory pages and essays: Page vi, photo by John David Fleck, courtesy of Pearson Craham & Fletcher Group. Page 6 right, photo by Greg Murphey Photography, courtesy of Browning Day Mullins Dierdorf. Page 7 left, photo by © Balthazar Korab Ltd., courtesy of HNTB. Page 9 left, photo by John David Fleck, courtesy of J. W. McQuiston. Page 13 left, photo by W M Photographic Services, Inc., © Wilbur Montgomery, courtesy of Schmidt Associates. Page 14 right, photo by Darryl Jones, courtesy of HNTB. Page 20 left, photo by J. F. Housel Photography, Seattle, courtesy of Danadjieva & Koenig Associates. Page 24 left, photo by Bass Photo Company, courtesy of Mansur Development. Page 24 right, photo courtesy of Mansur Development. Page 26 lower right, photo by Bass Photo Company, courtesy of the Indiana Historical Society. Page 26 upper right, photo by Marsh Davis, courtesy of Historic Landmarks Foundation, Inc. Page 26 left, photo by Bass Photo Company, courtesy of the Indiana Historical Society. Page 27 left, photo by Bass Photo Company, courtesy of the Indiana Historical Society. Page 27 center, photo by Bass Photo Company, courtesy of the Indiana Historical Society. Page 28 left, photo by Bass Photo Company, courtesy of Mansur Development. Page 35 right, photo courtesy of Simmons & Associates. Page 37 left, photo by W M Photographic Services, Inc., © Joe Vandersaar, courtesy of Duke Associates. Page 43, photo by Woolpert Geographic Information Services, courtesy of Duke Associates. Page 47 left, photo by John David Fleck, courtesy of CSO/Architects.

Mile Square: Page 54, photo by W M Photographic Services, Inc., © Wilbur Montgomery, courtesy of Schmidt Associates. Page 55, photos by Darryl Jones, courtesy of HNTB. Page 56 left, photo by Greg Murphey Photography, courtesy of Ratio Architects. Page 58 right, photo by John David Fleck, courtesy of Mansur Development. Page 58 center, photo by John David Fleck, courtesy of Mansur Development. Page 59 left, photo by W M Photographic Services, Inc., © Wilbur Montgomery, courtesy of Browning Day Mullins Dierdorf. Page 60 left, photo by Amy Henning Jobst, courtesy of Browning Day Mullins Dierdorf. Page 62 center, photo by Chilluffo Photography, courtesy of Ratio Architects. Page 64 left, photo by W M Photographic Services, Inc., © Wilbur Montgomery, courtesy of Woollen Molzan & Partners. Page 64 right, photo by W M Photographic Services, Inc., © Wilbur Montgomery, courtesy of CSO/Architects. Page 68, photo by Greg Murphey Photography, courtesy of Browning Day Mullins Dierdorf. Page 69 right, photo by W M Photographic Services, Inc., © Wilbur Montgomery, courtesy of Odle McGuire & Shook. Page 69 left, photo by John David Fleck, courtesy of CSO/Architects. Page 70 right, photo by Cornelius Alig, courtesy of Mansur Development. Page 70 left, photo by John David Fleck, courtesy of Mansur Development. Page 71 right, photo courtesy of HNTB. Page 71 center, photo by Amy Henning Jobst, courtesy of Ratio Architects. Page 71 center, photo by Bass Photo Company, courtesy of Mansur Development. Page 72 right, photo courtesy of Porter Paints and the Cooler Group. Page 73 left, photo by © Balthazar Korab Ltd., courtesy of HNTB. Page 78 left, photo by © Dan Francis/Mardan Photography, courtesy of Blackburn Associates. Page 83 right, photo by James Lingenfelter, courtesy of HNTB. Page 84 left, photo by W M Photographic Services, Inc., © Wilbur Montgomery, courtesy of HDG Architects. Page 84 right, photo by W M Photographic Services, Inc., Wilbur Montgomery, courtesy of Woollen, Molzan & Partners.

Regional Center: Page 85 left, photo by W M Photographic Services, Inc., © Wilbur Montgomery, courtesy of Schmidt Associates. Page 86 left, photo by John David Fleck, courtesy of Ratio Architects. Page 90 left, photo by W M Photographic Services, Inc., © Wilbur Montgomery, courtesy of Browning Day Mullins Dierdorf. Page 92 left, photo by © Balthazar Korab Ltd., courtesy of Woollen Molzan & Partners. Page 93 left, photo by John David Fleck, courtesy of Ratio Architects. Page 99 right, photo by W M Photographic Services, Inc., © Wilbur Montgomery, courtesy of HNTB. Page 103 left, photo by Donald G. Olshavsky, AIA, ARTOG/D G Olshavsky Photography, courtesy of HNTB. Page 106 center, photo by Amy Henning Jobst, courtesy of Browning Day Mullins Dierdorf. Page 107 right, photo by W M Photographic Services, © Mike Fisher, courtesy of Browning Day Mullins Dierdorf. Page 109, photo by W M Photographic Services, Inc., © Wilbur Montgomery, courtesy of BSA Design. Page I I O left, photo by George Lambros Photography, courtesy of HNTB. Page 110 right, photo by W M Photographic Services, Inc., © Wilbur Montgomery, courtesy of HNTB.

Northside: Page 116 left, photo by Greg Lucas, courtesy of photographer. Page 125, photo by Timothy Hursley, courtesy of Woollen Molzan & Partners. Page 133 right, photo by John David Fleck, courtesy of J. W. McQuiston. Page 142 right, photo by James A. Strain, courtesy of photoghapher. Page 142 left, photo by © Jim Hedrich, Hedrich Blessing.

Fall Creek Valley: Page 146 right, photo by W M Photographic Services, Inc., © Wilbur Montgomery, courtesy of BSA Design. Page 146 left, photo by Tim Hardin, courtesy of WareAssociates. Page 147 left, photo by © Dan Francis/Mardan Photography, courtesy of CSO/Architects. Page 147 center, photo by Greg Murphey Photography, courtesy of CSO/Architects.

Eastside: Page 150 right, photo by © Dan Francis/Mardan Photography, courtesy of HNTB. Page 150 left, photo by D. Trent Champ, R.A., Earth Ethic, Inc., courtesy of HNTB. Page 151 right, photo by © Dan Francis/Mardan Photography, courtesy of HNTB. Page 154 right, photo by W M Photographic Services, Inc., © Wilbur Montgomery, courtesy of BSA Design. Page 155 left, photo by W M Photographic Services, © Joe Vondersaar, courtesy of Schmidt Associates. Page 155 right, photo by Donald F. Amt, courtesy of Amt, Inc. /Architects.

Southside: Page 156 left, photo by W M Photographic Services, Inc., © Joe Vandersaar, courtesy of Schmidt Associates. Page 159 right, photo by W M Photographic Services, Inc., © Wilbur Montgomery, courtesy of HNTB. Page 161 left, photo courtesy of Schmidt Associates .

Westside: Page 166 right, photo by © Balthazar Korab Ltd., courtesy of Woollen Molzan & Partners. Page 171 left, photo by Mike Holmes Photography. Page 173 right, photo by © Dan Francis/Mardan Photography, courtesy of Odle McGuire & Shook. Page 175 left, photo by W M Photographic Services, Inc., Wilbur Montgomery, courtesy of J. W. McQuiston. Page 178 right, photo by W M Photographic Services, Inc., © Wilbur Montgomery, courtesy of Browning Day Mullins Dierdorf. Page 178 left, photo by John Traexler, courtesy of R W Armstrong and Sverdrup-Gilbane.

86th Street: Page 187 center, photo by W M Photographic Services, Inc., © Wilbur Montgomery, courtesy of Duke Associates. Page 188 right, photo by © Dan Francis/Mardan Photography, courtesy of CSO/Architects. Page 188 left and center, photo by Aker Photography, courtesy of Duke Associates. Page 189 bottom, photo by © Dan Francis/Mardan Photography, courtesy of Duke Associates. Page 190 left, photo by Dan Francis/Mardan Photography, courtesy of Citimark and CSO /Architects. Page 191 right, photo by W M Photographic Services, Inc., © Wilbur Montgomery, courtesy of HNTB.

From left to right: volunteer Merrie Molzan; members of the Editorial Review Board: Lynn Molzan, Val Williamson, Terry Bradbury, and Jim Kienle. Not pictured in this photo: Jim Lingenfelter.

EDITORIAL REVIEW BOARD MEMBERS

Lynn H. Molzan, FAIA

James T. Kienle, AIA

Terry L. Bradbury, AIA

Valentina G. Williamson

James E. Lingenfelter, AIA

Lynn Molzan, a practicing architect since 1963, is president of Woollen, Molzan and Partners. Since 1990 he has served as the executive director of the Indiana Architectural Foundation.

James Kienle is principal in charge of architecture of the Indianapolis office of the HNTB Corporation. He currently serves as president of the Indiana Architectural Foundation.

Terry Bradbury is the principal of Bradbury Associates, Inc. With 20 years of experience, he has been an officer in several local community organizations and was president of the Indiana Architectural Foundation in 1992.

Valentina Williamson, an architect, is a principal in the firm of Mozingo Williamson Architects, Inc. She has served on the foundation board since 1990.

James E. Lingenfelter is an architect with the Indianapolis office of Greiner, Inc. He currently serves as an officer of the Indianapolis chapter of the American Institute of Architects.

Indiana Architectural Foundation Board Members, 1991-1993

David Bowen, FAIA, Terry Bradbury, AIA, Kenneth Englund, Hon ISA, Kenneth Featherstone, Robert Fisher, AIA, Ronald Fisher, AIA, Stephen Ford, AIA, Dean Illingworth, AIA, James Jelliffe, AIA, James Kienle, AIA, Henry Meier, AIA, Ronald Menze, AIA, Lynn Molzan, FAIA, Michael Montgomery, AIA, Charles Tyler, AIA, Russell Wilhite, Valentina Williamson, Angelo Zarvas

Volunteer Recognition

The Indiana Architectural Foundation wishes to acknowledge the many volunteers who gave their time and expertise to this book. From researching buildings and drafting write-ups to the more mundane tasks of filing and phone calling, all efforts are sincerely appreciated.

Principal Volunteers

Daniel L. Everett
Mark Handy
Stephen J. Holzer
Steven H. Logan, AIA
Todd S. Rinehart
Helaine K. Robinson, CCS
Steven W. Robinson, AIA
Troy D. Thompson
Mary Olds Toshach

Additional Volunteers

Patsy G. Cram
Mary Domblewski
Robert Gadski
Jim Kiefer
Merrie Molzan
Todd Mozingo
Roselle Oyer
Stephanie S. Turner
Pamela Heos Zarvas

The foundation would also like to acknowledge the efforts of many people who were especially helpful in the course of their jobs: Susan Sutton, Indiana Historical Society; Craig Charron, Division of Historic Preservation and Archaeology; Nancy Grounds, Julie Fulford, and Jenni Jegen, Indiana Architectural Center; Suzanne Rollins, Historic Landmarks Foundation of Indiana; Phyllis Hamilton, IPS Karl R. Kalp Library; Graphic Design by Mary Ann Davis, and the librarians of the Arts Division, Central Library, and the Indiana Division of the State Library.

Associated General Contractors of Indiana, Construction Advancement Program of Central Indiana

List of Contributing General Contractors

The Associated Builders, Inc.

Batts Construction, Inc.

M. K. Betts Engineering & Contracting

Bowen Engineering Corporation

Bowman Construction Co., Inc.

Charles C. Brandt and Company, Inc.

Bruns-Gutzwiller, Inc.

Calumet Construction Corp. CDI, Inc.

A.B. Cochran & Son, Inc.

Dallman Industrial Corporation

Deig Bros. Lumber & Construction Co.

W. R. Dunkin & Son, Inc.

Dunlap & Co., Inc.

Force Construction Co., Inc.

Geupel DeMars Inc.

Arthur A. Gill & Son, Inc.

Glenroy Construction Co., Inc.

Hagerman Construction Corp.

Hannig Construction, Inc.

The Robert Henry Corporation

Huber Hunt & Nichols Inc.

Indiana Construction Corp.

Industrial Contractors, Inc.

Irmscher, Inc.

Jungclaus-Campbell Co., Inc.

J.R. Kelly Company, Inc.

Kettelhut Construction, Inc.

Larson-Danielson Construction

Macku Construction, Inc./R.H.C. Construction Company

Roy A. Miller & Son, Inc.

Oberle & Associates, Inc.

Parco Construction, Inc.

Repp & Mundt, Inc.

J.C. Ripberger Construction

Earl C. Rodgers & Assoc., Inc.

Shuck Corporation

Superior Lumber & Bldg. Co.

J.S. Sweet Company, Inc.

Taylor Bros. Construction Co.

The Gale Tschuor Co., Inc.

Verkler Incorporated

Weddle Bros. Construction Co.

White Construction, Inc.

F.A. Wilhelm Construction Co., Inc.

CAPCI is also supported by over 1,000 subcontractors in Central Indiana.

Index

Bold numbers refer to pages in the section on featured buildings.